About Island Press

Since 1984, the nonprofit organization Island Press has been stimulating, shaping, and communicating ideas that are essential for solving environmental problems worldwide. With more than 1,000 titles in print and some 30 new releases each year, we are the nation's leading publisher on environmental issues. We identify innovative thinkers and emerging trends in the environmental field. We work with world-renowned experts and authors to develop cross-disciplinary solutions to environmental challenges.

Island Press designs and executes educational campaigns, in conjunction with our authors, to communicate their critical messages in print, in person, and online using the latest technologies, innovative programs, and the media. Our goal is to reach targeted audiences—scientists, policy makers, environmental advocates, urban planners, the media, and concerned citizens—with information that can be used to create the framework for long-term ecological health and human well-being.

Island Press gratefully acknowledges major support from The Bobolink Foundation, Caldera Foundation, The Curtis and Edith Munson Foundation, The Forrest C. and Frances H. Lattner Foundation, The JPB Foundation, The Kresge Foundation, The Summit Charitable Foundation, Inc., and many other generous organizations and individuals.

The opinions expressed in this book are those of the author(s) and do not necessarily reflect the views of our supporters.

Autonorama

Autonorama

THE ILLUSORY PROMISE OF HIGH-TECH DRIVING

Peter Norton

◐ **ISLAND**PRESS | Washington | Covelo

Library of Congress Control Number: 2021937486

All Island Press books are printed on environmentally responsible materials.

Manufactured in the United States of America
10 9 8 7 6 5 4 3 2 1

Keywords: Autopilot, autonomous vehicle (AV), car dependency, *CenterCore*, Demo '97, Disneyland, driverless, electronic highways, EPCOT, Federal Highway Administration, Ford Motor Company, Futurama, Futurama 2, General Motors, next-generation technology, Intelligent Transportation Systems (ITS), Intelligent Vehicle-Highway Systems (IVHS), Magic Skyway, mass transportation, mobility, *motordom*, Partners for Automated Vehicle Education (PAVE), Rachel Carson, RCA, smart highway, *technofuturistic*, Tesla, traffic congestion, traffic safety, transport-driven data collection, USDOT, vulnerable road user, World's Fair 1939–40, World's Fair 1964–65

For Will and Paul, and for Debby

Contents

Not If but When

*Any sufficiently advanced technology is
indistinguishable from magic.*
        —Arthur C. Clarke

"Someday—and it may come surprisingly soon—a car
maker will introduce a radically advanced automobile, and
cash in on the giant market of tomorrow." So an American electronics firm seeks to entice automobile manufacturers' interest in its products. The advertisement depicts
a high-tech future: Four smiling occupants of a driverless
car travel a high-speed, zero-congestion highway, enjoying
one another's company in comfort and safety. They face
each other; none pays any attention to the road. Their geographic setting is nondescript; what matters are the fast
vehicles and their relaxed occupants, the delay-free roadway, the unseen electronics that purportedly make this

utopian future possible. In these respects, the promise is typical of countless others like it from the last decade. This example, however, is from 1958.[1]

Such promises of technofuturistic driving utopias, depicted vividly and with claims of credibility, have again been ubiquitous in the media and wherever tech companies and carmakers meet. They assure us of a future in which traffic congestion never slows vehicles down, and cars never collide with anything. These promises, in turn, become reasons not to commit too much money or attention to modes of transportation that are already safer today, and that are also spatially efficient, more sustainable, and much cheaper.

By promising perfection, the promoters of technofuturistic visions make ordinary sufficiency bland by comparison. According to the author of a blurb on the back of a 2018 book celebrating "our driverless future": "This book should be required reading for every city planner and for every taxpayer fed-up with wasted transit dollars."[2] It's an extraordinary statement, considering the public money that has been spent for decades in the pursuit of highly automated driving that still offers little besides some convenience benefits to some drivers—but it's not an unusual position. In a 2020 book called *Driverless America*, published by SAE International (the former Society of Automotive Engineers), the author forecasts: "By the 2030s, no one outside of New York City and a few other big U.S. cities will be investing much in bus or rail transit any longer. In fact, the smarter areas will have stopped making such investments much earlier."[3]

Though diverse, the visions of high-tech driving share a common claim: with sensor data, state-of-the-art hardware, machine learning, and digital networking, onboard computers in every car will drive for us, better than we can, and sooner than we think. Despite the extraordinary technological developments of the last twenty years, however, the practical possibility of widespread automatic driving remains elusive. High-tech "solutions," always just over the horizon, are supposed to offer the anticipated deliverance. The lack, however, lies not in technology but in the aspiration itself. Meanwhile the supposed solutions, in promising an eventual end to all our afflictions, divert us from transport sufficiency: an unspectacular state in which everyone can meet their practical needs.

The governing assumption is that a car-dependent future city that is efficient, safe, sustainable, and equitable is practically possible, or desirable enough to be pursued at any cost, to the neglect of less utopian but more feasible alternatives. When pressed, promoters of such futures point out the obvious deficiencies of the status quo, as if the universe of our choices is limited to just two possibilities: status quo car dependency or futuristic car dependency. We may hear that people prefer to drive. But in settings that offer no good alternatives to driving, we can't say what people prefer. More often, however, we hear that the technology, like the weather, "is coming"; for those of us not developing and selling it, our task is only to forecast and prepare for the inevitable.[4] According to an analyst from Kelley Blue Book, a firm that studies the auto industry for consumers and investors, "Like it or not, autonomous cars are coming, and coming fast."[5] More often than not, in the advocacy of machine autonomy there is an implicit denial of human autonomy.

There are no autonomous vehicles

Most of the autonomous cars we are presented with look a lot like conventional cars. Those that are coming are supposed to be electric, but an electric car can be human driven; the high-tech enthusiasm is about the cars' supposed autonomy. The implication is that cars' problems are not due to their spatial demands, their low passenger capacity, or their weight (and consequent energy requirements) but to their human drivers. In this case, then, the remedy is a driverless car, or rather a car that drives itself: an autonomous vehicle.

Yet the term *autonomous vehicle* (AV) is paradoxical. Engineers have specialized definitions for autonomous systems, but among wider audiences, something autonomous has a will of its own. AV promoters seem to welcome the association, perhaps because it suggests that the AV is in control, unimpaired by human deficiencies. A vehicle that is in fully autonomous mode accelerates, brakes, and steers without direct human supervision, but only in response to the dictates of sensor data and the program that processes them. An AV is controlled by its program just as a conventional car is controlled by its human driver. The program has been automatically trained on vast data through machine learning, but human beings decide how the car will respond to its environment. Will the AV be risk averse, and drive so cautiously it frustrates its human occupants? Will it take chances, thereby offering its passengers a better ride? Will it yield to all pedestrians—or will it first honk at those who are not in a crosswalk? Will it comply with all the rules of the road so scrupulously that it annoys the human drivers behind it? Will it apply its machine learning capacities to determine how much faster than the speed limit it can go without risking a penalty? The car does not decide. Decisions like these have already been made—by human beings.

Human decisions will continue to govern the behavior of so-called autonomous vehicles as their capacities improve. A responsible human driver's decisions can be influenced by pressures that encourage risk-taking: a driver who is late for an appointment may take more chances. The human decision makers who really drive "autonomous vehicles" take chances, too, because few people would pay for a ride in an AV that takes none. In such human decisions, a company's survival in a competitive environment is at stake.

Hence both a conventional car and an AV are driven by human beings—neither one is autonomous or driverless. And for both cars' human drivers, safety is not the only consideration. This means that an autonomous vehicle is really just a highly automated vehicle. Fortunately *AV* can mean automated vehicle, as it does in the pages that follow. Just as road safety experts learned to study the performance, psychology, and limitations of the human drivers who sit in the cars they drive, we must also study the human drivers who develop, sell, and drive AVs.[6]

The autonomous revolution is coming

Though even the promoters of AVs concede that the claims of a decade ago have proved far too sanguine, enthusiasm for autonomous or highly automated driving seems undiminished at tech fairs and auto shows—and not just among business enterprises. Failing promises are sustained interminably on the assurance that the next technological development will deliver what all its predecessors could not. Even the US Department of Transportation (USDOT) has been as committed as ever. In 2018, less than four months after a self-driving Uber vehicle struck and killed Elaine Herzberg in Arizona, the secretary of transportation, Elaine Chao, declared, "One thing is certain—the autonomous revolution is coming. As government regulators, it is our responsibility to understand it and help prepare for it."[7] In 2019 Chao's federal highway administrator, Nicole Nason, reasserted Chao's statement, quoting it at the Automated Vehicles Symposium in Orlando, Florida.

I was among Nason's audience in the cavernous Crystal Ballroom of the Orlando World Center Marriott hotel, about a ten-minute drive from Disney World. I was there to serve on a panel of "stakeholders" in the safe deployment of automated driving systems.[8] There were four of us; the other three were from the American Automobile Association (to represent drivers), the Association of Global Automakers (to represent motor vehicle manufacturers), and the Insurance Institute for Highway Safety (to represent insurers). My job was to represent the "vulnerable road user."

Though consideration of people who are not in cars or trucks as stakeholders is a kind of progress, *vulnerable* is not the adjective I would have chosen. It was accurate—given the status quo—but hardly fair. To make it fair, we'd have to call motorists "menacing road users." The road uses of vulnerable road users are generally the safest for others, and the most sustainable, efficient, and affordable. Compared with these essential attributes, their vulnerability is merely circumstantial. Indeed, many of those routinely classified as drivers—as if by identity—would welcome a good chance to join this category of road users, at least occasionally, if their choices were better and vulnerability were no longer mistaken for the defining attribute of any road user who is not in a car or a truck.

But the hotel itself was a reminder that vulnerability is the norm, or that walking has been denormalized. AVs may have many useful applications, but ubiquitous AVs as a new generation of car dependency can make sense only where walking is no longer practical or safe—including the long-distance walking that is often necessary to patronize public transportation systems in car-dependent settings. Within a triangle defined by Interstate 4 and two six-lane arterials, the hotel reflected the official assumption that accessibility means accessibility by car. It was there that

I had my only ride in an autonomous car so far. After I signed a waiver agreeing not to sue for anything, including my death, I sat in the front passenger seat, next to a "safety driver" to my left. We circled around slowly in a closed, roped-off parking lot, with two other passengers seated behind me.

The hotel could have been a metaphor for the autonomous vehicle I rode in and for the technology that was celebrated in the meetings. Its showy extravagance (the enormous outdoor pool is also an elaborate water park; swimmers can watch giant TV screens from the pool) mirrored the flashy high-tech vehicles on display in the hotel's exhibit hall. And for both the hotel and the vehicles, astonishing claims of sustainability were made. The hotel was awarded a Green Lodging certification by Florida's Department of Environmental Protection,[9] and the high-tech vehicles were supposed to be "green" too.

Nason assured her audience that USDOT "supports the safe, reliable and cost-effective integration of automation into all modes of American transportation," including "automated vehicle development." As for her own Federal Highway Administration (FHWA), Nason promised, "At FHWA, we've been busy in preparing the nation's roadway infrastructure for automated vehicles."[10] True to its word, that September, USDOT awarded $60 million in grants to projects "to test the safe integration of Automated Driving Systems (ADS) on our nation's roadways." The results would "inform rulemaking and foster collaboration amongst state and local government and private partners."[11] Government agencies' favorite justification of public support (including money) for the technology has been safety; common secondary reasons have been sustainability and congestion relief. But there was little good evidence that automated vehicles would or could ever come close to meeting expectations. Under the Biden administration, we may expect shifts of emphasis, but early indications are that AVs, backed by coalitions of tech companies, automakers, and investors, will retain their favored position.

By 2019 such commitment to AVs was remarkable, especially because developers had already fallen far short of the promises they had made just a few years earlier.[12] Proponents of highly automated driving brushed off these failures, arguing that despite unanticipated "speed bumps" along the way, all the trends still made the "self-driving revolution" inevitable.[13] In particular, technology costs decline, and machine learning improves. *Not if but when* remains a favorite turn of phrase: like a late guest, autonomous cars are still coming—it's just not clear when.[14]

The cost of short memories

The very novelty of the technology would warrant patience with missteps, and forbearance with unfulfilled promises. But the promises can appear novel only to those who neglect history, or who uncritically accept the constructed versions of history that justify their governing premise: that car dependency is merely the product of mass preferences. Given this supposed fact, the task that follows is to apply technology to make car dependency finally deliver on its elusive, century-old promise—ubiquitous, convenient, fast, efficient, affordable, and safe personal transportation.

This and other assumptions are historically dubious, but history is nearly invisible wherever AVs are the subject of interest, whether at tech fairs, at auto shows, or in research universities. If history is invoked at all, it is only as a simple progress story—a timeline of innovations that, if extended into the future, points inevitably to self-driving cars. While most AV developers are silent about history, Anthony Levandowski, a leading developer of the Google self-driving car, is an exception. In 2018 Levandowski said: "The only thing that matters is the future. I don't even know why we study history. . . . What already happened doesn't really matter. . . . In technology, all that matters is tomorrow."[15] Among AV promoters, Levandowski's statement has been an implicit credo.

From a long-range perspective, promises that "surprisingly soon" a carmaker may make "a radically advanced automobile" that drives itself, carrying passengers in safety and comfort on delay-free roads, are not new at all.[16] When it advertised this claim in 1958, TRW, a US electronics company, was seeking to interest automakers in its products by promising to give them a decisive innovation edge—much as Intel, Nvidia, Aptiv, and other tech companies have been doing more recently. TRW was then contracting with the Pentagon on its ICBM projects, but it wanted to diversify its customers in a highly competitive tech environment—a pattern that persists in the tech sector today.

In 2014 a German automotive parts company, ZF Friedrichshafen (ZF), bought TRW Automotive, which by then was all that was left of the company. Today ZF unites automotive and electronics development, and continues the message of TRW's 1958 ad. At the 2020 Consumer Electronics Show (CES) in Las Vegas, ZF pitched itself as a contributor to the radically advanced autonomous car that the 1958 ad described. By its own account, in 2020, "ZF is an attractive partner when it comes to the realization of automated and autonomous driving."[17] In 1958 the pitch was essentially the same: "Want to build a car that drives itself?"[18]

At CES 2020, ZF was in good company. Automated driving was more prominent there than ever before, and the promises were as extravagant as they have ever been. Yet the gulf between the promises and the practical possibilities remains forbiddingly vast, and the implicit assumption— that in the future, as in the recent past, car dependency must continue—is as dubious as ever.

Their promoters represent AVs as an essential departure from all past mobility models. A little history, however, reveals that AV promotion is merely a new version of a century-old sales technique developed within a coalition of North American automotive interest groups once loosely called motordom. This moniker, from the first half of the twentieth century, is a convenient label for companies and interest groups engaged in efforts to promote automotive transportation and roadbuilding, and is therefore worth reviving.

In the 1930s, motordom learned to depict an unachievable future utopia that is forever just over the next horizon, apparently always close enough to attract extravagant private and public investment, but somehow never actually achieved. The purpose, as some of motordom's leaders explained to one another, was not to satisfy personal transportation demands but to serve them while keeping them strategically unsatisfied, to stimulate consumption.[19] Transport sufficiency was never the objective. Motordom sold not personal transport but transport consumerism. The heirs of such transport salesmanship take the form of international partnerships of motordom and tech, which are still in this business of avoiding sufficiency for the sake of consumerism. To divert audiences from realistic transport sufficiency, promoters of car-dependent technofuturistic utopias promise instead unrealistic transport solutions, up to and including "zero crashes, zero emissions, and zero congestion."[20]

Autonorama

Such promises are attractive but hard to believe. They are also not new: the unfulfilled promise of a car-dependent city that is also safe, clean, and congestion-free is well over eighty years old. How then to keep the claims credible? For this purpose, motordom long ago developed the technofuturistic spectacle: a depiction of a future so vivid and appealing that it invites acceptance and approval. Essential to such displays are conspicuous evocations of high-tech and future-tech possibilities, which invoke the prestige of science and impart new credibility to old, unfulfilled promises. They are not ordinary marketing campaigns. They do not sell particular products; they sell idealized futures in which their products will be in endless demand. These futures are not meant to be achieved. They are to be pursued, for in the pursuit lies the endless demand for vehicles, technology, and pavement.

Unlike routine marketing, the promotion of these technofuturistic visions has been episodic. An astonishing, attractive, but far-fetched vision is presented; references to the wonders of state-of-the art technology and impressive demonstration projects deflect skepticism. The visions stimulate business partnerships, investment, policy support, and public interest, all of which reinforce one another. Years pass and the results disappoint. The promoters explain that their real goals were actually a lot more modest, but still worthwhile: congestion relief, not congestion-free driving; fewer crashes, not none. As results remain uninspiring, the promoters conclude that policy makers and the public must be educated, and a public relations effort is organized. A credibility gap has set in, however, and the public relations campaigns can't bridge it. But by then, there will be a new generation of state-of-the-art technology, and it will support impressive new demonstration projects and visions of the future.

In 2003 Jameson Wetmore—now an associate professor at the School for the Future of Innovation in Society at Arizona State University—joked that automated driving has been "'only 20 years away' for over 60 years."[21] It was an astute observation, derived from his study of the three waves of such promises that by then had come and gone. It was practically a forecast of the next wave of high-tech driving promises, which had not yet begun. On schedule, just a couple of years later, a fourth wave was rising. This time it has taken the form of the persistently extravagant promotion of automated or autonomous vehicles: cars that can drive themselves.

Of the many displays promoting technofuturistic tomorrows in which technology has delivered a driving utopia, the first and still the most famous was General Motors' *Futurama* exhibit at the New York World's Fair of 1939–40, where millions saw the city of 1960 as GM imagined it: a drive-only, drive-everywhere city free of collisions and traffic jams, made possible by highway engineering supplemented by the electronics of the vacuum tube era. Twenty-five years later, GM presented an updated vision, *Futurama II*, at the New York World's Fair of 1964–65. This time solid-state, transistorized electronics were to deliver what the first futurama had promised.

In the early 1990s, after another twenty-five years, automakers, technology companies, military contractors, and government agencies collaborated on a third exercise in technofuturistic enthusiasm. Microprocessors in digital computers would finally make possible the safe and congestion-free driving that the first two futuramas had depicted. They never called their vision *Futurama III* outright, but as the rightful heir of its two predecessors, it earned the title. Twenty-five years after that, in 2010, GM and its Chinese partner SAIC Motor Corporation collaborated on a monumental cinematic depiction of Shanghai in 2030, replete with computer-generated imagery. They presented their ambitious vision at Shanghai's Expo 2010. Finally, with state-of-the-art sensors, machine learning, and wireless network connectivity, autonomous vehicles will purportedly achieve what the first three futuramas promised but failed to deliver: a city of ubiquitous, convenient, safe, and delay-free driving. Their vision is as vibrant today as it was in 2010; variations on it are commonplaces at auto shows and tech conventions, and in online marketing. Though GM and SAIC chose to name this most recent depiction *2030 Xing!* they might well have called it *Futurama IV*—it was unmistakably in the tradition of its predecessors. Given the essential place of vehicular autonomy in this version, however, perhaps the most suitable name for the vision would be Autonorama.

These episodes have arisen with a seasonal regularity. In each, lavish promises are made: traffic congestion will be eliminated, collisions will cease, efficiency gains will reduce waste and pollution. Incredible claims are lent plausibility by the impressive new capacities of state-of-the-art technology. Exactly how the technology is to deliver the promised wonders is never precisely specified, but confident reassurances are associated with scientific authority. As Arthur C. Clarke noted in 1968, new technology is just like magic: defying the limits of what had been possible and thereby suggesting that anything is possible.[22]

Audiences (business partners, investors, politicians, voters, drivers) are warned that the trends are inevitable and that they should join them—or get out of the way. Skeptics are disparaged. The promised benefits are held to be about twenty years off: soon enough to attract interest, distant enough to sustain disappointing results for years.[23] But the disappointing results catch up in time, eroding the promoters' credibility. The claims are scaled back (congestion and hazards will be mitigated, not eliminated). The promoters argue that the public does not understand what they have to offer and must be educated to appreciate it, yet audiences grow skeptical and the technofuturistic vision retreats. But memories fade and new technology lends credibility to new promises. A new vision may then emerge. While it lasts, each vision is the excuse for diverting resources from commonsense, affordable transport techniques that are of proven efficacy but cannot credibly promise the miracle cures that sell the technofuturistic visions.

Strictly speaking, *Futurama* and *Futurama II* were General Motors exhibits. In a more general sense, however, futuramas were visions of a version of car dependency that works thanks to state-of-the-art technology. Similarly, as a phenomenon, Autonorama was not confined to Expo 2010, and is as ubiquitous today as ever. Autonorama's technofuturism is borrowed from the first three futuramas, to which were added essential new elements: sensors, machine learning, and networked digital automation. Defined in this more general way, Autonorama has been hard to miss wherever transportation futures have been the

Since 1940, technofuturistic visions of crash-free, congestion-free driving have emerged roughly every 25 years (author). Each invokes new technology to gain new credibility.

technofuturistic vision	era	transformative technology
Futurama 1	circa 1940	*engineering*: highway engineering, steel-reinforced concrete, vacuum tube electronics
Futurama 2	circa 1965	*electronics*: solid-state, transistorized electronic systems; jet-age and space-age hardware
Futurama 3	circa 1990	(*advanced*) *technology*: "smart" systems, microprocessors, digital computers
Futurama 4 (Autonorama)	circa 2015	(*data-driven*) *autonomy*: "next-generation" technology, "disruptive innovation," sensors, machine learning, wireless network connectivity

subject of interest over the last dozen years: in the media, at trade shows, in corporate annual reports, in public policy forums, in private investment venues, and at research universities. Though promotional in its origins, Autonorama survives, adapts, and thrives by working its way into "sponsored" articles in media, policy white papers, and academic research proposals.

Not all high-tech transport is from Autonorama. Where high-tech automation is a tool chosen selectively from the wide sociotechnical spectrum of tools—from zero tech to future tech—serving transport purposes chosen with equal selectivity, high-tech transport is just high-tech transport. Self-driving road vehicles may well serve as useful and valuable tools in versatile transport systems. But Autonorama is evident wherever AVs are represented as inevitable solutions, or as ends in themselves rather than as means to ends.

Autonorama is the place where old-fashioned car dependency is lent new credibility through the application of a fresh gloss of high-tech novelty, where simple possibilities are neglected not because of their inferiority but because of their simplicity, and where implausible promises of perfection divert attention from practical possibilities of actual improvement. In Autonorama, transportation research looks like public relations (and vice versa), theoretically possible performance is equated with actual performance, and technology is less a human means to human-chosen ends than a mysteriously willful entity that inevitably delivers ever-better solutions, the merits of which are proportional to their technological sophistication.

Selling driving

In his 1921 film *The Kid*, Charlie Chaplin has a two-person business. As the Tramp, Chaplin is a glazier who repairs broken windows. His adoptive child, the Kid, stealthily throws stones to break windows, thereby sustaining demand for the senior partner's services. As a business model, it's an obvious winner. What's less obvious is that among its real-world analogues are the businesses that sell cars, including those selling cars with automated driving systems.

Since the 1920s, automotive enterprises have been in the business of not just selling cars but sustaining and expanding demand for driving as well. Like the Tramp, these businesses propose to sell solutions to problems that they also create. In neither case, however, is the solution real. The Tramp's customers can expect their windows to be broken again. Motordom's customers—not only the car-buying public but also the public policy makers motordom depends upon—are caught up in a perpetual consumption machine, pursuing expensive but elusive solutions in vain.

Vehicles with advanced automated driving systems, misleadingly called autonomous vehicles,[24] are nowhere near to being the solutions their promoters claim them to be. Yet AVs do work exceedingly well in one essential respect. Such vehicles credibly pretend to be categorically different from their predecessors. Though AVs are really just automatic cars, they are indeed different enough to persuade many to trust them to do what their predecessors could not: deliver safe, sustainable, affordable, and efficient mobility. In this respect, AVs have been working superbly. A future of sustainable mobility, however, will require seeing AVs for what they are: more of the same.[25] They offer nothing really new. Instead of car dependency, they offer only high-tech car dependency.

Automakers and tech companies present AVs as categorically new. This portrayal is essential to the promotional effort, because AVs are supposed to cure the ills that conventional cars caused. But the promises that AVs will be safer overall, that they will be cleaner, and that they will be more efficient do not bear close scrutiny. Nevertheless they retain a credibility that far exceeds their actual possibilities. In this way, too, they are a continuity.

AVs may be useful, but they can't solve all our problems, and can even make them worse. Far from bad news, however, this fact is a heartening starting point. It frees us from untying the Gordian knots that tie shut the gates to the promised AV future. Once we turn our attention from that thankless task, we will find that much simpler, more affordable, and more practical possibilities surround us. We do not have to equip two billion personal cars with lithium-ion batteries, lidar, and other sensors. We do not have to find sustainable ways to manage a doubling in grid load to supply enough electric power for them all. We do not have to apply machine learning to develop algorithms that can predict a pedestrian's path as reliably as a human driver can. High-tech tools are useful, but we have vastly more at our disposal.

Suppose today's medical experts could travel back in time, taking supplies along, and offer people of 150 years ago three modern medical techniques. Which three would yield the best medical benefit: MRI systems, dialysis machines, and stents? Or sanitation, vaccines, and antiseptics? The question is not which three are the most technically impressive but which would make the greatest difference for the most people. The answer is obvious. Yet we are being asked to accept transport boons from the future that (we are assured) will be breathtaking in their technical capacities—when our most essential mobility needs can be better met with tools we already have.

If most people could walk to a convenience store, we wouldn't have to figure out how to get everyone access to a robotic car that would take them there. If most children had safe ways to bike to school, we wouldn't have to design school driveways long enough to accommodate driverless car lines for dropping them off and picking them up. If most bus stops were sheltered and equipped—thanks to technology—with digital signs telling bus riders exactly when the next bus will arrive, we wouldn't have to commit so much research effort and money to developing high-tech systems that can fit more driverless cars in a given road lane. By recognizing the promise of high-tech driving as illusory, we have our best chance of recognizing all that we can do. When we rescue innovation from the technofuturists and recover the tools they have dismissed, we will find that we can do today, at far less cost, what the they have promised to deliver for unlimited dollars at an ever-receding future date.

CHAPTER 1

Futurama 1: New Horizons

There will always be new horizons.
—*General Motors*, Research Looks to
New Horizons

In the early 1920s, American automobile manufacturers feared that demand for their vehicles was approaching saturation.[1] Most people who wanted and could afford a car already had one. Most sales would be replacements for worn-out cars. Unpaved rural roads were one limitation, though Ford's Model T was equal to most of them. But in cities—despite their paved streets—sales were disappointing. Cities were unwelcoming environments for drivers. Parking was scarce and speed limits were low. Pedestrians, including children, felt entitled to walk in streets. Drivers had to drive slowly and watchfully. Traffic casualties were high, and in cities, most of those injured or killed were on foot. Many of the victims were children. The press, the law, and public opinion generally blamed drivers. In cities, drivers were easy to caricature as a privileged minority. Personal passenger cars were typically called pleasure cars, and extensive electric railways generally made driving unnecessary. The conventional wisdom was that passenger cars would never serve most urban transportation needs.

In the 1920s, American automobile manufacturers, auto clubs, and their allies organized to improve conditions for drivers. They learned to cooperate, sometimes even under a common name. As motordom, they backed gasoline taxes on condition that the revenues go to paved roads. They organized to win priority for drivers on city streets, discouraging jaywalking with publicity campaigns and city ordinances. They used press releases to shift blame for street casualties from drivers to pedestrians, and from speed to reckless driving. They also worked to influence developing standards of traffic and highway engineering in ways that were favorable to drivers.

Keep the consumer dissatisfied

General Motors emerged as a leader in this effort. GM saw no reason to wait until its customers' cars had worn out to sell them a replacement. By redesigning each model every year, it induced some customers to come back to the showroom sooner. GM offered its customers opportunities to show off their success too. A Chevrolet owner who got a promotion and a raise need not be lost to another carmaker. GM could offer an Oakland or a Pontiac, then an Oldsmobile or a Buick. At the top of GM's "ladder of success" was the Cadillac.

The genius behind these techniques was Charles Kettering. In 1929 Kettering distilled his advice into an article, written for *Nation's Business*, with a memorable title: "Keep the Consumer Dissatisfied." "If everyone were satisfied," he explained, "no one would buy the new thing."[2] To Kettering, transport sufficiency was a threat to motordom's future. He advocated perpetual insufficiency, propelled by an ever-receding promise of future perfection. In short, Kettering was advocating not transport but transport consumerism. At GM the idea developed and acquired a name: futurama.

Motordom applied the technique to sell not only cars but driving too. Its leaders learned that in order to sell cars where sales resistance was high—particularly in cities, where cars were blamed for congestion and casualties—driving had to be reframed as the solution instead of the problem. By the standards of the early 1920s, motor vehicles clogged traffic and made streets dangerous. In the 1930s, motordom guided the development of highway engineering to redefine traffic congestion and traffic safety in ways that exonerated motor vehicles. In the 1920s, automobiles were the worst offenders in traffic congestion because of their high spatial demands per passenger. In the new field of highway engineering, funded by gasoline tax revenues and guided by its promoters in motordom, vehicles' capacity for speed made them potential congestion relievers, provided highway capacity was sufficient to permit speed. Conversely, wherever motor vehicles slowed one another down below the road's designed speed limit, this was to be defined as "delay," and though delay was caused by the vehicles themselves, it was to be regarded as an economic burden on the public measurable in terms of the value of vehicle occupants' time. Wherever traffic slowed vehicles down, the consequent delay was therefore grounds for building new road capacity.[3]

With motordom's help, a similar transformation redefined traffic safety.[4] In the 1920s, speed made motor vehicles dangerous. But highway engineering promised to make speed safe, and to redirect blame for crashes to deficient highway design. A leading proponent of motorage highway engineering, Miller McClintock, developed the idea and gave it expert standing. In 1934 McClintock described "the fool-proof highway of the future," where collisions would be practically impossible. Writing for *Safety Engineering*, McClintock asked: "Are fool-proof highways possible?" He had a straight answer: yes.

McClintock characterized "education of drivers and the punishment of offenders" as necessary but insufficient efforts that tended to distract safety experts from the key: foolproof road design. "The highway, itself, must be built in such a way that accident will be impossible." Such roads offered drivers "safe speeds up to fifty miles per hour to the very centers of congested cities." The essential design features? "Traffic streams moving in opposite directions are physically separated. All intersections are eliminated." There is "no connection with any abutting property and entrances and exits . . . are arranged at convenient intervals by specially designed structures."

McClintock could cite no actual performance data, but he confidently resorted to commonsense reasoning: "In 1933 nine hundred people were killed in the City of Chicago in traffic accidents. An examination of the cause of each of these accidents reveals that only seventeen of them would have been possible if all traffic had been moving on limited ways." For example, "about half our fatalities are the result of collisions between motor cars and pedestrians. There are no pedestrians on limited ways and, hence, no pedestrians can be killed on such a structure." McClintock did not speculate about how the hoped-for speed of limited ways might make the rarer collisions more deadly. He nevertheless assured readers that such roads promised "permanent safety."[5]

According to McClintock, vehicular hazards were due to four kinds of "friction": medial friction (between opposing traffic streams), intersectional friction (where streets crossed each other); marginal friction (along the roadside); and internal stream friction (between vehicles in the same lane traveling at different speeds). Well-designed motor highways would practically eliminate the first three frictions. To reporters, McClintock promised that with such highways, "we could eliminate 98 per cent of all accidents and practically all congestion."[6]

The urban highway projects of the 1930s and 1940s were, in theory, responses to a growing demand for driving. But especially after the Great Depression reduced driving substantially, the projects were sold as ways to stimulate demand for cars. For example, to Harry Hollingshead, a Nash car dealer and president of the Chicago Automobile Trade Association, building elevated highways was a way to sell more cars, plain and simple. In 1938 Hollingshead told his colleagues that with a network of elevated highways in Chicagoland, residents would spend 21.8 percent more money each year buying new cars and maintaining them.[7]

"It is obvious," Hollingshead said, "that with elevated highways for safe and rapid travel there would be more inducement for a person to own an automobile." Congestion limits "the sale of automobiles and supplies. Many Chicagoans and suburbanites now using other forms of transportation would prefer to use the more convenient automobile were it not for the congestion encountered within city limits. It is simple mathematics to estimate that a man who uses his car going to business six days a week will buy more automobiles and will buy more parts than the one who uses it only on Sunday." He concluded: "Every one interested in the growth of the automobile industry will want elevated highways built as speedily as possible."[8]

To sell cars where cars were a poor fit, motordom learned to sell driving. But selling driving is hard. A dealer can sell a paying customer a good car in an hour, but promises of congestion-free driving, in safety and convenience, cannot be fulfilled quickly. Meanwhile traffic jams, casualty lists, parking tickets, and other woes make driving unattractive, even in a fine new car. Motordom could not sell driving as most people knew it. It had to sell a vision of driving, one that appeared credible while being attractive enough to persuade people to accept short-term dissatisfaction in the hope of future contentment. In the 1930s, motordom learned to depict attractive, car-dependent futures and to sell them.

The drive-everywhere, drive-only city

The promises of safe and congestion-free driving remained elusive. In the United States, though the Great Depression diminished both congestion and crashes, these maladies returned with economic recovery. In 1935, as traffic casualties rose, *Reader's Digest* published a vivid exposé of the horrific effect of road crashes on the people they maimed and killed.[9] In terms of risk of death per vehicle mile driven, the worst year in US history was 1937, when thirty-eight thousand Americans were killed on roads and streets. And though motordom was convinced of the merits of its new models of congestion and safety, older attitudes persisted in the press, in legislatures, and among the public.

Under these pressures, motordom developed a new strategy. No matter what the expenditure on roads and highways, in no given year could it deliver marked improvement. What was needed was a clear vision of a more distant and idealized future toward which motordom was striving. The promise of future perfection can buy tolerance of present affliction. And if the promise is both visually convincing and far into the future, it can even win confidence. Beginning separately in the mid-1930s, sources within motordom began to conceive of and present the drive-everywhere city of the future. By 1939 they were showing it to millions at a monumental scale.

In 1936 General Motors launched its first *Parade of Progress*: a traveling exhibition of eight bus-sized vehicles called Streamliners that toured the country, visiting fairgrounds and displaying visions of transportation to the public. Exhibits portrayed the past, present, and future of transportation as a progress story culminating in universal driving.[10] Also in 1936, the Shell Union Oil Corporation (later Shell Oil Company) was looking for a way to expand its small US market share. Gasoline was just nineteen cents a gallon at the pump, and a future of greater demand for gasoline was naturally of interest. Shell turned to legendary advertising agency J. Walter Thompson, a pioneer of subtle advertising that attracted readers.

Thompson executives saw an opportunity to use McClintock's "fool-proof highways" concept in an ad campaign to promote driving. To depict a future city, where everyone drove but there were no delays and no hazards, Thompson hired Norman Bel Geddes. A former stage designer, Bel Geddes had reinvented himself as a versatile practitioner of modern design; he had recently designed interiors and furnishings for Thompson's offices.[11] Thompson teamed him with Miller McClintock, with a notion of developing a series of advertisements illustrating the City of Tomorrow—a place where everyone drove everywhere (thanks to Shell gasoline)—and at 50 miles per hour with no traffic lights. For use in Shell ads, Bel Geddes built an elaborate model of the future drive-everywhere city.

McClintock offered advice and, above all, the value of his endorsement as the nation's leading traffic authority.[12]

Shell's model was built for an ad campaign, but on June 1, 1937, weeks before the first ad appeared, Miller McClintock presented it in a photographic slide show to the National Planning Conference in Detroit. The conference was a joint meeting of the American City Planning Institute, the American Planning and Civic Association, the American Society of Planning Officials, and the National Economic and Social Planning Association. McClintock called his address "Of Things to Come."[13] "The city of tomorrow," he told his audience, "will be an automotive city."[14] As he showed the audience photographs of the City of Tomorrow, McClintock never mentioned Shell's sponsorship. In his address, the model was all city planning, not marketing.

At the conference, McClintock made an eloquent plea for a city worthy of the "automotive revolution." He invoked the "vision, initiative, and boldness of American planners." He appealed to them above all on the grounds of public health, referencing the "annual toll of 36,000 lives and more than a million injuries." But he also contended that the automobile's practical benefits were hampered. Liberating them safely would require correcting "basic maladjustments in automotive transportation which will never yield to palliatives but can be cured only by major surgery." McClintock called for an alternative to "'stop-and-go' traffic" through the separation of opposing traffic streams, generous road shoulders, and grade separation at intersections. Such "limited ways" would eliminate the "frictions" between traffic streams "from which all accidents and all congestion arose."[15]

The City of Tomorrow still had no estimated date of arrival. The model included Manhattan's 1913 Woolworth Tower as an indication of how the new would pervade the old. McClintock, projecting himself into the future, described the building as "a monument to man's architectural daring a hundred years ago," suggesting that the model was set in the early twenty-first century. Beneath a network of limited ways lie streets "not unlike those of the old city except that there is no pedestrian traffic, as this is raised to an upper level along the streets and bridging the intersections." Parking garages "are a natural, integral part of every building." Pedestrians would thrive in the City of Tomorrow. "All of the land uses are so arranged and interconnected" so that a pedestrian can walk "with some degree of security and dignity. No longer is he required to fight his way across roadways filled with uncongenial vehicles. He moves on his own level raised above the flow of vehicular traffic." McClintock closed by asking his audience, "Are we to have an opportunity to utilize the full efficiencies of the automotive revolution or are we to continue to suffer the inconveniences and hazards of the present day? The answer to these questions lies largely in the hands of the planning profession."[16]

The model toured the country; elsewhere, where it was not on display, McClintock presented the slideshow of it. It was a sensation at the Milwaukee auto show that

November, where it was described as a model of Milwaukee in 1960—"when traffic problems will be a thing of the past."[17] Now tiny cars traveled in slots along the highways. In the summer and fall of 1937, magazines and newspapers carried Shell's ads. The largest were two-page spreads. The copy introduced Bel Geddes as an "authority on future trends," and ambitiously set the City of Tomorrow in 1960, promising that "motorists of 1960 will loaf along at 50—right through town."[18] Perhaps noticing the attention the model attracted, *Popular Science* ran an illustrated feature on the "Highways of the Future."[19]

In 1938, as GM was planning its exhibits for the 1939–40 New York World's Fair, the company's initial plan was to renew its exhibit at the 1933 Century of Progress fair in Chicago: a full-scale mockup of a Chevrolet assembly line. Bel Geddes, hoping to build upon his success with Shell, pressed GM executives to consider expanding his City of Tomorrow model instead, developing it into an exhibit. GM agreed, and under Bel Geddes's direction, the company began planning one of the greatest exhibits ever presented. The enormous *Futurama*, housed within GM's Highways and Horizons pavilion, would bring millions of fairgoers a breathtaking look at a future city where everyone drove everywhere. Motordom was learning to sell not just products but a future in which demand for its products would be permanently assured. It was a fitting response to an economic depression blamed on insufficient demand. Before the decade ended, an oil company, auto manufacturers, and road builders would all be using the technique.

Highways of Tomorrow

As its 1939 annual meeting approached, the American Road Builders Association, a trade association representing contractors, joined the trend of depicting a utopian future. ARBA's theme for the conference was "Highways of Tomorrow."[20] Held at San Francisco's Civic Auditorium, the vast convention drew twenty thousand participants. To unite the road builders' vision of the future, the auditorium housed a model divided highway with grade-separated intersections. ARBA's leaders, Charles Upham and Murray Van Wagoner, proposed an increase of one cent per gallon in the federal gas tax to finance such roads.

To open the convention, ARBA's president, Van Wagoner, presented a vision of a future of superhighways—the "highways of tomorrow."[21] As Michigan's highway commissioner and a future governor, he was well positioned to promote his cause. He declared that "the intolerable traffic congestion and shameful accident record in modern America constitutes a public disgrace." He proposed "a nation-wide program of superhighway construction" leading to "a new national system of superhighways." He cautioned his audience: "There will be those who accuse us of dreaming. But 25 years from now, our children will look back with the same recollections of horror of present-day traffic congestion that we recall in reflecting upon the nightmare of mud roads of our own youth."[22]

In proposing a network of long-distance motor highways, ARBA conferees took their example from Germany's new highways. Van Wagoner could speak from experience:

"It has been my pleasure to travel over these autobahns, which certainly give to Germany an outstanding leadership in the development of limited access highways."[23] Such roads served both military and employment needs while operating as commercial arteries. ARBA's engineer-director, Charles Upham, praised the German example as well: "Germany is our test tube or laboratory."[24] He said, "The German program is outstanding because it is a complete system of highways connecting the greater centers of population of the entire nation."[25] Another speaker also extolled German "super-roads."[26]

Unlike the German highways, however, American highways should go through the centers of cities, according to the speakers. Van Wagoner said: "I cannot overemphasize the urban phase of superhighway development. It is certainly the most important." Superhighways "should be started in our larger cities and the industrial sections of our country where the traffic volume is the greatest." Such highways were for "getting people in and out of our cities at moderate speeds rather than with the present intolerable delay and congestion," including "the smaller cities with as few as 50,000 population."[27]

Addressing ARBA conferees, L. I. Hewes of the Bureau of Public Roads (BPR) concurred: highways should run "from the country into the heart of the city, and particularly into the centers of the larger cities."[28] Hewes quoted his boss, BPR chief Thomas H. MacDonald: "Special motor roads in congested areas" should lead "from the hearts of the cities through metropolitan areas, designed to permit free flow of traffic separated from cross-traffic."[29]

Conferees heard from an ARBA committee on elevated highways, which recommended such routes for cities. The committee was headed by V. G. Iden, secretary of the American Institute of Steel Construction, and included Miller McClintock as a member. The committee found that "traffic congestion is crying out to high heaven for a solution which seems to become simple and economical with the elevated highway."[30] Besides congestion relief, the projects were justified by the demands of safety. According to one speaker: "The surest way to reduce the bloody orgy on our highways is to incorporate every known possible safety device in the highway. This means an era of constructing roads with safety built in the highway itself."[31]

ARBA's ambitious public relations team was learning from consumer marketing techniques. Included on the program in San Francisco was a public relations man, E. W. Moeller of Minneapolis. Moeller attributed road-builders' past successes to "mass selling" that "succeeded in molding public opinion in conformity with the ideology of these organized minority groups."[32] But "the call of the hour" for motor-age highways was in trouble: "The demand for improved roads comes only from the highway engineers and the highway commissioners. . . . It is not now the voice of the people." Only "a public relations program" could "secure public support." Americans had to "be informed, educated, propagandized, if you please, on the subject of roads." Road builders had much to learn about marketing, Moeller said. "Today, our industry is competing with 'Grape-Nuts,' 'Charlie McCarthy,' Campbell's Tomato Soups, sinus medicants, beer, a skin you love to touch, tooth powders that whiten the teeth, and cigarettes that satisfy, are toasted, easy on the throat, ad infinitum, ad nauseam." The highway industry had to join in the public relations fray or risk losing popular and political support. "You know what this means? It means decreased revenues."[33]

Conference goers could visit the recently opened Golden Gate Exposition on Treasure Island, where yet another industry was unveiling the city of the future. In the U.S. Steel exhibit, a thirty-five-foot-long moving diorama imagined the San Francisco of 1999: a city of steel-framed skyscrapers and steel-supported, grade-separated elevated highways.[34] According to the *Oakland Tribune*, the model demonstrated "the solution of traffic problems" through "cloverleaf intersections, elevated highways . . . and subway lines instead of surface cars," all requiring structural steel.[35]

"Keep the consumer dissatisfied" can work only if the seller can persuade the consumer that eventual satisfaction is forthcoming, and that the seller has it on offer. What is impossible today is possible tomorrow—such is technology's promise. In the 1930s, motordom developed the technique; by 1939 it had a name: futurama. Futuramas depict utopian futures of about twenty years hence: soon enough to be relevant to consumers, but sufficiently distant to avert distrust and disillusionment when reality disappointed—as it always did. Each successive generation of promise makers could invoke new technological developments as indications that this time, success was assured—even inevitable. In 1939 and 1940, at the New York World's Fair, millions of Americans encountered futurama for the first time. It has been with us ever since; today it is selling the "self-driving future."

Ever-receding horizons

"Keep the consumer dissatisfied" was a message directed by business to business, not to the general public. However valid as a principle of business success at the dawn of consumerism, it had to be stated in other terms for consumers themselves. How could business palatably impart the notion that there can be no state of lasting contentment, when only replacement purchases are necessary? How could it positively entice consumers to tread on, seeing each achievement as but a step of transitory satisfaction on an infinite trail of acquisition? In the 1930s, General Motors' answer lay in the metaphor of the horizon. As one approaches a horizon, it recedes, yielding ever-new horizons. The rewards of consumption lay in the journey itself, which never ends.

The word *horizons* appears with striking regularity throughout the history of the City of Tomorrow. Bel Geddes called his 1932 book on design *Horizons*. In a 1934 history of General Motors, Arthur Pound celebrated GM cars for making America "a nation of travelers moving on ever improving highways at an ever increasing tempo toward wider and wider horizons, higher and higher standards of living."[36] The 1937 planning conference in Detroit, where McClintock presented Shell's model to planners, published its proceedings as *New Horizons in Planning.*

As it planned its massive exhibit for the 1939–40 world's fair, General Motors developed the theme. It used the term in a small book called *Research Looks to New Horizons*, celebrating GM's innovations. "One of the hardest things to understand about a research man's work is that it's never ended. There is always something more to do. . . . Ever he works with an eye to the future, constantly pressing to new horizons for discoveries which will make better living available to growing numbers of people." According to the book's final sentence: "There will always be new horizons."[37] On April 19, 1939, GM dedicated its new Highways and Horizons pavilion at the New York World's Fair at an exclusive dinner it called Highways to New Horizons.[38] The guests were among the first to see the World of Tomorrow, including the city of 1960, in the massive *Futurama* (a diorama of the future) exhibit. That June, in a letter inviting GM dealers to a preview of *Futurama*, board chairman Alfred P. Sloan used the word *horizons* twelve times.

Sloan concluded: "It is the hope of General Motors that the visitor to HIGHWAYS AND HORIZONS at the New York World's Fair will be inspired with a greater realization of the fact that the 'World of Tomorrow' can be made an infinitely better place in which to live, with greater opportunities for all; that industry is moving forward toward that objective." If American business can "broaden the highways of research and science that lead to better things, better methods and new opportunities, we can begin to unfold the possibilities of the 'World of Tomorrow' and more rapidly move forward along the true HIGHWAYS TO NEW HORIZONS OF BETTER LIVING."[39] Sloan repeated these appeals in the official *Futurama* booklet.[40] With every advance, the horizon recedes, enticing the consumer to press on toward the promised land.

According to an editorial in an engineering journal, "The entire Futurama and encompassing building is a masterpiece in the application of engineering skill, architectural finesse, and directed psychology."[41] GM's public relations director, Paul Garrett, explained to his fellow GM executives what the company hoped *Futurama* would achieve: "It may well mark the beginning of a new era in road construction which will greatly stimulate the use and sale of cars, at a time when the saturation point may have been reached." *Futurama* would induce "a public enthusiasm for improved highways."[42]

Within GM, *Futurama*'s purpose was to stimulate the use and sale of cars. The message to visitors, however, was quite different: Demand for cars was so high, and growing so fast, that road capacity had been left far behind. Road building would have to follow. Hence road building was necessary not to stimulate latent demand for cars but accommodate actual demand for them. In the entry hall of *Futurama*, before they could sit in the comfortable chairs that would carry them to the World of Tomorrow, visitors saw an enormous map of the United States with lighted roads. A voice warned: "During the next twenty years, motor traffic on some of our main highways is expected to increase by as much as 100 per cent—particularly in and about metropolitan areas. The number of motorcars by 1960 may reach from between 35,000,000 to 38,000,000." The voice offered a solution. "The 1960 congestion may conceivably be relieved through the development and use of Motorways—particularly through and between our larger cities."[43]

Futurama was by far the most popular exhibit at the New York World's Fair. It could handle about twenty-five thousand visitors a day, and lines to enter the Highways and Horizons building were often hundreds of yards long. Footsore visitors enjoyed the relief that came with sitting in the exhibit's cushioned, moving chairs. The "carry-go-round" of 552 seats transported them along a winding rail track three-tenths of a mile long, from which they observed the World of Tomorrow below them as through an airplane window. As they watched during their sixteen-minute flight, a man's soothing voice described the wonders below.

The equipment required for synchronized recorded sound was prodigious; according to GM, it was called "twenty-tons-of-voice." The model was vast. Covering four-fifths of an acre, it included a million tiny trees, half a million buildings, and fifty thousand automobiles—ten thousand of which actually traveled along slots in the model highways. At the end of the ride, visitors rose from the carry-go-round and left the building, only to find themselves overlooking the full-scale Street of Tomorrow. From elevated pedestrian sidewalks, visitors looked to a pedestrian-free street intersection below, crowded with GM cars (1940 models).[44]

Earlier, in the comfort of their "sound chairs" on the carry-go-round, visitors saw the "wonder world of 1960" pass beneath them as they approached a "magic city of progress."[45] The voice coming from a speaker in each chair explained what they saw:

"Here we see one of our 1960 express Motorways. . . . This superb one-direction highway, with its seven lanes accommodating traffic at designated speeds of 50, 75 and 100 miles an hour, is engineered for easy grades and for curves that require no reduction in speed." From a "traffic control tower . . . experts advise drivers by radio control signals when and how they may safely move from one traffic lane to another." As the model disclosed its wonders, the voice asked: "Strange? Fantastic? Unbelievable? Remember, this is the world of 1960!" The horizons theme was repeated. "This vision of 1960 dramatizes possible highway progress—highways to new horizons of a country's welfare and happiness. . . . This 1960 drama of highway and transportation progress is but a symbol of future progress in every activity made possible by constant striving toward new and better horizons."[46]

As the highway approached a great city, the traffic on it did not slow. Through highway design, engineers had achieved "the elimination of congestion and bottle-necking of the various converging Motorways and feeder

Fairgoers viewed the first *Futurama* as if they were traveling to the future by air. Below they saw a "city of tomorrow" in which car dependency works. (General Motors, LLC)

roads." The city has been "replanned around a highly developed modern traffic system, and, even though this is 1960, the system as yet is not complete." It's a slumless utopia, and this is no accident: "Whenever possible, the rights of way of these express city thoroughfares have been so routed as to displace outmoded business sections and undesirable slum areas."[47] Though Shell's City of Tomorrow made some provision for parking, in the *Futurama*, parking was never shown and never mentioned. The ten thousand moving vehicles merely disappeared at the end of their journey, to travel back underneath the model and return to the beginning.

When the fair closed in the fall of 1940, *Futurama* was dismantled. Only fragments were preserved. GM, however, distributed films of the *Futurama* ride, including a color movie called *To New Horizons*. Its almost hypnotically soothing narrator delivered a variation on the voice visitors heard in *Futurama*. "Old horizons open the way to new horizons," yielding "the promise of more tomorrow. . . . More desires have developed to be satisfied." Of the roads themselves, the narrator said, "The keynote of this motorway: safety. Safety with increased speed," in part because "safe distance between cars is maintained by automatic radio control."

The narrator's conclusion was rhapsodic: "Every forward outlook reminds us that all the highways of all research and all communication—all the activities of science—lead us onward to better methods of doing things, with new opportunity for employment and better ways of living, as we go

on, determined to unfold the constantly greater possibilities of the world of tomorrow, as we move more and more
rapidly forward, penetrating new horizons in the spirit of
individual enterprise, in the great American way."

The theme of endless striving carried even into the closing text: instead of THE END, it read "Without END."[48]

There was irony in the appeal to "individual enterprise."
Writer Walter Lippmann did not miss it. "General Motors
has spent a small fortune to convince the American public
that if it wishes to enjoy the full benefit of private enterprise in motor manufacture it would have to rebuild its cities and its highways by public enterprise."[49] In the decades
that followed, motordom embraced the paradox. Motordom would strive, through public policy, and with public
money, to destroy and rebuild American surface transportation around motor vehicle travel, in ways that deprived
travelers of a marketplace of competing modes, with the
express intention of promoting demand for motor vehicles. All the while, motordom would propagate the notion
that public policy was merely following mass preferences,
and that the entire conversion was the consequence of the
free market.

As they left *Futurama*, visitors received a lapel button
reading simply: I HAVE SEEN THE FUTURE. It was not *a*
future—one of many countless possible futures—but *the*
future, according to General Motors. GM had long ago
abandoned mere selling in response to demand. It aspired
to construct a future that would produce the new demands
necessary to reach it.

CHAPTER 2

Futurama 2: Magic Highway, USA

Automatic driving of automobiles is desirable for the prevention of accidents, and what is desirable is in this case possible.
—Vladimir Zworykin, RCA

In the 1940s, '50s, and '60s, true to Kettering's precept, motordom continued selling unattainable futures. In its usual form, the technique meant annually unveiling futuristic mock-ups, publicizing new features, and applying jet-age design aesthetics. By keeping automobile consumers dissatisfied with last year's models, companies hoped to spur demand for next year's lineup.

But many businesses in motordom, GM and Ford in particular, also sold futures of congestion-free driving. They offered apparently plausible visions of a drive-everywhere, drive-only city—a city where all motorists could drive anywhere at any time, without delay, and park for free when they got there. That such a future was not a practical possibility was no reason not to sell it. Credibly presented, attractive but impossible tomorrows justify spending—both personal spending on cars and public spending on roads. What they needed was a vision of perfection in a future soon enough to attract interest, but far enough away to forestall accountability. In 1939 GM set this horizon at twenty years; it has remained there ever since.

Magic Highway, USA

The examples are many. GM resumed its *Parade of Progress* in 1953, beginning a three-year tour. Included in the traveling exhibit was a model of an urban highway that somehow magically eliminated traffic congestion even though it could not possibly have served a city of the extreme density depicted. Millions saw this roadshow in the 1950s, but GM's postwar futures found much more vivid forms elsewhere. GM staged the most elaborate auto shows of the era, typically presenting them at the Waldorf-Astoria in New York. Beginning in 1953, the GM show took the name Motorama, evoking the futurism of GM's 1939–40 *Futurama* exhibit. Occasional Motoramas were held at the Waldorf-Astoria and other venues from 1953 to 1961.

At the 1956 Motorama, GM presented a film, later distributed nationally, that again depicted a collision-free, congestion-free, drive-anywhere future.[1] The crash-free highway promise was developed much more fully than it had been at the 1939 World's Fair, and presented this time on film in a new, high-resolution, wide-screen format called VistaVision. In *Key to the Future*, a family of four gets stuck in a traffic jam because of inadequate highway capacity. The teenage son sets the radio to 1976, magically transporting the four twenty years into the future. They find themselves in a gas-turbine Firebird II (a GM concept car), where the father, assisted by a traffic-control officer in a tower, guides the car onto a "safety autoway." There he lets go of the steering wheel as the car drives itself at high speed with perfect safety. An onboard electronic "autopilot" keeps the car on "autocontrol" for "hands-off steering" in a "high-speed safety lane."[2]

Motorama visitors could see an even more fanciful film, *Design for Dreaming*.[3] In a dream, a woman is whisked away by a mysterious man to the Waldorf-Astoria to attend the GM Motorama spectacle. He shows her—and even buys her—GM cars and invites her on a drive to "the place where tomorrow meets today." Again in Firebird II, they travel "the electronic highway of the future." Ethereal voices sing, "Tomorrow, tomorrow, our dreams will come true. / Together, together, we'll make the world new."

The nation's general-purpose trade association, the US Chamber of Commerce, followed GM's lead in presenting utopian futures to be delivered twenty years hence by technological consumerism. In 1955 it released a film called *People, Products and Progress 1975*, hosted by its executive vice president, Arch Booth.[4] Seventeen businesses contributed animated segments, each depicting its part in the utopia of 1975. Among them, RCA promised "electronic devices to alert the driver to road conditions far ahead—plus an automatic brain that will park the car." In a self-driving "highway cruiser . . . electronic guidance and obstacle warning devices will keep the car under control, and will eliminate the need for a driver once the car is on the highway and headed in the right direction." The film's ending evoked the ever-new horizons that GM had promised in the 1930s and '40s: "Each new threshold we attain will be only a springboard to still another threshold." The closing frame was much like that of GM's *Futurama* film: "THE END—or is it only the beginning?"[5]

The Portland Cement Association's contribution to the film included high-tech concrete highways, promising safe, congestion-free driving at high speeds. Booth narrated, calling the scene "a preview of the city of tomorrow, as envisioned by the cement industry," with "ever-expanding use of concrete." The film presented "the future heavy-duty superhighway, separated by multilevel structures, and offering high-speed travel at maximum safety." Beneath a reinforced concrete arena was "a mammoth parking garage."

The Portland Cement Association developed its highway idea further, embedding it in an episode of *Disneyland*, a popular prime-time television show. The trade association sponsored a 1958 episode, which was called "Magic Highway, U.S.A."[6] Besides the cement industry, others in motordom contributed to the film, among them the Automotive Safety Foundation (funded by the Automobile Manufacturers Association, to which the greatest contributor was General Motors), the Ford Motor Company, and Ingersoll Rand (a manufacturer of road-building equipment).

Walt Disney hosted the program, telling viewers that "the most important symbol in the progress of our nation is the highway." A narrator explained: "Yes, more and more new highways are being opened each day, but we're still not building them fast enough." Disney added: "There are highway experts—men of vision who try to predict . . . what the highway of the future will be like." He then introduced an animated sequence, characterizing it as "a realistic look at the road ahead and what tomorrow's motorist can expect in the years to come."[7]

The narrator of this part of the film promised viewers, "Speed, safety, and comfort will be the keynotes of tomorrow's highways." Drivers would enjoy "dashboard panels featuring built-in safety controls and electronic operating devices. A teletype panel shows up-to-the-minute traffic bulletins. The recommended safe driving speed is automatically indicated. Our rearview mirror is actually a television picture." The cars can drive themselves. "As Father chooses the route in advance on a push-button selector, electronics take over complete control. Progress can be accurately checked on a synchronized scanning map. With no driving responsibility, the family relaxes together. En route, business conferences are conducted by television."

With "a punched-card system . . . the car is automatically operated and guided to preset destinations. Highly specialized pleasure vehicles will have every convenience of home." Motorists would drive far more, because "the shape of our cities will change as expanded highway transportation decentralizes our population centers into vast urban areas. With the advent of wider, faster expressways, the commuter's radius will be extended many miles." Such roads would usher in a new and better age. "These giant arteries will link together all nations and help create a better understanding among the peoples of the world. As in the past, the highway will continue to play a vital role in the progress of civilization. It will be our magic carpet to new hopes, new dreams, and a better way of life for the future."[8]

Electronics

Like the Portland Cement Association, RCA also further developed the promises it had contributed to *People, Products and Progress 1975*. In promising better tomorrows, RCA had an advantage over the cement industry. It could invoke state-of-the-art electronics. Before World War II, RCA vacuum tubes had transformed mass entertainment in the form of broadcast radio. As radar, electronics was celebrated for its part in the victory by Allied forces. After the war, electronics transformed entertainment again through broadcast television. Large computers—or, as the press called them, "electronic brains"—performed extraordinary feats. In 1952 a big vacuum tube computer named UNIVAC predicted the results of the presidential election on live television, and did so much more accurately than human experts. The stunt attracted extraordinary attention.[9]

In 1947 the transistor—a solid-state substitute for much bigger, fragile, and energy-hungry vacuum tubes—introduced new possibilities in miniature, portable, and durable electronics. By the 1950s, some speculated that the transistor might enable a kind of autopilot for cars. In June 1953, *Mechanix Illustrated* ran a story called "Why Don't We Have Crash-Proof Highways?" Apparently unaware of any actual research project to automate driving, the author reasoned that "recent advances in the printed radio circuits and the use of transistors instead of radio tubes" would make an onboard autopilot system for drivers practical and affordable, making crash-proof highways possible.[10]

By then, RCA was quietly developing a model electronic highway to demonstrate how transistors could make driving safe. The project was led by RCA's Vladimir Zworykin, famous for his part in the development of electronic television. On the cement floor of a basement at RCA's Research Laboratories in Princeton, New Jersey, Zworykin set up a test rig. In summer 1953, Zworykin showed off the setup to John Lear, a reporter for *Collier's* magazine. Zworykin told the reporter: "Automatic driving of automobiles is desirable for the prevention of accidents, and what is desirable is in this case possible." He led Lear to the basement and started one of the electric cars.[11]

"There on the floor before us," Lear recalled, "faithfully following the path of a thin strand of insulated wire taped to the concrete, the five-foot-long red motorcar was driving itself round and round a circle of perhaps 100 feet in circumference." The shiny red car, about one third the size of a production sedan, was occupied: "Seated nonchalantly behind the steering wheel, reading a magazine which squarely blocked any view through the windshield, was a midget-sized dummy, fashionably dressed, with a cigarette dangling from its lips." The car could detect an obstacle in its path; in this case, if the wire offered the car a passing lane, it passed. In the absence of a passing lane, it stopped. Lear was impressed. "I left the place convinced, as Dr. Zworykin was, that we had been testing a small-scale model of the motorcar of the future," he wrote, adding: "I see no reason why the vehicle should not relatively soon take over all the driving on the turnpikes and express roads which are beginning to carry the burden of long-distance travel across the United States." Drivers would drive their cars normally until they reached the electronic highway, when they would flip a switch to let the system take the wheel. Reflecting on the demonstration, Lear wondered "what America's highways might be like 30 years from now"—in 1983. His conclusion: "You will be able to read your newspaper while your auto takes you to work without human guidance."[12]

Time magazine's reporter was impressed, too, and anticipated a day when "cars will speed along the Zworykin highway in a wide and orderly stream, passing and repassing like strands in a braided belt." Released from their task, "the drivers will have nothing to do; they can sleep or play cards or stare at the flowing road." But a note of caution in the story proved prescient in its significance for the automation developments of later decades. "Apprehensive critics point out that Zworykin may be increasing the very hazard he is trying to diminish. Drivers on the New Jersey Turnpike become hypnotized because the beautiful highway demands too little from them to keep them alert. If the highway itself does their driving for them, they may fall even deeper into drivers' coma." Even with full automation, "some irregularity—an electronic failure or a blown front tire" might disrupt the system, and the inattentive drivers would be too slow to respond.[13]

Despite *Time*'s misgivings, divided highways with grade-separated interchanges were being sold as the way to prevent collisions and to relieve—or even eliminate—traffic congestion. While Zworykin was showing off his electronic test track, motordom was lobbying hard for a vast new federal highway program, promising that the roads would prevent deadly crashes and traffic jams. They had a friend in President Eisenhower, who said in 1954 that "metropolitan area congestion" could be "solved" by "a grand plan for a properly articulated highway system."[14] Later the president added that interstate highways would also "save four thousand American lives a year."[15] For this claim, he cited the Automotive Safety Foundation, an interest group established by the Automobile Manufacturers Association.

A wide industry coalition backed a big interstate highway program. They argued that the high cost of building the new roads would be less than the high cost of the congestion and collisions they would prevent. In 1953 a Chrysler vice president told a congressional subcommittee that congestion and collisions on American roads wasted $3 billion every year. New highways could erase this loss, he said—and prevent "about 2 in every 5 traffic deaths." "We pay for good roads whether we have them or not," he told the subcommittee. "And we pay less if we have them than if we do not."[16] With bipartisan support, Congress passed the Federal-Aid Highway Act of 1956 that summer, allocating $25 billion over ten years for a forty-one-thousand-mile Interstate Highway System. The network was to be funded by a new federal Highway Trust Fund, sustained by gasoline and other motor excises committed to right-of-way acquisition and road construction. With this money, the federal government would bear 90 percent of the construction costs of the new Interstate Highway System.[17]

As the vast road projects got under way, RCA worked with the Nebraska Department of Roads to develop a full-scale experimental electronic road: a "highway of the future." The state temporarily closed a four-hundred-foot segment of public highway for the project, just outside of Lincoln. Triggered by the vehicles passing above them, loop detectors embedded in the road pavement transmitted radio signals that operated indicator devices in the car, alerting drivers to deviations from the lane and to approaching hazards. There were no automatic controls; the human drivers managed all the steering, acceleration, and braking. They did so, however, in response to automatic signals that could in principle be used to guide electronic controls. Even for human drivers, the automatic signals promised safety benefits under conditions of poor visibility. They could also get the attention of a drowsy driver (and thereby encourage a driver who should pull over and rest to instead press on).[18] Project personnel told reporters that in a more developed system, drivers could be oriented by voice through the car radio; it might tell them, for example, where the upcoming highway exits could take them.[19]

On Thursday, October 10, 1957, RCA ran a public test of the road, ensuring that the experiment had a large audience of "nearly 100 state and federal highway Officials, representatives of automobile manufacturers, and the press."[20] The test, though successful, did not yield practical results that could be applied on ordinary roads anytime soon. Nevertheless, RCA publicized it as "the first long step" toward the "automatic highway of the future," when, "selecting your lane, you settle back to enjoy the ride as your car adjusts itself to the prescribed speed. You may prefer to read or carry on a conversation with your passengers—or even to catch up on your office work"[21]

Vladimir Zworykin explained: "We are looking into a relatively far distant future in which the human factor will have been entirely removed as a cause of accidents."[22] In the press, such statements could be interpreted generously; according to one reporter, for example: "Electronic highways—on which drivers will be able to doze, watch television or read a book while traveling at prescribed speeds—will become a reality in the foreseeable future."[23]

Meanwhile, at the General Motors Technical Center in Warren, Michigan, a project was already under way to apply the basic vehicle automation demonstrated in Princeton in full-size production cars. In 1957, inspired by the imaginary Motorama highway, Joe Bidwell and Roy Cataldo of the Engineering Mechanics Department began developing a prototype electronic highway that would actually control the car—or at least the steering.

They fitted a 1958 Chevrolet with pickup coils on the front bumper to detect a powered cable embedded in a slit in the pavement of a mile-long concrete test track. Guided by the signals, a small computer in the Chevrolet's glove compartment controlled the steering wheel. Cataldo drove the car, operating the accelerator and the brake, but leaving his hands off the steering wheel even around curves. Steering was the only automated control, but engineers anticipated developing full automation. Tests in January and February 1958 yielded mixed results; in particular, turns were difficult and required very low speeds. By April, however, the automatically steered Chevrolet was reaching 30 miles per hour, and tests were getting flattering reviews in the press.[24]

In 1959 two engineers from Westinghouse's electronics labs near Baltimore, Yaohan Chu and Phillip Buford, announced that they had a radar-based automatic driving system in development. The *Baltimore Sun* reported: "They predict that such driving will be in practical use within five years." It was not a company project; the two worked on their idea on their own time, from their homes in College Park, Maryland, with Westinghouse's approval. Radar on the vehicle would track a strip of metal or metallic paint on the road surface, sending signals to control devices on board. According to the *Sun* reporter, Chu and Buford "believe that within a few years after it is ready for everyday use, the new idea will revolutionize driving in this country and throughout the Western world."

On equipped stretches of limited-access highway, drivers would enter their destination as encoded instructions, then enjoy "looking at the scenery or at television," getting work done, or sleeping. Chu and Buford foresaw "programmed coast-to-coast automatic driving." According to the *Sun*, Chu said that experimental "radar-equipped cars will be a fact within two years," leading the reporter to conclude: "It seems sure that in one way or another the automobile driver's importance will be greatly minimized by automation within the next few years."[25] But much like autonomous vehicle developers of recent years, Chu and Buford found the theorizing far easier than the practical application.

In 1960 RCA and General Motors joined forces to achieve fully automated driving in full-size GM cars on a circular, quarter-mile test track at RCA's Princeton Laboratories—close to the site of Zworykin's demonstrations with miniature electric cars seven years earlier. According to RCA, "the developmental system combined for the first time the electronic vehicle detection and guidance techniques developed over the past seven years by RCA Laboratories, and the automobile control equipment developed by the General Motors Research Laboratories to respond to signals from the RCA roadway circuits." Electrical circuits in the roadbed responded to a conventional car passing above them, relaying radio signals to a specially equipped car following behind. The signals controlled the following car's acceleration and braking, so that it automatically kept at a safe following distance behind the lead car; it was steered automatically too, by the same method that had been used two years earlier on a GM test track in Michigan. One of the test cars in Princeton was the same 1958 Chevrolet that had been automatically steered along the GM test track.[26]

On Sunday, June 5, RCA demonstrated its "electronic highway" for an audience of reporters, highway engineers, and other guests. In one of the tests, a "specially equipped convertible" followed a conventional car, "accelerating, braking, and maintaining a center-of-the-lane course, without assistance from the engineer in the driver's seat." Then a second equipped car "joined the parade, and it too proceeded to perform as if a well-mannered expert driver were at the wheel." The driver of the automatic car kept his hands on his lap as it automatically followed the lead car around the circular track. At the demonstration, Dr. James Hillier, Vice President of RCA Laboratories, told the press and other guests: "We could proceed by gradual steps to an eventual system of fully automatic driving as demonstrated in this pilot system." The test was a glimpse, Hillier said, of a better future: "a new era of convenient, efficient, and safe travel for vehicle drivers and passengers." Proclaiming "tomorrow's thruway is here today!" RCA's company magazine, *Electronic Age*, claimed the test was an advance look at "fully automated travel on superhighways of tomorrow."[27] A *New York Times* reporter raved that system opened "a new world of highway safety." Highway engineers in the audience were also impressed; according to the *Times* reporter, "Many engineers attending the tests gave the opinion that the complex multiple stage system was about 15 years away from mass expressway use."[28]

The promises found expression in the popular press, in news items and advertisements. In a 1961 ad campaign, the Commonwealth of Pennsylvania's Traffic Safety Program urged drivers to keep driving cautiously until electronics eliminated all hazards and congestion. Over the governor's name, the ad assured readers that "science promises a future free of traffic accidents." Credit was due to "the nation's finest automotive and scientific brains," who "predict that someday in the future automobile accidents will be eliminated completely"—in part because of "miraculous electronic devices." Engineers would develop the safe "electronic highway" and the congestion-free "jam-proof expressway." Such highway technology "prevents accidents," plus "radar controls steer the car, setting speeds and making crashes impossible." By "cancelling out the possibilities of human error in the operation of motor vehicles, the scientists and engineers expect to solve most of the problems" of driving, "and move more people greater distances at unprecedented speeds in safety and comfort."[29]

By 1964 RCA was explaining to readers of *Fortune* "how RCA transistors will run your 'electronic' car of tomorrow." Drivers of the future would "sit back and let transistors take over." Onboard electronics would "guide you safely along the electronic lanes of super highways," automatically steering, braking, and accelerating as needed.[30]

Futurama 2

These 1950s developments supported visions of high-tech, car-dependent futures, culminating in exhibits at the 1964–65 New York World's Fair. It was held at the same site in Queens as the world's fair of twenty-five years earlier. Its president was Robert Moses, New York City's veteran parks commissioner and power broker. Moses refused to comply with the standards of the Bureau of International Expositions, so the "world's fair" title was unofficial. Many nations declined to participate, so Moses compensated by raising the profile of major corporations at the fair.

At the 1964 fair, the biggest pavilion again belonged to General Motors. At its giant *Futurama II* pavilion, seated fairgoers were transported through the new exhibit as GM's latest version of the automotive future unfolded before them. The ride could accommodate seventy thousand visitors a day. As before, a solemn recorded voice guided them on a "journey into the future," though this time it was dated only as "the near tomorrow." In a mock-up of an Antarctic research station, the narrator pointed out Weather Central, where scientists were "forecasting to the world the great climatic changes borne in the Antarctic's never-ending winds."

The implicit theme was one of mastery over the natural world—including deserts, rain forests, the ocean floor, and the moon—through technology. Thanks to high-tech roads and vehicles, "people live today where they will, neither terrain nor distance a deterrent to where the men of the city build their homes." In "electronically paced" cars, motorists "travel routes remarkably safe, swift, and efficient." In the "city of tomorrow," we see "plazas of urban living" that "rise over freeways." "Towering terminals" offer ample parking. As usual, the close is rhapsodic: "Its traditions and its faiths preserved, there is new beauty and new strength in the city of tomorrow. Technology can point the way to a future of limitless promise, but man must chart his own course into tomorrow—a course that frees the mind and the spirit, as it improves the wellbeing of mankind."[31]

People who missed *Futurama II* could get a close look at its vision of the future city in a booklet called *Metro-Mobility*.[32] In a preface, Frederic Donner, chairman of General Motors, called for urban transportation "of maximum flexibility." He offered concessions to the advocates of mass transportation. "In some cities a combination of rail and expanded highway systems may be needed," he wrote. "In many of our cities, however, the expanded

The City of Tomorrow, according to *Futurama II*. (General Motors, LLC)

requirements can be met by the prompt completion of planned freeways under the interstate highway program." The goal, he said, was "improving what might be called Metro-Mobility."

In the pages within, the booklet explained how the "advance of science" can "make our highways safer and more pleasant." Readers learned of GM researchers' work on electronic highway systems, which might "automatically and safely steer, brake and accelerate cars, and control the spacing between vehicles on the highway." Cars would follow "a magnetic path" generated by a cable embedded in the pavement along the road. Such a system "would substantially increase highway capacity by safely reducing the space between vehicles" traveling at "normal freeway speeds." Drivers would enter the highway on a conventional lane to the right; they could then transition to the automated "Autoline" lane to the left. As they neared their exit, they would shift back to the conventional lane. Of course, higher-capacity highways would mean more cars flooding cities with drivers searching for parking. The booklet proposed eight-story parking garages that sorted and shelved cars automatically. Exclusive bus lanes were also recommended. It ended by advising readers: "Highway progress is everyone's responsibility. . . . If communities throughout America act with energy and vision, they—and America as a whole—can look forward with confidence to meeting future highway needs."[33]

The Magic Skyway

Ford Motor Company had a popular pavilion at the fair too. Unlike GM's *Futurama II*, Ford's futuristic *Wonder Rotunda* offered fairgoers a chance to ride in real cars along a congestion-free "automated turnpike of tomorrow." The Ford exhibit's main attraction was the Magic Skyway: an indoor ride along a winding track. It was designed by WED Enterprises, Walt Disney's design team, which was named for his personal initials. In the designers' vocabulary, their projects at Disneyland were works of Imagineering, for which they developed "audio animatronics": lifelike, moving human and animal figures that populated scenes along the rides.

In designing Ford's Magic Skyway, WED designers

applied these skills. Brand-new Ford, Mercury, Falcon, Thunderbird, Comet, and Lincoln convertibles—160 of them, all with their tops down—were slowly and silently pulled along an automated "turnpike of tomorrow" by spinning, rubber-tired wheels mounted in the roadway in fixed positions near the centerline of the track; as a car passed over them, the embedded wheels contacted a panel attached to the vehicle's undercarriage, pulling it forward. The cars maintained 4 miles per hour, never stopping. Pavilion personnel escorted fairgoers into the moving Fords from moving platforms that kept pace with the vehicles.

As visitors found their seats in the driverless cars, the recorded voice of Henry Ford II, a grandson of Henry Ford and the company's chairman of the board, introduced the occupants of the driverless cars to the twelve-minute journey they were beginning. Ford called it "a voyage through time and space, from a dark and distant yesterday to a bright and promising tomorrow." The cars soon entered dim "time tunnels," where "flashing Strobe lights and stereophonic sound effects" imparted "the sensation of speeding through the sound barrier." Seated in their new convertibles, they passed moving dinosaurs, then cave-dwelling people. They saw the invention of the wheel.

The ride took its passengers "from the Stone Age to the Space Age," then across the "threshold of tomorrow," offering them a view of the futuristic Space City. The travelers had "the feeling of moving at great heights over the city on a vast skyway." In Space City, they saw "a brilliant kaleidoscope of towering structures, sky highways, strange hovercraft and seemingly suspended landing platforms." At the end of the ride, the travelers stepped out of their cars onto a platform moving in sync with the ride. They had the feeling of stepping into Space City, where they found an exhibit of futuristic Ford concept cars.[34] In the fair's first year alone, 6.6 million people rode Ford's Magic Skyway.[35]

Ford's Magic Skyway was but one of four big projects that Disney's WED Enterprises developed for the 1964–65 World's Fair, but Disney himself was frustrated by the experience. At Disneyland he was the boss, and his decisions were final. At the fair, however, Disney had to report to Robert Moses. In particular, Moses rejected Disney's proposal to install a full-size monorail that would serve fairgoers' practical needs as they explored the vast fairgrounds, and serve Queens residents thereafter. Disney had been operating such a system at Disneyland for almost five years when the world's fair opened, and he was convinced that such systems were not just fun to ride but practical means of mass transportation.

Moses, however, settled for a small monorail installation with just one stop; riders disembarked where they had boarded. It was an amusement, not a mode of transportation. For practical transportation at the fair, Moses supplied buses.[36] Disney did not subscribe to the drive-everywhere, drive-only vision. He wanted to demonstrate that modes of mass transportation, from local people movers to elevated rail lines, were essential to the city of the future. He would have to realize this ambition elsewhere.

Ford's Magic Skyway and GM's *Futurama II* were different in detail, but they were still of a kind. Both invoked scientific authority and technofuturistic spectacle to suggest that their visions of the city of the future, while entertaining, were also realistic and desirable. It is therefore useful to refer to both by a common name—one that captures their common version of the high-tech car dependency. Futurama can serve the general purpose well, and as a more specific term for the postwar decades' iteration of futurama, Futurama 2 is convenient.

The drive-everywhere, drive-only city was never easy to sell—otherwise, the lavish efforts to sell it would have been unnecessary. To sell it, motordom enlisted the authority of science. In such persuasive efforts, the futuramic sales force had the advantage of frequent news reports about research achievements. Confidence in futurama was not solely due to public demonstrations of "electronic highways." Marketing and press coverage of research reinforced the authority of experts in all fields—even in those cases in which the applications would later prove troubling.

In retrospect, postwar developments such as DDT, nuclear power, and the polio vaccine confirm that while research developments can be godsends, some can bear long-term costs that may ultimately exceed the benefit. The 1964–65 New York World's Fair opened just two years after Rachel Carson exposed the hazards of DDT and other potent toxins in *Silent Spring*. Researchers' confident promises still retained most of their authority, but scientific prestige was beginning to recede. Nevertheless, in each generation, technological innovations can renew confidence in old promises. Two decades after the New York World's Fair closed in 1965, new technology was again the basis for claims that high-tech highways would prevent collisions and solve congestion.

CHAPTER 3

Futurama 3: From CenterCore to Demo '97

Although their vision of transportation in the 21st century may seem like science fiction, the guardians of our highways expect to spend billions of dollars trying to make this fiction a reality.

—Elizabeth Pennisi

There was no *Futurama III*—at least not by this name. But twenty-five years after *Futurama II*, there was indeed such a phenomenon: a new wave of extravagant promises that state-of-the-art technology would deliver an automobile utopia, a city where technology would make car dependency liberating, safe, and inclusive. By the 1980s, the failed promises of the first two futuramas had mostly been forgotten, and recent technological innovations offered a basis for renewed credibility.

As in Futuramas 1 and 2, technofuturistic spectacle

joined with engineering, interest group politics, and corporate marketing to sell the drive-everywhere city, the future place where everyone drives to every destination safely, without delay. Safety remained a major selling point for Futurama 3, and even reductions in pollution or carbon emissions were routinely claimed.[1] But Futurama 3's persistent refrain was congestion relief through more efficient use of road capacity—or greater "throughput."[2]

New terms were introduced and promoted, among them *smart cars* and, especially, *smart highways*. As in Futurama 2, the technology invoked was still primarily electronics—only this time, as if to distance themselves from the disappointments of Futurama 2, the promisers of a future in which car dependency works used the word *electronics* much less often, preferring *technology* (sometimes *advanced technology* or *high tech*). While no single name united this wave of spectacle and marketing, it may fairly be called Futurama 3.

The credibility gap

To work, technofuturistic spectacle must be both imaginatively conceived and well executed. It must also be favorably timed. For over a decade following Futurama 2, the times were not encouraging. Credibility was in short supply, and invocations of scientific authority were less reliable.

In 1957, soon after the Soviet Union launched Sputnik into orbit, news reports of a "missile gap" between the United States and the Soviet Union circulated, alleging that the USSR had more and better offensive missiles. Together, Soviet satellite launches and the supposed missile gap raised alarm about the state of national security. In the 1960 US presidential election, Senator Kennedy and his supporters made much of the gap, but in 1961, when President Kennedy had his secretary of defense look into the matter, the secretary found that the United States had the advantage in missiles.[3]

The episode made *gap* a versatile and overworked metaphor, a fashion that the 1964 film *Dr. Strangelove*, a Cold War parody, made grim fun of by introducing *doomsday gap* and *mineshaft gap*. One of the first serious variants was *credibility gap*, which emerged in 1961. Originally it was about the credibility of Cold War deterrence. To deter attack, the United States and NATO had to convince the USSR that a Soviet attack would provoke retaliation. Deficient resolve, this line of reasoning went, risked inviting attack. This was the original credibility gap.[4]

In 1965, months after the New York World's Fair closed for good, *credibility gap* began to gain far more circulation in a new usage. In December a staff writer for the *Washington Post*, Murrey Marder, wrote a column about "creeping signs of doubt and cynicism about Administration pronouncements" from President Johnson's White House, especially in matters of foreign policy. "The problem could be called a credibility gap. It represents a perceptible growing disquiet, misgiving or skepticism about the candor or validity of official declarations."[5]

Credibility gap soon proliferated, in part because it suited so much more in the 1960s and 1970s than just presidential assertions. In 1962, when Rachel Carson's *Silent Spring* cast doubt on chemical companies' "little tranquilizing pills of half truth" that their insecticides were safe, numerous others had already been questioning authorities in other realms. By then, the Committee for Nuclear Information and Women Strike for Peace were eroding the credibility of the Atomic Energy Commission's repeated (but false) promises that aboveground nuclear weapons tests in Nevada were harmless to residents downwind. In 1964 the surgeon general's report on smoking and health exposed decades of false reassurances from tobacco companies, many of them presented with an aura of scientific authority. The next year, Ralph Nader's *Unsafe at Any Speed* had a similar effect on automakers' habitual assertions about the safety of their vehicles. In 1970 Helen Leavitt's *Superhighway—Superhoax* gave readers ample cause to distrust experts from the coalition of industries engaged in automaking, roadbuilding, and related enterprises.[6]

In popular science fiction, technofuturistic spectacle endured, but typically with an edge of mistrust. In *2001: A Space Odyssey*, the more astonishing technology is, the more it imperils those who develop and naïvely trust it. The film complemented popular demands for humility, simplicity, and balance. *Silent Spring* was, above all, a call for balance against those who promised perfection. The ecology movement, inspired in part by Carson, was almost by definition a commitment to balance. In 1973, E. F. Schumacher's *Small Is Beautiful* extended Carson's thesis, paradoxically concurring with Charles Kettering's 1929 contention that to work, consumerism must "keep the consumer dissatisfied."[7]

Official assertions of many kinds were up against a broad credibility gap. Technofuturistic spectacle depends on credibility, but from the mid-1960s to the mid-1980s, this resource was in short supply. A version of the mistrust was directed against close relationships between government and corporations. Disturbed by the growing political influence of big military contractors during the Cold War, President Eisenhower delivered a famous warning to Americans. Three days before he left office, Eisenhower, by live television, suggested that a "military-industrial complex" could make government more accountable to big contractors than to voters, and in ways that ensured contractors steady streams of public money.[8]

Eisenhower's warning was generalizable; in the 1960s and 1970s, it was applied to other industries that depended upon public spending—including the coalition of automakers, road builders, and related industries that had been striving to sell car dependency since the 1920s. In 1970 such a charge was even made in the *Wall Street Journal.* In a favorable review of *Superhighway—Superhoax,* Alfred Malabre declared that "the military-industrial complex has a big brother who is just beginning to get the attention he deserves." Comparing their respective shares of the economy, Malabre concluded that, next to the military-industrial complex, "the highway-auto-petroleum complex is a giant."[9]

Ironically, perhaps the most spectacular technological feat the twentieth century, Project Apollo, contributed to a shift in values that further constrained the possibilities of technofuturistic spectacle. Inaugurated in 1961, when experts' credibility was high, Apollo survived into the 1970s on the strength of bureaucratic momentum and its astounding successes. But when astronauts orbiting the moon on Apollo 8 photographed an earthrise over the lunar surface in 1968, they accelerated an appreciation for Earth as a fragile oasis in the cold, colorless vastness of space. Titled *Earthrise*, the photograph became an emblem for a growing movement that questioned some predominant values. Now suspect were representations of technological wonders as "weapons" in a "war against nature." *Earthrise* was an inspiration for the first Earth Day in 1970, provoking questions about the commitment of vast resources to feats of scientific daring. In 1972, Apollo 17 yielded a second photograph, called *Big Blue Marble*, that became emblematic of the ecology movement.[10] Thereafter, NASA had to settle for far more modest missions.

The US supersonic transport project demonstrates the importance of timing. As a federally funded enterprise, development of a supersonic passenger airliner began in 1963, before the credibility gap. By 1970 the SST—a project as technofuturistic as any—was in trouble. There was still no working prototype, and congressional support was falling. The project was canceled in 1971. A television

editorial on ABC's evening news program set the cancel-
lation firmly in the era's mistrust. The program's science
editor, Jules Bergman said: "The SST forces charge that
the airplane became a scapegoat—not for itself, but for all
that is wrong in our society. It became a whipping boy for
the anti-technology movement that has grown out of the
charges of a military-industrial complex."[11]

Even within computer science a credibility gap
emerged, casting doubt on expectations that computers
could take over complex human tasks. In the summer
of 1956, about twenty computer scientists gathered at
Dartmouth College in New Hampshire to pursue their
common aspiration for computers that could perceive,
learn and make judgments. It was the beginning of a new
field in computing: artificial intelligence. Throughout the
1960s, expectations were high, and research grants were
generous. But artificial intelligence could seem creepy
and threatening—an anxiety best exemplified by the
polite but willful (and ultimately homicidal) computer
HAL in *2001: A Space Odyssey*. Computer scientists were
less inclined to see danger in artificial intelligence—in
part because by the end of the decade, many of them
doubted AI's practical possibilities. Disappointing results
appeared to confirm their skepticism, and research funding for AI projects ebbed. Computer scientists later called
the 1970s an "AI winter": a decade in which AI projects
could attract little support.

The credibility gap of the 1960s and '70s deterred lavish projects promoting utopian futures. It also afforded a

breathing space for overlooked perspectives—including those that yielded Earth Day (1970), the US Environmental Protection Agency (1970), the banning of television commercials advertising cigarettes (1971), and the DDT ban in the United States (1972). But as memories of broken promises recede, credibility gaps decrease. By the 1980s, the broken promises of Futurama 2 were fading.

The Florida Project

Among Futurama 3's origins were 1960s plans for a city where people could live, work, and play without driving anywhere. This vision was entirely inconsistent with the guiding principles of Futuramas 1 and 2, but by the 1980s, those had been transformed beyond recognition, into a third iteration of motordom's promised land.

When the New York World's Fair closed in 1965, Walt Disney sought a giant canvas where he could begin an experimental city in which walking and transit were so convenient that no one would need a car. Traces of this vision were evident at Disneyland, where, from the park's opening in 1955, a walkable Main Street U.S.A. was served by horse-drawn streetcars. Visitors could ride a train from one attraction to the next. In 1959, in a sector of Disneyland called Tomorrowland, Walt Disney opened the park's monorail, the first in North America.

Disney hoped the monorail and other transit innovations at Disneyland would serve as examples for cities to emulate. He tried, without success, to interest Los Angeles in such a project.[12] Disneyland did indeed achieve some influence in city planning, as Disney had hoped; in 1963 James Rouse, an influential planner, told an audience at the Harvard Graduate School of Design: "I hold a view that may be somewhat shocking to an audience as sophisticated as this, and that is, that the greatest piece of urban design in the United States today is Disneyland."[13] But Disneyland was an amusement park. It could not serve as the example of everyday car-free living that Disney envisioned. He wanted a real car-free city.

Disney called his idea the Experimental Prototype City of Tomorrow—EPCOT. The city would include a second Disneyland park, called Disney World. But Disney World was to be just one sector in a much larger, working city. To design it, Disney learned from the example of a prominent Austrian-American architect and city planner, Victor Gruen.[14] Gruen, like Disney, was torn between pragmatic concessions to the automobile's preeminence and a visionary commitment to the possibility of a better city, where people could get where they wanted without driving, and vibrant public spaces were unblemished by parking lots and expressways.

Before they met, both Gruen and Disney had separately arrived at similar compromises. For Disney, the result was the original Disneyland—a walkable, transit-friendly place surrounded by vast parking lots. To enjoy Disneyland's promise of car-free mobility, sociability, and fun, most visitors arrived by car. Gruen's compromise was much the same. He pioneered the shopping mall: a place where most shoppers arrived by car, but where they went from shop to shop on foot, amid pleasant surroundings. Gruen assailed "the insane arrangement by which hordes of mechanical monsters fight for every square inch of space with others of their own kind and with human beings on foot."[15] He intended malls to include attractive public spaces and civic amenities, such as libraries and post offices.

Gruen's first shopping mall projects coincided almost exactly with the construction of Disneyland. In 1954, while Disneyland was being built, the first shopping mall of its kind opened in suburban Detroit. In 1956, in Disneyland's second year, the first fully enclosed shopping mall opened: Southdale Mall in suburban Minneapolis. Much like Disneyland, both Gruen projects were planned, inviting, walkable clusters of destinations, free of motor vehicles—but encompassed by acres of parking lots.[16]

Both Disney and Gruen were frustrated city planners. Gruen, the professional, found himself limited for a time to shopping malls, where retail inevitably crowded out the civic amenities he favored. Disney, who aspired to design not just amusement parks but cities, studied Gruen's work. While Walt Disney was working on projects for the 1964 World's Fair, Victor Gruen was on assignment, redesigning central Fresno, California, to make it a welcoming place for people on foot. That year, Gruen's book *The Heart of Our Cities* was published. Gruen's new book was the statement of principles Disney needed. The two men were divided by some specifics—Gruen, for example, saw monorails as "highly overrated."[17] But they were united by their essential values: above all, that urban vitality depends upon people, who must not be confined within vehicles or crowded out by them.

Applying Gruen's principles and his own intuitive values, and prepared to risk the vast resources at his disposal, Disney planned a utopian city where no one would have to drive. He put his design team to work developing an enormous model of his urban vision: EPCOT. It was much smaller than the 1939 *Futurama* model, but at 60 by 115 feet, it was still vast, and it rivaled GM's model in its detail.[18]

For EPCOT, Disney found the blank slate he wanted in Central Florida, where he bought a parcel of land amounting to almost twice the area of Manhattan. To work with, he had land equal to 170 times the area he had purchased in 1953 for Disneyland. In 1966, in a film shot seven weeks before his death, Disney presented his Florida Project to a limited audience, including the state legislators whose approval he needed.[19] As in a Gruen design for a shopping mall or a pedestrian zone, motor vehicles were to remain essential but peripheral, and entirely excluded from the center—only in this case, the center was a whole city.

The film's off-screen narrator explained: "Here the pedestrian will be king, free to walk and browse without fear of motorized vehicles." Everyone would use public transit, including a monorail for longer journeys. According to the narrator: "Most EPCOT residents will drive their automobiles only on weekend pleasure trips." Fanning out from monorail stations were local transit routes, served by a people mover system of small electric vehicles in continuous motion along a fixed guideway. This local transit system was called the WEDway (after Disney's design firm, WED Enterprises). Transit systems of both kinds had been in service at Disneyland for years. The narrator told viewers, "Automobiles and freeways will not be EPCOT's major way of entering and leaving the city. The transportation heartbeat of EPCOT will be the two electric powered systems—monorail and WEDway."[20]

EPCOT, as Disney envisioned it, was not the opposite of futurama. Motor vehicles were to be essential to connect EPCOT to the rest of the country. But the plan was based on Disney's conviction that successful public spaces are car-free, and that everyday mobility needs are best served by public transport systems. He did not subscribe to the drive-everywhere, drive-only urban vision. Yet Disney's Florida Project was never realized. EPCOT would instead become the site of an exhibit that did for the 1980s and the 1990s what Futuramas 1 and 2 did for their eras: present, for millions, an attractive vision of high-tech car dependency.

In December 1966, before any construction had begun, Walt Disney died. The extravagant, high-risk project had depended on Disney's personal commitment to survive; after his death, his company took a far more cautious path. It kept the theme park, but abandoned the EPCOT vision entirely, retaining only the name. The company made EPCOT a permanent commercial technology fair, funded by corporate sponsors. It finally opened in 1982, as the Epcot Center. Apart from the monorail connecting the site with other destinations in Walt Disney World, there was no trace of Walt Disney's "experimental prototype community."

In an exhibit building called World of Motion, however, an ambitious vision endured—though it was nothing like Walt Disney's experiment. World of Motion was General Motors' pavilion—shaped like an enormous wheel lying flat, with a curved exterior wall sixty-five feet high. It opened in October 1982. The *EPCOT Center Guide Book* promised that visitors to World of Motion would see "how tomorrow's transportation will change the face of our cities."[21]

General Motors must have been impressed by Ford's Magic Skyway ride at the 1964–65 New York World's Fair, because its World of Motion exhibit was a remarkably close imitation. Visitors to GM's new exhibit did not ride in real cars; otherwise, the ride was an update of Ford's. The pavilions' shapes were similar; both were squat, vertical cylinders. In both, visitors were carried in an upward spiral, then into a tunnel with lighting effects; they passed a series of scenes populated by Disney animatronics—purported milestones in the history of transportation. The solemn didacticism of GM's first two futuramas was out; most of the scenes along the World of Motion ride, like those at the Magic Skyway, were humorous. And in both, the culminating scene along the ride was set apart from the rest: a giant model of a technofuturistic city, a place where car dependency finally works. In both pavilions, when visitors left the ride, they entered an exhibit hall of prototype cars and similar attractions.

At World of Motion, visitors boarded moving "chair-cars" to perpetually looped recorded voices singing "It's fun to be free, to be on the move / You go where you please, with comfort and ease / To see all there is to be seen / It's fun to be free." These voices recurred occasionally during the fourteen-minute ride. Seated through the darkened exhibit, visitors traveled through time. They witnessed illuminated scenes of transportation advancement, brought to life with the help of electromechanical characters (animatronics) commissioned from Disney workshops.

A narrator's recorded voice explained each scene as visitors passed it on their ride.[22] At the outset, the first message is that walking has been obsolete since the Stone Age. "Throughout the ages, we have searched for freedom to move from one place to another," the narrator says. "In the beginning, of course, there was foot power. But with our first wandering steps, we quickly discovered the need to improve our basic transportation." Animatronic cave dwellers sit, blowing on and fanning their sore feet, as if they had forgotten to wear sensible shoes. The invention of the wheel is depicted humorously, with animatronic characters—as on Ford's Magic Skyway. The narrator comments: "The wheel! Now things really get rolling. It's fun to be free."

Thereafter, a distorted, Eurocentric, and cliché-bound transportation history unfolds—with comic book levity and simplicity—as linear progress, and always as the extension of freedom. Nevertheless, at every stage, visitors see the latest transportation modes failing travelers, in contrast with the narrator's optimistic comments. The transportation mishaps continue until the final stage, when automobiles finally deliver the freedom humanity has sought since prehistoric times.

Visitors' chaircars take them from ancient Rome to Renaissance Europe, then across the sea to North America. There they see transportation progress as a steam riverboat called the *Cotton Queen.* As their ride continues, the narrator tells visitors they are going "beyond the Mississippi," where settlers "enjoy the scenic West with the freedom and adventure of the open road." Circled wagons come into view, menaced by hostile natives, but a US Cavalry detachment rescues the pioneers. Visitors next see a locomotive bringing "fast, dependable, safe travel to the new frontier"—but the train has been stopped; a holdup is in progress. The passengers stand helplessly beside the track as robbers take their valuables at gunpoint.

Soon visitors see bicyclists. "Ah, the peaceful countryside," the narrator says. "What more romantic way to enjoy it than with that infallible combination of man and machine: the bicycle!" But again, the scene tells a different story. One cyclist, menaced by an aggressive dog, has climbed a tree. Another man has taken a spill; he sits in a pool of mud, his white suit ruined. His cycling companion has dismounted; she stands holding her bike, giggling at the sight. On a screen projection, visitors see other bicycle scenes, including one in which a woman has been stopped by her bike's flat tire. A man with a pump is trying to inflate it. Until the automobile, nothing works.

The narrator tells visitors: "The call of the open road brings us a new wonder: a carriage without a horse. Yes, with the horseless carriage, we thunder full speed into the twentieth century!" The "new wonder" is introduced with another mishap: in a chaotic scene at a small-town intersection, an iceman's motorized truck has collided with a horse-drawn produce wagon, spilling fruits and vegetables. But thereafter the problems cease. We see a Sunday drive in the country, now with none of the nuisances that afflicted the cyclists. Airplanes join the scene. "Mobility is the byword of modern transportation," the narrator says—suggesting that while there are many modes of transportation, only cars and planes offer mobility. At last travelers have "a way to move from here to there, for every need and every care. Now it's *really* fun to be free!" The visitors are taken past a parade of vintage General Motors cars, each populated by smiling, fun-loving figures enjoying what humanity had striven for since the Stone Age.

Approaching the end of the ride, the visitors are whisked through a tunnel with flashing light effects, suggesting time travel. They then pass the climactic scene: an elaborate, sixty-foot-tall model of the futuristic, high-tech, car-dependent city of tomorrow. It occupies the full height of the building's center, making a spectacular end to the ride.

GM called the model CenterCore. It bore an umistakable resemblance to Space City, the climactic scene at the end of Ford's Magic Skyway. Both were relatively abstract models, and both were presented in darkened settings that gave the scenes a dreamlike atmosphere. In both, colored lights evoked activity and mobility. In CenterCore, lines and points of light, some made by cadmium lasers, suggested radial access routes to a dense center zone of lofty skyscrapers.[23] Somehow technology had reconciled extreme density and car dependency. As visitors took in the scene, the narrator told them: "Yes, our world has indeed become a World of Motion. We have engineered marvels that take us swiftly over land and sea, through the air, and into space itself. And still bolder and better ideas are yet to come. Ideas that will fulfill our age-old dream to be free. Free in mind. Free in spirit. Free to follow the distant star of our ancestors to a brighter tomorrow."

Like Space City, CenterCore was an enormous and highly stylized night view of the city of the future. Unlike Space City, however, GM's model could also have been taken as an abstract depiction of the electronic signal paths in a computer processor. The name CenterCore associated this technofuturistic vision with a new age of electronics, when discrete transistors had been outclassed by integrated circuits and microprocessors. Microprocessors, introduced in 1970, were essential to the microcomputing revolution of the 1970s and 1980s; they released computing from its inaccessible confines in research universities, corporate headquarters, and government agencies.

A microprocessor's core executes computer operations;

in the processors of the 1970s and 1980s, a processor had just one central core. In GM's technofuturistic vision, the city of the future had a high-tech central core as well. CenterCore envisioned the city of the future as high tech and high speed, like the latest processor. When World of Motion opened in 1982, the heavily advertised IBM PC had been out for a year; sixteen months later, the Apple Macintosh was released. Microprocessors made both of them work, and CenterCore suggested that in the city of the future, microprocessors somehow make the drive-everywhere, drive-only city work.

When the ride ended, visitors stepped out of the chaircars, finding themselves in the TransCenter: an exhibit of GM vehicles and prototypes—including, presumably, some of the vehicles that would populate the high-tech roads of CenterCore. The exhibit ran for more than thirteen years, and was seen by millions of visitors, many of them children, before GM closed it for good in 1996.

Mobility 2000

World of Motion was not merely an amusement park ride. General Motors was committed to pursuing high-tech car dependency, and it strove to build a coalition of partners in business and government to join in the effort. In the late 1980s and early 1990s, four trends combined to encourage GM and other proponents of transport consumerism to unite behind a new means of pursuing it: First, the Interstate Highway System was nearing completion. As the project ended, Congress might scale back federal road funding—unless it could be convinced that a new generation of high-tech roadwork was necessary. Second, as Gorbachev's Soviet Union first disarmed and then dissolved, the Pentagon's budget was expected to fall steadily. Many anticipated a "peace dividend" that could support domestic priorities, and such rhetoric could prove useful for vast new transportation projects. Third, with defense expenditures falling, military contractors were scrambling for new big-budget government customers, and they saw opportunities in high-tech road transportation. In Congress, the weapons makers had friends who were eager to help them find new markets, and they gave the effort an attractive name: defense conversion. Finally, military contractors took advantage of the Gulf War of 1990–91, not only to sell weapons but also to showcase "smart bombs" and other high-tech weapons systems. Military contractors soon used these displays of digital prowess to seek markets for other kinds of high-tech systems—including systems for applications in transportation.

In 1988 *Automotive News*, a trade publication and news service for people in the automotive business, reported that "highway congestion is growing so rapidly some think it soon will be serious enough to violently rock the world's auto industry and all its offshoots."[24] By then, informal working groups were coalescing to respond to this threat; participants included auto industry representatives, state and federal transportation officials, and university researchers. They agreed that state-of-the-art technology, integrated into road systems and vehicles, could make car dependency finally work. Their term for this vision was Intelligent Vehicle-Highway Systems. IVHS was "a collection of technologies that would manage the flow of traffic in cities and on freeways to increase capacity, enhance safety, and ease congestion."[25] More often, the idea was called smart highways.

In 1988, at a meeting in Washington, DC, the growing IVHS coalition gave themselves a name: Mobility 2000. They met just ahead of a two-day conference hosted by the Transportation Research Board called "Look Ahead to 2020." There, the Mobility 2000 group presented their vision. The conference theme and Mobility 2000's message were in close accord: Car dependency is a given. Congestion is costly and worsening, but advanced technology can make car dependency work.

In choosing a name for themselves, Mobility 2000 joined a trend that was already well under way among promoters of high-tech car dependency. An early example was General Motors' term Metro-Mobility, introduced in a booklet about a display at *Futurama II*.[26] Though automobiles were clearly modes of passenger transportation, *mobility* suggested freedom of movement—transportation unimpeded by schedules, terminals, and other constraints. By using the word, automotive enterprises and their partners could distinguish cars from other modes. But drivers seeking this kind of freedom were likely to face complications that negated the car's advantages—complications they and other drivers caused. Traffic congestion and scarce parking could make driving feel constrained, like other modes of transportation. They made driving a mode of transport, not a means of mobility. Mobility 2000's vision was to apply technology in a quest to make the car a means of unhindered mobility, not just another constrained mode of transport.

Mobility 2000 held meetings again in 1989 and 1990, then renamed itself IVHS America: a growing coalition of industry, government, and universities committed to intelligent vehicle-highway systems. Member companies included military contractors (Lockheed, Rockwell International, TRW, and Allied Signal), technology and telecommunications companies (AT&T, Texas Instruments, and Motorola), and automakers (GM, Ford, and Chrysler).[27] According to one reporter, General Motors was "by far the IVHS leader among U.S. automakers," committing sixty-five researchers and engineers to the work and "spending an estimated $10 million a year" on it.[28] As its executive director, the members of IVHS America chose James Costantino, sixty, the director of the Transportation Systems Center in Cambridge, Massachusetts, a research center of the US Department of Transportation.

In the 1950s, motordom had won support for the vast Interstate Highway System on the promise that the network would solve America's road transport problems. Finished decades late and billions over budget, the problem now was to build political support again for a renewed federal effort. This was no easy task. IVHS America could not characterize the Interstate Highway System as a success story, because if the system had solved transportation problems as promised, no new massive effort could be justified. In 1965 GM's chairman had told Americans that "expanded requirements can be met by the prompt completion of planned freeways under the interstate highway program."[29] If the experience of ensuing decades proved the claim false, this would be grounds for doubting new claims; on the other hand, if time had proved the claim correct, no new, massive, national effort would be needed.

General Motors managed the dilemma by keeping attention on the future, by invoking the wonders of state-of-the-art technology, and by making a massive new project appear cheaper than doing nothing. In June 1989, William Spreitzer of General Motors Research Laboratories told a House of Representatives subcommittee that GM was funding research projects toward a national "future highway program" and that it would invite the USDOT to join it. In his written statement for the subcommittee, Spreitzer warned that American drivers wasted "more than two billion hours of delay a year" in congested traffic, costing "$73 billion a year in lost productivity." Without a major new federal effort, the problem would get far worse: "Traffic delays on the Interstate System are expected to increase in the range of 400 to 500 percent by the year 2000."

By 1992, IVHS America had raised the guessed annual cost of congestion to the rounder figure of $100 billion.[30]

Rather than blame state and federal transportation spending that gave most people few or no choices besides the most spatially inefficient mode of transportation available, Spreitzer proposed instead "a national cooperative effort by government, industry and our intellectual community as represented by the universities." A ten-year high-tech project, funded at $100 million a year in federal money, would do the job, Spreitzer promised. He assured the subcommittee that "GM is committed to serving major roles in that effort."[31]

Spreitzer's reception in Congress was friendly, and committee members spared him hard questions. They did not ask him, for example, why congestion was so extreme just as the Interstate Highway System was approaching completion. The highway network was often characterized as "the biggest public works project in history."[32] In the 1950s, it was justified primarily as a means of relieving traffic congestion, and GM had been second to none among its proponents. Four decades and $100 billion later, GM was claiming that congestion was worse than ever, and getting worse still.

Why, then, given the apparent failure of the system to relieve congestion, should Congress trust GM's advice again? Had the system in fact exacerbated the problem it was purportedly intended to relieve, by directing overwhelming federal support to space-hungry cars, to the neglect of other modes? Wasn't a new federal effort to make car dependency work also doomed to fail, and for the same reason? That is, wasn't the problem due to the car's inherent properties: its space demands relative to people moved, its storage demands, and the cost of accommodating them? Wouldn't federal support for spatially efficient modes serve the purpose better?

New technology, new promises

Had committee members asked such questions, Spreitzer would have been ready with answers, which lay within his written testimony. Why would congestion relief work this time, when it had come up short before? His answer was "advanced technology." The term was an update of Futurama 2's preferred answer: electronics. Since Futurama 2, impressive and conspicuous new electronics—much of it enabled by the microprocessor—offered credibility to those who could associate their agendas with it. Personal computers, video games, and even cordless phones were everyday reminders that technology delivered new possibilities. It was all still electronics, but as a word, *electronics* had lost its magic. *Technology* inherited it.

Word counts from works in English that have been scanned and digitized indicate that *electronics* reached its peak frequency, relative to other words, circa 1986.[33] The word's fortunes had risen with the celebrity of the transistor, until the words *transistorized* and *solid state* on a television or a radio assured consumers that they were getting the best. In the new era of integrated circuits and microprocessors, electronic devices continued to proliferate, but they were now more often called technology.

Historically *technology* had been far too general a term to specify state-of-the-art electronics, so during the transitional decades, *advanced technology* and *high tech* distinguished new technology from old. But today the modifiers are seldom used: in many circles, technology is state-of-the-art electronics.

Spreitzer was unspecific about how electronics (or advanced technology) would curtail or eliminate congestion in a drive-everywhere, drive-only city. He cited off-vehicle "sensors and centralized controllers" and onboard navigation guidance for drivers. Why not improve transit systems instead? "Public transportation," Spreitzer's written statement asserted, "has not proven to be the solution to transportation problems."[34] A more skeptical committee member might have asked how Spreitzer could possibly know, since decades of anemic investment in public transportation, coinciding with decades of massive highway projects, had led many to turn to driving not by choice but by necessity. Once transportation policy deprived most people any good choice besides driving a car, whether they could afford one or not, the recourse to driving was then routinely interpreted as grounds to ignore everything but cars. "The increasing reliance on the automobile," wrote an IVHS proponent, "demonstrates that Americans prefer the independence and privacy of the automobile over public transit."[35]

General Motors' preferred talking point was the claim that the cost of doing nothing far exceeded the cost of its proposals. To spread the word, GM sent William Agnew of its Research Laboratories on the road. Weeks after Spreitzer's testimony, Agnew addressed a meeting of the Institute for the Advancement of Engineering in Los Angeles. "There are two billion vehicle-hours of delay per year attributed to congestion," he said, "and an estimated $73 billion loss to the nation because of congestion." The answer, Agnew said, was IVHS: the application of technology to better coordinate traffic. "You might think of this system as a grand extension of the highway traffic advisory system based on helicopters and commercial radio used today," Agnew explained. "The system consists of a navigation system on the vehicle, a traffic-control center, two-way communications between the vehicle and the center, and sensors on the highway to detect traffic densities and vehicle speeds." IVHS was "the system of the future"; in it, a control center would "receive information from individual vehicles and adjust the signals, signs and ramp gates to balance traffic densities. The center would advise drivers of congested areas, or any other blockage. And it would suggest alternate routes."[36]

GM's pitch succeeded. IVHS America's position earned the favor of the US Department of Transportation. In 1990 the department's Federal Highway Administration sealed its endorsement in a twelve-minute video called *Intelligent Vehicle-Highway Systems: A Smart Choice for the Future*.[37] The narrator took car dependency as a given: "The automobile continues to be the dominant form of personal transportation." The solution was not a diversified transport system promoting more efficient modes of travel but high-tech car dependency: "Fortunately, we're entering an era of new solutions. The electronics revolution has produced integrated circuits, microelectronic chips and other products featuring miniaturization technology."[38]

IVHS would not only solve congestion; it was also supposed to make the roads much safer. In 1989 Lester Lamm, the president of the Highway Users Federation for Safety and Mobility, a lobby representing road transportation interest groups, warned: "We're moving in the wrong direction. If traffic keeps going up, the best we can do is hold at today's fatality rate, or make very minor gains. If this happens, by the year 2000 we may have as many as 75,000 traffic deaths, which is totally intolerable."[39]

In the 1990s, the safety claims for IVHS grew bolder. In 1994 Rodney Slater, the Federal Highway Administrator, assured a House subcommittee that "this technology will initially provide partial control or control assistance to the driver, and will eventually lead to fully automated control on selected, high priority highways." This in turn would mean almost perfect safety: "By reducing human error, an automated driving system could prove a nearly accident-free driving environment." Drivers would enjoy "fully automated control on selected, high priority highways." These roads would offer "a significantly enhanced level of safety, traffic flow efficiency and trip quality." Incidentally, smart highways would "also spawn innumerable commercial opportunities for U.S. electronic and communications firms, as well as many other large and small high-tech companies," plus "enormous opportunities for the American automobile industry to develop and market new products."[40]

As early as 1991, some were anticipating that IVHS would deliver driverless cars, as the developers of the "electronic highways" of the 1950s had promised. Electrical engineer Ronald Jurgen speculated: "The various IVHS technologies in various stages of demonstration throughout the world are paving the way for the introduction one day of a truly autonomous vehicle. It would be capable of operating in any traffic situation, while traveling from one point on a freeway to another, without driver intervention."[41]

High-tech navigation

General Motors engineers reasoned that one means to make more efficient use of existing roads was to improve navigation. A driver who could, while driving, find the car's current location, get directions, hear traffic reports, and learn of alternative routes, would save time—and by driving more efficiently, would save others time too. In 1966 GM engineers developed a prototype system called Driver Aid, Information and Routing (DAIR), installing it in two test vehicles. The DAIR computer sat under and in front of the center of the dashboard, in easy reach of the driver's right hand. DAIR was intended to offer drivers automatic reports on local road and traffic conditions, plus two-way communication with information centers. More impressive, it would also have given drivers turn-by-turn directions to destinations on at least some routes, in the form of lighted arrows on the DAIR console.

DAIR was a direct application of the principle RCA had demonstrated in Nebraska in 1957. For such guidance, however, drivers had to begin the journey by inserting punch cards into the DAIR computer, and to work DAIR required magnets and relays embedded in roadways for the system's computer to follow.[42] A second-generation system, called Electronic Route Guidance System (ERGS), operated on essentially the same principle and was also never implemented; General Motors had developed it with support from the federal Bureau of Public Roads.[43] In 1978 the first satellite of the Pentagon's Navstar Global Positioning System was launched, but civilian access to GPS satellites was not granted until 1993. Until then, electronic navigation for drivers was limited to much cruder alternatives in which an onboard computer kept track of distances and turns to locate the vehicle on a stored electronic map.

In the 1980s, a small Silicon Valley start-up finally developed a system that did not require any hardware outside the vehicle, and GM became its first big customer. Satellite navigation was still the monopoly of Navstar, the US military system. The company was called Etak, founded by electronics expert Stan Honey. In 1983 Honey, age twenty-eight, told Nolan Bushnell, a developer of Pong and the founder of Atari, about an idea he had for an onboard navigation device for drivers. Bushnell was impressed and gave Honey $500,000 to start

Etak. Honey based the new company in Sunnyvale, California; for its name, he used a Micronesian word for a traditional navigational technique.

Introduced in 1985, the Etak navigator got its bearings, one journalist explained, "through a roof-mounted electronic compass and magnetic sensors, mounted near the car's wheels, that monitor the distance and direction traveled." Calculating distance traveled by counting wheel revolutions, and following the car's turns, the Etak computer plotted the car's location on a black screen, its green-line map displayed on a 4.5-inch CRT monitor that could be mounted to the driver's right. The car appeared as a fixed cursor on the map; the map itself changed to reflect the car's changing location.

The system itself cost $1,400, but there was more to buy. Drivers needed stored electronic maps that had been laboriously entered into cassette tapes, and at first the maps were available only for large metropolitan areas in California. The cassettes were $35 each; installation of the Etak could cost another $200. For all that money, the driver got a system that was useful only where cassette maps were available. As the driver traveled, location error in the system accumulated until the driver manually recalibrated it.[44]

In 1985 General Motors licensed the Etak navigator, planning to include it as a high-end option in some future GM cars. GM's Jon Bereisa, who would later lead the company's electric vehicle effort in the 1990s, recognized Etak's limitations, but saw a big future for it. "In ten years" he said in 1985, "a navigator like this will cost about $500 and be as common as air-conditioning. . . . You'll be as plugged into the wired society when you're in your car as in your office or home."[45]

Displays of high-tech prowess

Despite Etak's constraints, GM made it the first working electronic component of the anticipated smart highway of the future. In 1988 General Motors, the California Department of Transportation (Caltrans), and the Federal Highway Administration teamed up on a $2.25-million experiment called the Pathfinder Project. For IVHS's first large field test, an intensely busy fourteen-mile stretch of the Santa Monica Freeway in Los Angeles (I10) was selected. GM equipped twenty-five Oldsmobile Delta 88s with Etak navigators, which by then used CD-ROMs to store maps, instead of cassette tapes. For Pathfinder, the Etaks received traffic data from the Caltrans Traffic Operations Center in downtown Los Angeles; besides displaying real-time maps, the Etaks also indicated congested routes. A synthesized voice recommended driving directions through the car radio's speakers. Drivers' choices were few; to avoid congestion ahead, they could exit the freeway, but little else.[46]

On Monday, June 25, 1990, Elaine Chao tested the system. Chao was then deputy secretary of transportation; she later served as secretary of transportation under President Trump. After a drive along the freeway in one of the test Oldsmobiles, Chao offered reporters a favorable review:

"With this Intelligent Vehicle Highway System, Los Angeles leads the nation in revolutionizing transportation in the 1990s." State workers served as the primary test subjects. Hundreds took turns driving the Oldsmobiles on their daily commute for six months.[47] The system worked as intended, but drivers were generally unimpressed with it as a congestion beater. Two-thirds reported that it did not save them time on their commute.[48]

In April 1990, twenty-five years after the *Futurama II* exhibition reopened for its second season at the New York World's Fair of 1964–65, Transportation Secretary Samuel Skinner announced an $8 million IVHS project to be conducted by General Motors and the American Automobile Association. Skinner revealed the plan at AAA's annual meeting in Palm Desert, California. The total budget, which would soon grow to $12 million, included $2.5 million from the Federal Highway Administration. The new project, which was more ambitious than Pathfinder, was to be conducted in the vicinity of the Epcot Center. The Florida Department of Transportation and the City of Orlando joined in.

In the project, called TravTek, 100 specially equipped Oldsmobile Toronados operated in a vast, 1,200-square-mile test sector around Orlando, each receiving road data from Orlando's traffic management center. Of the 100 cars, 75 were driven by tourists (all of them AAA members) as Avis rental cars; the rest served local drivers who knew the region. Over the course of the yearlong test, about three thousand drivers rented the equipped

Oldsmobiles. The navigation system, like Etak, required magnetic compasses and wheel direction sensors mounted in the vehicle, plus roadside video cameras and sensors embedded in the road; unlike Etak, it was recalibrated intermittently by signals from GPS satellites. In 1992 and 1993, drivers in Central Florida received real-time route and destination advice, via synthesized voice and a dashboard map display. Drivers could select from menus of destinations or enter a street address; they could also get live assistance from a desk at AAA's national head-quarters, at Heathrow near Orlando. For the voice com-mands, TravTek used a voice synthesis program called DECtalk, which had given Stephen Hawking his famous synthesized voice. In 1988 Hawking's *Brief History of Time* made him a worldwide celebrity; four years later, some test drivers would have enjoyed the illusion of hav-ing the world's most famous physicist as a navigator.[49]

As in Pathfinder, the technology generally worked as planned. Tourists said that TravTek saved them time plan-ning routes to destinations and helped them avoid getting lost. Once drivers were on the road, however, the system's traffic reports seldom saved drivers time, suggesting that TravTek could do little to speed anyone's daily commute. Though a *New York Times* reporter gushed that TravTek, "at long last, could make reality of the future that was fore-cast [for 1960] at the 1939 World's Fair," its practical ben-efit was limited to route planning and guidance.[50] Unlike Walt Disney's original vision of EPCOT, TravTek was a Florida project committed to high-tech car dependency.

Federal support for IVHS was obtained on a promise of congestion relief and safety. But Pathfinder and TravTek primarily offered navigation guidance and traffic information, which were of only marginal help. Developments seemed to have more to do with what was technically feasible than with what would actually prevent collisions or traffic jams. For General Motors, however, its major parts in Pathfinder and (especially) TravTek gave it a lead in automated navigation that helped it introduce the first commercial driver navigation systems based on Global Positioning System technology. As a $2,000 option, buyers of a 1994 Oldsmobile 88 could have their new car equipped with GM's Guidestar GPS system, developed by Rockwell International, Zexel Electronics, and GM's Delco Electronics.[51] A decade earlier, GM's Jon Bereisa had predicted that by the mid-1990s, a driver navigation system would "cost about $500 and be as common as air-conditioning." The reality was much more expensive and far less common, but with federal money GM had at least put itself in the lead.

Among IVHS's few modest successes, electronic toll collection was the only one that offered a credible means of substantially relieving road congestion. Road capacity is valuable; when users pay less than what it's worth, and pay only very indirectly (through gasoline taxes), congestion is as predictable as a long line for free pizza. Tolling can correct for this—if the toll collection system is neither too expensive nor too intrusive.

In 1989, emulating some early examples in Europe, Texas introduced electronic tolling on the Dallas North

Tollway. Drivers who purchased a special windshield tag did not have to stop. Instead, as they drove through the tollgate, the battery-powered tag transmitted a unique radio signal that was locally received, then relayed to the toll authority; the toll was deducted from the driver's account. The contractor for the system was a local Dallas company called Amtech.[52] Impressed, the Oklahoma Turnpike Authority contracted Amtech to implement the system. On January 1, 1991, Oklahoma's PikePass system went into effect; it was the first long-distance route in the United States with electronic toll collection. Drivers with a yellow windshield tag and a positive balance in their account could drive through the tollgate at 60 miles per hour; the toll was deducted automatically.[53] Electronic toll collection proliferated in the 1990s and early 2000s; with license plate recognition systems, even drivers without windshield tags or transponders drive through tollgates without slowing—though often at a high premium.

But automated tolling was a paradoxical success for some members of the IVHS coalition. Tech companies and road builders were generally eager to get in line for toll road projects, but General Motors and the American Automobile Association had long opposed them. In 1932 GM and AAA, together with other allies among automotive interest groups, banded together in common cause to protect drivers' interests and, by extension, those of their own organizations. Calling themselves the National Highway Users Conference, they opposed financial burdens on motorists, including toll roads and allocations of gas tax proceeds to anything but roads.[54] As long as toll collection was slow and expensive, requiring drivers to stop to pay human toll collectors, the Highway Users Conference and its successor, the Highway Users Federation, had an advantage over tolling advocates. But by 1990, General Motors' favorite justification for expensive IVHS projects was the $73 billion (or $100 billion) a year that congestion allegedly cost Americans. To this problem, an ideal answer was to charge drivers for their part in contributing to the bill. As "congestion pricing," unintrusive, automated tolling could be the means to finally charge drivers for the cost of the road capacity they used—something gasoline taxes, at best, could only very crudely approximate.

Congestion pricing could ease congestion by charging drivers for road capacity like a business charges for a service. Gasoline taxes could not approximate such pricing—and to automotive interest groups, that was their virtue, because even the most expensive road capacity would be accessible without charge. In the 1920s, automotive interest groups, recognizing that gasoline taxes committed to road projects were the ideal means to ensure that road capacity would grow to accommodate ever more driving, backed them in all forty-eight states, with provisions to prevent "diversion" of revenues into anything other than roads. Now automated tolling and the possibilities it offered threatened this model. Consequently, interest groups representing road users, including the Highway Users Federation (of which GM was a member) and the American Automobile Association, opposed congestion pricing and accepted toll road projects only where toll-free projects were not politically feasible.[55]

In June 1994, a major study from the National Research Council strongly endorsed automated tolling to implement congestion pricing, but the report's authors admitted that "congestion pricing faces significant public and political resistance."[56] They were right. Though congestion pricing was IVHS's greatest practical opportunity to relieve congestion, thirty years later, the United States still had no citywide congestion pricing. In 2019 a historic plan was approved for New York City; some of the revenues would fund public transportation. Implementation has been delayed, but the plan's prospects have much improved since the 2020 election.[57]

From smart bombs to smart highways

It was never obvious how IVHS technology was supposed to transform car dependency into a safe and efficient surface transportation mode, or even just mitigate the stresses of the daily commute to work. Inherent limitations of the personal automobile itself constrained the possibilities. But in 1991, the Defense Department featured high technology in an extraordinary spectacle that drew the world's attention. The displays suggested that in so-called smart systems, high tech makes the unimaginable possible. Though the United States had used such weapons in the Vietnam War, they remained little known to the public until the Gulf War.

In January, US and coalition forces began a devastating air campaign against Iraq. The featured event at Pentagon press briefings was aerial video of laser-guided bombs, soon known to almost everyone as smart bombs. Television news welcomed the video as a visually interesting relief from the conventional news conference; for the Pentagon, the video was an effective way to persuade Americans that military targets were selected and destroyed with surgical efficiency—even though such guided bombs accounted for only about 8 percent of bombs dropped by coalition forces. For the contractors who built guided weapons, the videos were lavish free publicity that they could use to cultivate civilian markets.[58]

By March 1991, the Gulf War was over; before the year ended, the Soviet Union had dissolved. Military contractors sought a reliable new market for technology that was generally much too expensive for the consumer market and not cost-effective enough for customers in industry. For its part, the growing IVHS coalition needed tech so impressive that it could make their extraordinary promises credible. Both parties stood to gain if military technology companies joined the IVHS coalition, which had already won the support of the Transportation Department. The next step was to get Congress to shift its attention from the Cold War to a renewed war on congestion, waged with new smart weapons. "Defense contractors," wrote one observer, are "offering to use smart bomb technology in smart cars."[59] From their point of view, the problem was not "How do we make transport safer and more efficient?"

It was "How do we find new customers for our expensive, high-tech systems?"

The Interstate Highway System was practically complete. Military contractors and transportation interest groups, with the backing of USDOT, urged Congress to undertake a new national transportation effort by committing substantial funds to IVHS. They succeeded. In December 1991, President George Bush signed into law a massive new highway act, the Intermodal Surface Transportation Efficiency Act, known as ISTEA (pronounced *ice tea*). ISTEA made IVHS America an official advisory committee to the US Department of Transportation. Under Title VI, the act immediately authorized $234 million for IVHS; total IVHS funding for the ensuing six years was to be $660 million. During the first term of the Clinton administration, funding grew; Congress authorized $924 million for fiscal years 1994 through 1997.[60] But IVHS America anticipated a far greater total market, including the states, the private sector, and consumers (drivers); it estimated a total expenditure of $209 billion over the following twenty years, or $350 billion in thirty years—more than enough to beat the Interstate Highway System's record as "the largest public works program in United States history."[61]

By some accounts, "ISTEA was regarded as the first transportation bill of the post-Interstate era."[62] The ISTEA money included funds for a prototype highway, to be demonstrated by 1997. Like President Kennedy's public commitment in 1961 "to achieving the goal, before this decade is out, of landing a man on the Moon and returning him safely to Earth," the deadline was intended to spur rapid innovation.

Two weeks after President Bush signed ISTEA into law, the Greater Los Angeles Auto Show, sponsored by the Greater Los Angeles Motor Car Dealers Association, was about to open at the city's downtown convention center. On Friday, January 3, 1992, one day ahead of the show's opening, a preview was held for the press. The keynote speaker was James Costantino, executive director of IVHS America. Costantino was confident. With four hundred businesses as members, the IVHS coalition was growing and ISTEA committed federal support to their cause. He offered his audience of reporters and auto industry people a vision of thirty years hence—of 2022. According to an Associate Press reporter's summary, Costantino predicted that "within 30 years, drivers may be superfluous as sensor-laden, computer-controlled vehicles cruise highways."

The audience welcomed the forecast until Costantino guessed the cost: "$350 billion over 30 years." At this, the reporter noted, "some heads in the audience shook skeptically."[63] By comparison, the thirty-five-year Interstate Highway System had cost about $100 billion. Some of the press coverage treated the figure as an absurdity. For the AP story it carried about Costantino's speech, one California newspaper used this headline: "Automated Cars and Roads? No Problem. Got $350 billion?"[64] Over the following months, IVHS America moderated its cost estimates.

In the spring, it prepared a strategic plan;[65] according to Costantino's summary, "the plan estimates $210 billion will be spent by the public and private sectors for IVHS products and services over the next 20 years, with the public sector accounting for 20 percent of the spending."[66]

In 1992 a science journalist, Elizabeth Pennisi, observed: "Although their vision of transportation in the 21st century may seem like science fiction, the guardians of our highways expect to spend billions of dollars trying to make this fiction a reality." But "oh, what a vision they foresee. Cars will drive themselves, sometimes at high speeds, and compute new routes to bypass congestion as it develops. People who prefer not to carpool can travel in one-person vehicles that link together for expressway travel." Eventually "fully automated cars will drive themselves everywhere."[67]

Military contractors, expecting declining military spending and attracted by federal money for IVHS, rushed to offer their services to the smart highway cause. In April 1993, at the third annual convention of IVHS America in Washington, DC, a reporter found that IVHS was "shaping up as the second California gold rush for many defense firms on the West Coast." Companies wanted in on this "billion-dollar bonanza," hoping that "as military contracts dry up, . . . the technology they sold to direct Gulf War smart missiles is the right stuff for automated traffic management systems and cars that drive themselves." At the convention, "exposition space and meetings were jammed with members of the defense and avionics community." According to industry insiders, the cost "for developing and deploying smart highways and vehicles over the next 20 years" would be "$215 billion."[68]

At such events, though there was still no clear path from the military technology to better traffic conditions, there were few doubters. At the Washington IVHS America convention, however, one participant offered a skeptical assessment. Randall Jones of Chicago's SEI Information Technology, referring the military contractors, told the reporter: "Much of the military stuff is technology looking for a marketplace. What they offer is not really what consumers are looking for." But most IVHS insiders claimed certainty: tech would soon make highways much safer and much more efficient. The military contractors returned for IVHS America's 1994 convention in Atlanta. According to the coalition's board chairman, "Of the more than 120 exhibitors, over half were defense and aerospace contractors striving to apply their technology to the surface transportation system."[69]

Competing for a leading position in IVHS, some military technology contractors resorted to big advertising campaigns. In ads run in numerous business and investment publications, Rockwell International told readers that "Rockwell battles gridlock with military technology" by "converting our defense electronics to create smart highways for tomorrow." The company, which had put almost $100 million into its IVHS effort by 1994, promised that its "new transportation systems will eliminate highway congestion, reduce pollution and increase safety." It was unspecific about how its technology would perform these feats, apart from asserting that its GPS systems would "revolutionize civilian and commercial navigation."[70] Lockheed, known for its military aircraft, promised that its systems integration prowess, demonstrated in military satellites, gave it "expertise in integration and operation of . . . 'smart highways.'"[71]

Demo '97

ISTEA, the 1991 highway act that put substantial federal money behind high-tech driving, included funding for a test smart highway, to be in operation by 1997. The law mandated "an automated highway and vehicle prototype from which future fully automated intelligent vehicle-highway systems can be developed."[72] To compete for about $160 million in federal project money, General Motors assembled a team from industry, government agencies, and research universities, calling it the National Automated Highway System Consortium. *Automated highway systems* (AHS) was another of the many terms for high-tech highways and the technology they required. NAHSC included military electronics contractors (Bechtel Group, Martin Marietta, and, later, Lockheed Martin), a top research university (Carnegie Mellon), and two GM subsidiaries (Hughes Aircraft and Delco Electronics). A competing group consisting of Ford Motor Company, TRW, and Motorola submitted a rival bid, but in October 1994, USDOT awarded the money to the GM team.[73] NAHSC proposed to not only build the mandated prototype by 1997 but continue on to develop a more advanced version by 2002.[74]

By the time the award was announced, insiders considered Intelligent Vehicle-Highway Systems too restrictive a term; thereafter, they used Intelligent Transportation Systems (ITS). Within NAHSC, there was no apparent effort to take advantage of ITS's most promising congestion-mitigation technique: congestion pricing by means of electronic toll collection. Instead, NAHSC strove to develop means to automate vehicle guidance for hands-off driving, and to permit cars to travel closely together in coordinated "platoons." In a platoon, cars follow one after the other, safely but at speed, thereby increasing road capacity; sensors in the vehicles send signals to apply the brakes or the accelerator as needed. The project's program manager, James Rillings of General Motors Research Laboratories, explained how its systems were to relieve congestion: "A typical freeway lane can handle about 2,000 vehicles per hour, but a lane equipped to guide traffic automatically should be able to carry about 6,000, depending on the spacing of entrances and exits."[75] Rillings did not explain how tripling the volume of cars exiting highways was to relieve congestion on urban arterial routes, city streets, and parking lots.

The USDOT award to NAHSC made big winners of the consortium's members—above all, General Motors. But it also made other automakers and tech companies losers who had no more incentive to play along with GM's and NAHSC's lavish claims for automated highways. With no chance at getting the federal money committed to the prototype smart highway, they commented frankly about it. In 1995 William Spreitzer, now technical program director of GM ITS, told a reporter about a day when drivers would read the newspaper as they drove, adding that "when every vehicle on the road has an intelligent cruise-control system and it is used intelligently, you won't have any accidents." The reporter took this claim to others in the business, including an ITS expert from Siemens. Siemens was collaborating with Chrysler on ITS, and neither company was part of NAHSC. Asked to comment on Spreitzer's assertion, the Siemens engineer flatly disagreed with it. Crashes might fall markedly over time, he said, but, "I don't think there is any way all accidents can be avoided."

A Ford executive concurred: "The driver must stay in control of the vehicle. The human brain is a much better computer than anything we can build to deal with adaptive situations." Chrysler's ITS program manager, Ivy Renga, was optimistic about automated safety systems but considered smart highways a distracting and wasteful dead end. "Chrysler has not participated in automated highways," he said. "We don't think it's practical and don't think it will ever happen. It appears to be a sinkhole for U.S. tax dollars."[76]

NAHSC publicized its planned experimental smart highway as Demo '97. By 1996 the consortium had selected its test road: a 7.6-mile stretch of Interstate 15 about 12 miles north of San Diego. The highway offered a pair of high-occupancy vehicle lanes, separated from the other lanes, that NAHSC could refit at off-peak hours. As in the Pathfinder Project in Los Angeles and the TravTek project around Orlando, the specially equipped test cars included GM models—this time, ten Buick LeSabres. Sponsored research teams entered other cars as well; in all, twenty-one semiautomated vehicles were tested. About 1,300 rides were given to guests as passengers.[77]

Magnets—about ninety-three thousand of them—were installed into the roadbed, along the centers of the travel lanes. The Buicks could sense the magnets; onboard systems then steered the cars to keep them in their lane. The cars were also equipped with video cameras and radar linked to automated braking and acceleration systems, permitting them to follow each other closely, single file.[78] The demonstration was more than a field test. "Of course, the technical content has to be there, but educating our stakeholders is also a big part of the success of the demo," said a NAHSC representative. "Once highway users understand the true benefits," he added, "they're likely to become excited about its potential." Referring to automated highway systems as AHS, NAHSC announced that it was committed to "supporting Demo '97's exciting array of activities" through "a broad-based public education program designed to activate AHS stakeholders in this effort, maximize demonstration attendance, build support for continuing the AHS Program, and promote the vision and potential benefits of AHS deployment to likely system users, operators and implementers."[79]

A year ahead of Demo '97, however, intelligent

transportation systems had a public relations problem. Automakers and tech companies generally agreed that technology offered practical opportunities, but only those in NAHSC were consistently optimistic about automated highways. As NAHSC raced to get its smart highway demonstration ready, James Costantino, president of ITS America (the renamed IVHS America), admitted that "the intelligent transportation industry" had been facing "an identity crisis" requiring professional help. In an article for government and industry insiders in *Public Roads*, the magazine of the Federal Highway Administration, he told readers what they already knew: "Attempting to explain the benefits of intelligent transportation systems (ITS) has been a difficult task." ITS America's treasurer had told Costantino that among its own members, ITS "was the dawn of a whole new era in transportation"—but "unfortunately, we didn't know how to describe it to anyone other than ourselves."

By summer 1996, Costantino explained, he and his associates realized they would have to "educate the public." ITS America needed "a coordinated, well-researched national public relations and advertising campaign." It hired two public relations firms. It adopted a new tagline (New Thinking in Transportation) and a new logo: in blue and white, an arrow signifying movement lay over a stylized printed circuit suggesting technology; the arrow was prominently marked *IntelliTrans*. It launched a major advertising campaign that included, for example, a seven-page special advertising section, called "Super Smart Transportation," in *Fortune*.[80] It hired a former congressman, Bob

Carr, putting him in charge of a new "national awareness campaign." In Congress, Carr, a Michigan Democrat, had earned Costantino's confidence as "a champion of the ITS industry, especially as the chairman of the House Transportation Appropriations Subcommittee."[81]

Costantino and other smart highway industry leaders attributed their image problem to the technology's low profile. ITS "is behind the scenes," Bob Carr explained. It's "all so user-friendly that the technology's invisible."[82] As a diagnosis, it was a flattering humblebrag. There was a far more obvious explanation, though it was harder to admit. From the start, the proponents of high-tech driving had been lavish overpromisers. Technology could and did inform drivers, automate tolling, and offer other conveniences. But it had no chance of solving rush-hour congestion or releasing driving from its last-place position in transport safety. The coalition could not even unite behind congestion pricing, a technique that implicitly demoted driving from its privileged position among transport modes.

In 1997 the most technically impressive achievement— driver navigation systems—was still an expensive option out of the reach of most drivers, and even it depended on access to a satellite network developed by the military, not by ITS projects. In heavy traffic, GPS could offer some drivers useful alternatives, but it was no solution. Still, the industry could not let go of its addiction to promises to solve congestion. Even in a confessional admission that the industry had an "identity crisis," Costantino's article included a photo of a highway traffic jam with the caption: "Through the use of ITS technologies, such scenes of traffic gridlock will soon become a thing of the past."[83] It was another empty promise.

The ITS industry had, in fact, achieved modest successes. In 2011, USDOT researchers found that "dynamic message signs" that alert drivers to congestion and hazards were ITS's greatest single congestion reliever; in preventing collisions, they were second only to onboard collision avoidance systems.[84] Dynamic message signs were an ITS success, but cast in the shadow of the industry's gigantic promises, they were unimpressive. Of greater significance to American transportation, however, was the diversion of resources. At a tiny fraction of their actual cost, smart highway projects might have been limited to what they could actually deliver: some practical navigation guidance, information about current traffic conditions via dynamic roadside messages, and especially charging drivers for the road capacity they used. Instead, because they were sold as systems that could relieve or even eliminate congestion and make roads much safer, smart highways attracted big public money, diverting resources that could have gone to the transit systems that can move people safely and efficiently.

Demo '97 could have been a display of the possibilities of congestion charging, bus rapid transit, updated arrival times on dynamic bus stop signs, separated bike lanes, integrated transit and bike-share services, and so on, and the technology that ITS America sold might have contributed to the success of such a demonstration. But as the coalition's founders had admitted from the start, they took car dependency as a given.

In 1989, when William Spreitzer of General Motors told a House of Representatives subcommittee that GM sought "a national cooperative effort by government, industry and . . . universities" to use "advanced technology" to make car dependency safe and efficient, he cautioned subcommittee members against the temptation to make public transportation part of the answer: "Public transportation has not proven to be the solution."[85] The statement implied that high-tech car dependency could work better. One decade and billions of public and private dollars later, smart highway technology had scarcely made a difference. It would have been interesting to see how the money might have improved other modes of transportation.

The smart highway industry's invisibility problem had less to do with invisible technology than with an invisible vision. The coalition was adept at organizing and getting political support, including funding. Strangely, however, Futurama 3 never developed attractive, technofuturistic visions of the car-dependent utopia they promised. Demo '97 was intended to be an impressive publicity-generating display, but it could show only what was possible with existing technology, and even the most ambitious feats planned for it were expensive stunts. There was no vivid depiction of twenty years hence, as fairgoers had seen at Futurama 1 and Futurama 2.[86]

Following the credibility gap of the 1960s and 1970s,

technofuturistic spectacle was harder to pull off, but it was not impossible; films such as *Star Wars* (1977), *Tron* (1982), and even *Back to the Future Part II* (1989) might have suggested how to do it.[87] The closest that Futurama 3 ever got to technofuturistic spectacle was the CenterCore display at GM's World of Motion pavilion at Epcot Center. But as a partner in the smart highway coalition, General Motors never used it to depict the future that the coalition sought. GM evidently learned from the experience. In the twenty-first century, Futurama 4 has been a renaissance of technofuturistic spectacle, and in these imaginative and impressive displays, GM was the early leader.

Demo '97 was both a federally funded research project and a public relations effort. Thursday, August 7, 1997, was day one; four days of demonstrations followed. In all, 3,500 people attended. Working in Southern California ten miles inland from the Pacific coast, NAHSC's personnel risked oppressive heat—but they were lucky. Daytime highs did not reach 90 degrees F, and by day four, the high was only 77.[88] Project researchers tested lone cars and buses, which easily followed the magnetic path while their drivers kept their hands off the steering wheel—often sticking both hands out the driver's side window to confirm the fact.

Equipped vehicles could stay in their lanes; with radar, they also kept a safe distance from other vehicles. They detected and steered around road obstacles, and reported obstacles to vehicles following behind. In the most impressive test, a column of eight Buicks, beginning at rest, accelerated to highway speed. Without their drivers' help, the cars kept themselves in a dense line, at first maintaining intervals of about twelve to fourteen feet between them. At 65 miles per hour, they stayed about twenty feet apart. Drivers could depart and rejoin the platoon.[89]

Commenting on Demo '97, Mike Doble, concept vehicles and technology manager for Buick, said, "The Automated Highway System is a reality." Eventually it "will allow cars, trucks and buses to operate automatically. Drivers will be free to do other things, such as writing or reading." High-tech highways will relieve "congestion and overcrowding, and provide for a safer, more relaxed and productive commute." Ken Baker, vice president of GM Research and Development, concurred: "Automated vehicle technology has the potential to significantly improve throughput and safety on our nation's highways. That will reduce traffic accidents, conserve energy, improve U.S. productivity and make driving more enjoyable."[90]

Soon after the demonstration, NAHSC released a ten-minute video presenting Demo '97 to wider audiences. "A crisis is looming on the nation's four million miles of streets, roads and highways," a narrator explained. "The National Automated Highway System Consortium brings hope." NAHSC is "at the helm of a breakthrough in transportation technology" that will save "lives, time, money, and the environment." GM's Jim Rillings, as NAHSC's program manager, appeared on camera to tell viewers: "Ten years down the road from now, we'll have the actuators in place, we'll have many of the sensors in place, and it will just take a little bit of additional electronics and

At Demo '97, eight Buick LeSabres drove automatically up to 65 miles per hour in a closely spaced platoon, following a path of magnets in the roadbed. Their drivers stuck both hands out their windows to show that they weren't steering the cars. An impressive stunt, it fell far short of the promises of congestion-free driving that had persuaded Congress to put big money into high-tech highways. (Photo: UC Berkeley California PATH Program)

a little bit of computer programming to make it possible to have completely automated travel."[91]

But ten years later, highway driving was much the same. Some vehicles were equipped with navigation systems or adaptive cruise control, but these developments simply made driving more convenient; they were not revolutions in transportation. None of the technical capacities on display in Demo '97 could do much to relieve congestion or improve safety. The demonstration's showpiece—platooning—was no congestion buster. Platooning at speed could make better use of highway capacity, but it was the high capacity of divided highways that caused congestion in the cities the highways led to. At its best, vehicles platooning at speed emulated a railway train—but the most inefficient train in the world, with just one or two passengers per train car, and each car requiring its own engine and high-tech systems.

High-capacity conventional highways with no electronic gadgetry had already proved sufficient to channel so many cars into American cities that whole blocks of real estate had been cleared for car storage. Platooning threatened to double cities' parking woes. Far from a cure for gridlock, platoons of vehicles lining up along highway exit ramps during the morning rush hour, to fill overburdened city street grids, would have often backed up into the highway itself. Under such conditions, spacing between vehicles would have been minimal with or without state-of-the-art technology. Five weeks after Demo '97, James Costantino, after leading the ITS coalition for seven years, announced that he would step down as president late the following year; James Rillings handed off leadership of NAHSC to return to GM.[92]

Unkeepable promises

Jameson Wetmore, who attended Demo '97, called it "the showcase of the 1990s efforts to envision an automated highway system," but concluded "it also marked the end of an era."[93] As a display, it was uninspiring. It came nowhere close to demonstrating the feasibility of "fully automated intelligent vehicle-highway systems," as the 1991 mandate had provided.

The fallacies in the smart highway vision were apparent early on to those whose judgment was not clouded by the business opportunities. In 1993 Marcia Lowe of Worldwatch Institute called attention to the "obvious flaws," warning that "smart cars and highways may well exacerbate the very problems they are supposed to solve." If IVHS doubles highway capacity, we have to ask, "What happens when all those cars reach their exits"? But in 1993, hardly anyone asked. "A nation of highways packed bumper to bumper," Lowe wrote, "can lead only to a 21st century hell—no matter how fast the traffic is moving." She was dismayed at the misallocation of resources. "Any improvements in public transit or other options are doomed to be erased by the much larger effort aimed at cars."[94]

Some in the insurance industry questioned the safety claims of the smart highway salesmen. In 1994 a reporter, Bryan Gruley, asked Brian O'Neill, president of the Insurance Institute for Highway Safety, to comment on the extravagant assertions about safety. "The safety claims being touted for intelligent vehicle-highway systems," O'Neill replied, "are based on flawed research or no research at all. With the money that's changing hands in the race to develop IVHS, it's worth taking a closer look. This has the potential for becoming a big government boondoggle." The Insurance Institute had just issued a report, coauthored by O'Neill, that was critical of the assertions about safety.[95] Citing the report, O'Neill said: "I question why the government is pouring so much money into it. You often get the feeling that we're dealing with technology looking for problems to solve." Gruley, the reporter, turned to James Costantino, executive director of IVHS America, for comment. Costantino "used an unprintable epithet to describe the Insurance Institute report," Gruley wrote.[96]

Despite Demo '97, and despite ITS America's national awareness campaign, the smart highway industry's public relations problem persisted. Through their own extravagant promises, the proponents of high-tech car dependency had dug themselves into a new credibility gap. "Oh, what a vision they foresee," wrote Elizabeth Pennisi in 1992.[97] Reality could not compare. The smart highway coalition had promised that their high-tech systems would make driving much safer, with much less congestion. With advanced technology and a steady stream of public money, nearly accident-free driving would be achieved, followed by fully automated control on select routes.

But as the 1990s closed, smart highways looked more like the expensive "boondoggle" that Brian O'Neill had cautioned a reporter about. In 2005 the congressional Government Accountability Office issued a report that criticized ITS projects for poor implementation and performance evaluation.[98] President Eisenhower's warning about government-industry partnerships that become insulated from public accountability applied as much to the ITS industry as to the military contractors he had in mind—indeed many of the same military contractors applied the skills they'd developed building the military-industrial complex to their work in the ITS coalition.

NAHSC had intended to continue after Demo '97 and develop a more advanced automated highway prototype by 2002, but in 1998 USDOT ended its financial support, and the consortium dissolved. In April 1998, NAHSC held its final meeting, which was sponsored by the Federal Highway Administration. Conference participants reexamined the future of high-tech driving. They called the meeting the Cooperative and Autonomous Workshop, and there was a new emphasis on autonomous vehicles. Participants in the meeting defined "an 'autonomous' vehicle system . . . as one that is expected to work reliably without help, regardless of the ambient or external state." It was an admission that high-tech highways had been an expensive disappointment. But insiders' faith did not vanish; instead it was redirected to high-tech cars.[99]

In 1991 a true believer in high-tech driving had warned the smart highway coalition that congressional support would not be enough. "Convincing Congress to support a national IVHS program" was essential, he told them, "but the public must also be convinced" that the projects "are needed" and "do offer a solution to transportation problems, such as congestion." But "without public acceptance . . . the advanced technologies that may be offered in future automobiles will appear to be nothing more than expensive, high-tech, electronic gadgetry left over from a James Bond 007 movie."[100]

The warning proved prophetic. After Demo '97, word frequency counts from digitized databases confirm that the term *smart highway* fell out of fashion. In the early 2000s, there was a lull in the showmanship promoting a car-dependent future through high tech. But about a decade after Demo '97, as memories of the extravagant promises began to fade and the latest technology validated a new generation of promises, selling high-tech car dependency returned with all the vibrancy and glamour of the previous three futuramas. This time the promise was that cars could be so smart that the roads they drive on could remain dumb. Robotics, sensors, and processing would make cars autonomous, and autonomy would somehow free cars of their deficiencies. By 2010, industry salesmen were again pointing to the horizon, telling us what lay just beyond it: the advent of efficient, safe, and sustainable car dependency, delivered this time by robotic cars. They were promising Futurama 4—Autonorama.

CHAPTER 4

Futurama 4: Autonorama

Twenty years in the future, cars not only shorten the distance between us, they also shorten the distance between our hearts.
— GM and SAIC, *2030 Xing!*

In the early 2000s, as the smart highway promises of just a decade earlier proved extravagant, lavish promises grew scarce. The promoters had delivered some practical benefits, but at high cost. Big claims that smart highways without congestion pricing would diminish traffic jams and improve safety were proved wrong. A new credibility gap deterred more promise making. The interval afforded breathing space to other ideas, including some enthusiasm for privatized roads (paid for by drivers through automated tolling), public-private partnerships, and urban light rail systems.

But the lull was brief. Cell phones, laptop computers, and the internet ensured that new technology retained the power to make the impossible seem possible. If smart highways had been a disappointment, then maybe the wizardry had been misdirected. If a car were smart enough, it wouldn't need a smart highway. It could perform its feats on ordinary roads, even driving itself. Technology still had persuasive power despite the unkept promises, but to reinforce its credentials, high-tech driving proponents enlisted buzzwords from marketing departments and consultancies. In frequency among all words in works in English scanned by Google, *next-generation* surpassed *advanced technology* in 2015.[1] Particular favorites have been *data* and the quasi-magical term *data driven. Innovation* and *solution* have been popular too. Informed guesswork would favor the existence of something purporting to be an "innovative, data-driven solution," and search engines confirm that such things are indeed abundant.

Much as the Gulf War had stimulated interest in so-called smart systems, the response to the attacks of September 11, 2001, spurred interest in so-called autonomous systems. The Pentagon's vast commitments in Afghanistan, Iraq, and elsewhere supplied more enduring support for high-tech military systems that would have extensive civilian applications. Between 2000 and 2005, the Defense Department's total research and development budget soared from $59 billion to about $92 billion.[2] Over the same period, the budget of the Defense Department's high-tech R&D arm, the Defense Advanced Research

Projects Agency (DARPA), rose from about $1.8 billion to nearly $3 billion.[3]

DARPA committed some of its growing budget to projects that stood a chance of developing vehicles that could drive themselves in war zones, sparing personnel from exposure to enemy action. Instead of making roads smart, now the task was to make vehicles so smart that they could operate on ordinary roads, and off roads entirely. To this purpose, in 2002 DARPA began planning Grand Challenges: open competitions of prototype driverless vehicles.[4]

In March 2004, at the first DARPA Grand Challenge, driverless vehicles were to finish a 142-mile course in the Mojave Desert. The team entering the first vehicle to complete the course in under ten hours stood to win $1 million. But none came close—the best performer completed just 7.4 miles.[5] DARPA doubled the prize to $2 million, inviting teams to compete for it on a new, 132-mile desert route in October 2005. Among twenty-three vehicles, five completed the course.[6] DARPA spent $9.8 million on the 2005 competition.[7] In 2007, competitors navigated a complex, simulated "urban" route; six vehicles finished the 60-mile course. The first-place team, sponsored by General Motors and Carnegie Mellon University, took home $2 million. The second- and third-place competitors won $1 million and $500,000 respectively.[8]

In the 2005 Grand Challenge, the best-performing vehicles—including the winner—were equipped with arrays that sensed their environments with lasers. The devices, called lidar, work like radar, only instead of transmitting and receiving radio waves, they use beams of laser light. The result is a high-resolution map of the immediate environment than radar can produce. Lidar has disadvantages too—it's very expensive, and rain or snow degrade its performance. In the DARPA Grand Challenges, however, neither disadvantage was import-ant. The big prize money and the favorable publicity made the expense worthwhile, and the tests were con-ducted in deserts, where the chance of precipitation was near zero. With a heavily modified Volkswagen Touareg equipped with roof-mounted lidar, a team from Stanford University, led by Sebastian Thrun, took home the $2 million prize.[9] To many, lidar was the key to a future of autonomous vehicles.

Just as important, however, were better means of inter-preting the things that lidar and other sensors detect. After the 2005 Grand Challenge, computer scientists began to achieve breathtaking artificial intelligence gains through deep learning: prodigious machine learning in which programs emulating neural networks train themselves on vast datasets, learning without direct instruction. Such machine learning gave us, for example, language transla-tion programs that are good enough to be useful. Until these developments, the reputation of artificial intelli-gence had never fully recovered from the AI winter of the 1970s. By 2010, however, AI was finally delivering impressive new applications—and lending new prestige to high-tech driving.

Tech entrepreneurs sniffed opportunity in the rapid performance improvements, and the media eagerly transmitted their enthusiasm. Word was out that, as TRW had put it in 1958, a radically advanced automobile was coming, and surprisingly soon.[10] To sell it, techno-utopian futures were back. Since 2007 the examples have been abundant; most have been remarkably similar. Pristine CGI imagery presents car dependency as liberating, and also as safe, delay-free, and efficient. Thanks to steep improvements in battery technology, the futures were also purportedly sustainable. The claims, though ubiquitously presented as inevitable, research-based, and "data driven," were usually at least two parts hype to one part engineering. Because the promised proof lay always in the future, the assertions went unsubstantiated. The presentations now took the form of website images, shareable videos, and the tech-guru stage talk.

The cult of disruption

In the 1990s, government money sustained Futurama 3 from start to finish. In the early 2000s, government money, now from the Defense Department, got Futurama 4 off to a start as well. This time, however, business and investor interest was high even without guaranteed streams of public funds. The smart money was hunting for the next "disruptive innovation," and autonomous vehicles fit the description.

In 1995 *Harvard Business Review* published "Disruptive

Technologies: Catching the Wave," written by Joseph Bower and Clayton Christensen.[11] The article was a hit, and Christensen quickly followed up with a bestselling book: *The Innovator's Dilemma*.[12] Thereafter, Clayton Christensen was a business prophet, and his vocabulary pervaded trade shows, consultancies, and investment portfolios. In 2011 *The Economist* included *The Innovator's Dilemma* in its list of "six of the best" business books "of the last half century or so."[13] Bower and Christensen warned business executives that big, established companies learn what their customers want, ensure that they deliver it reliably—and grow cautious. They invest in "sustaining technology": the means of improving whatever they have already been doing. They strive to keep the consumer satisfied—but this is an error. "Leading companies succumb" to dogma, Bower and Christensen wrote; "They stay close to their customers."

Meanwhile small, risk-taking start-ups introduce innovations that seem to have few or no customers. Yet such supposedly disruptive technology can eventually transform markets, leaving the big, cautious companies struggling to stay relevant. "Managers must beware of ignoring new technologies that don't initially meet the needs of their mainstream customers," Bower and Christensen advised.[14] Instead, established companies should behave like small start-ups: invest in impressive innovations of disruptive potential even before they have a market. Christensen cast technology as the driver of history, and innovation as a constant threat to the status quo. Successful businesses hitch themselves to the right technology, but are always on the lookout for the next so-called disruptive innovation.

Disruption theory was an old idea whose time had returned. Neither the 1995 article nor *The Innovator's Dilemma* mentions Charles Kettering, yet the General Motors executive had been a proponent of disruptive innovation seven decades earlier. He did not use the same vocabulary, but in 1929, when he urged his colleagues in business to "keep the consumer dissatisfied," Kettering, too, was warning them against "sustaining innovation" and against doing the same thing better, and recommending continuous change instead. Constant innovation is necessary because supplying existing demands only slackens demand.[15]

"There are no places where anyone can sit and rest in an industrial situation," Kettering wrote. "It is a question of change, change, change, all the time—and it is always going to be that way.[16] Both Christensen and Kettering agreed that a company that seeks only to respond to customer demands is vulnerable to a more innovative competitor. Kettering knew what he was talking about. In 1929 General Motors had just passed Ford as the world's top automaker. From his perspective, Ford's error was to strive to satisfy customers. GM introduced and marketed frequent innovations intended to stimulate ever-new demands. In twenty-first-century business speak, GM disrupted Ford.

GM's achievement in Kettering's day, however,

demonstrated that disruption is not always about better technology, or even about technology at all. Faced with a competitor that kept its customers satisfied, GM introduced annual model changes that appeared innovative enough to qualify, in Kettering's words, as "the new thing." Appearance mattered more than reality—or appearance *was* reality. The high-tech cars that drove themselves along desert test tracks for the DARPA Grand Challenges were overwhelmingly vehicles of century-old technology, but equipped with state-of-the-art systems, they qualified as "the new thing." They were, indeed, no longer just cars but "autonomous vehicles."

Autonomous vehicles retained the same fundamental constraints they had without the expensive new systems, including high cost, high energy demands, and low spatial efficiency, but their marriage to state-of-the-art technology made them appear innovative enough to be disruptive, and thereby made them targets of investment. To go in big for autonomous vehicles, smart investors did not have to believe the "disruptive innovation" hype themselves; they just had to notice that others believed it. Advanced sensors, better machine learning, and electric drive will not absolve AVs of the inherent limitations they have as passenger cars. They may make cars better at those tasks for which cars are well suited, but they will not make car dependency work.

To promote autonomous vehicles and the systems they depend on, tech companies and automakers presented them as disruptions. By 2012 Sebastian Thrun, who had led the team that developed the first vehicle to win a DARPA Grand Challenge, was working for Google on its driverless car project. At a business conference, he told the audience: "This is the age of disruption."[17] Reviewing the 2015 Consumer Electronics Show, *Forbes* magazine classed autonomous vehicles as a "big bang disruption."[18] Later that year, Mary Barra, the CEO of General Motors, insisted that her giant, century-old company was as disruptive as anyone else. "We are disrupting ourselves," Barra told *Business Insider*. "We're not trying to preserve a model of yesterday."[19] Four months later, GM announced it was buying Cruise Automation, a three-year-old tech start-up that retrofitted conventional cars for automated driving. It paid about $1 billion in cash and stock for the company.[20]

Great Togetherness

As the DARPA Grand Challenges generated interest in the next technological disruption, General Motors eyed rising car ownership in China as a chance to sell cars—and high-tech driving. China was unwilling to open its market to car imports, but also unprepared to meet demand with domestic makes. So GM and the Chinese motor company SAIC (Shanghai Automotive Industries Corporation) negotiated a deal that gave the companies joint access to the rapidly growing car market. Together the two companies developed a technofuturistic spectacular for the twenty-first century. There would be a new futurama, promising everything that

Futuramas 1, 2, and 3 had depicted, but now also promising sustainability. GM and SAIC intended to overtake their less imaginative tech competitors. They would present an imagined carbon-neutral future of total car dependency, and bring it all together in a short, narrative-rich movie that made their vision appear credible in a megalopolis of twenty million people. As in 1939, the future depicted would be twenty years hence—soon enough to attract interest, distant enough that the extravagant implausibilities could be excused for years. And as in 1939 and 1964, the vision would be unveiled at a world's fair.

For Shanghai's Expo 2010, GM and SAIC designed a sleek pavilion that architecturally echoed both the famous Bird's Nest pavilion of the recent 2008 Olympics in Beijing and the GM's Highways and Horizons pavilion from the 1939 World's Fair. It also bore a striking resemblance to GM's World of Motion pavilion at Epcot. As at the older pavilions, there was lots to see, but one featured centerpiece. This time it was a twelve-minute movie called *2030 Xing.*[21] According to the director of the new pavilion, "'Xing' is about travel and movement."[22] The head of GM's China Group explained that the film depicted "a vision of future driving that is free from petroleum, free from emissions, free from accidents, free from congestion, and at the same time fun and fashionable. We are proud to be showcasing solutions that will make this vision a reality."[23]

For a panoramic effect, the curved screen itself was monumental: 21 feet tall and 125 feet long. The audience had to turn their heads across a visual angle of 144 degrees to peruse the future wonder city, letting them "become fully immersed in the experience." Sounds came from distinct directions, and the 488 seats rocked or swerved in sync with the visuals.[24] Like the first two futuramas, the film depicted a city of tomorrow: this time Shanghai in 2030. It was innovative not only in presentation but also in content. In just twelve minutes, it deftly interwove three heart-tugging stories about separation and reunion, about birth and death, about struggle and achievement, and about life and love—even fitting in some patriotism in the form of a successful Chinese space mission.

The stories were united by a single persistent theme: togetherness. The film promised that 2030 will be "the Great Togetherness." In the intertwined stories, separation causes hurt. In all three, futuristic digital communications mitigate but never resolve disharmony, which requires physical togetherness. Ubiquitous driverless cars restore harmony by bringing people together. As the film begins, a narrator explains: "Twenty years in the future, cars not only shorten the distance between us, they also shorten the distance between our hearts. Freedom of mobility brings people closer together. Great togetherness." Text on the screen reiterates the point: FREEDOM OF MOBILITY BRINGS PEOPLE CLOSER TOGETHER.[25]

Like previous futuramas, *2030 Xing!* promised audiences a future of total car dependency that paradoxically liberates all. The superb visual qualities, achieved by state-of-the-art digital techniques and by the enormous panoramic screen, invited the suspension of disbelief. The scenes were, on reflection, quite incredible. At best, the future the film presents could reach only a superrich elite, and then only decades after 2030. But in themes and in detail, the film suggests a future of inclusivity and universality: all will share in these technological blessings. Your car will arrive at your door (even if you live many floors up in an apartment tower), and you'll have parking wherever you go. Distance will be no object; routes will be high-speed and congestion-free even in a city of twenty million in which everyone rides in a car. Islands of quaint, human-scale pedestrianism will thrive.

Most incredibly, the energy for this super-energy-intensive world will come entirely from wind, the sun, and even the car's roof. We see a GM-SAIC YeZ with a roof that looks like a giant leaf. It is, according to GM, a concept for "a vehicle that can absorb CO_2 and water molecules in the air and, like an actual leaf, convert them into power for the vehicle through a series of chemical reactions. It would work during both sunny and overcast days while also being able to leverage wind power. This would enable mobility with zero greenhouse gas emissions."[26] Like a tree, the car gets most of its energy from the sun through photosynthesis, supplementing it with power from wind.

2030 Xing! was the most popular attraction at the most popular pavilion at Expo 2010. Visitors to the pavilion totaled 2.2 million during the expo's six-month duration.[27] Lest its extraordinary claims be mistaken as merely inspirational, a useful if unrealistic ideal, GM insisted that the depiction was a realistic forecast of 2030. "The 2030 vision portrayed in the movie is achievable," GM predicted in a press release. "The vision portrayed in the movie is already on the road to being realized."[28]

Next-generation car dependency

2030 Xing! might well have been named Futurama 4, or more specifically Autonorama. It is a futurama, unmistakable in its descent from the GM futuramas of 1939 and 1964; what's new in Futurama 4 is that fully autonomous vehicles supposedly make utopia possible where it had proved impossible before. In all four, futuristic and implausible technology and design make ubiquitous car dependency affordable, safe, efficient, and convenient. Futuramas 1 to 3 failed dismally by all standards, and more than half of the way to 2030, Autonorama is failing as well. All four presented themselves as revolutionary departures from outmoded ways, but all four, as defenses of car dependency, were actually conservative. High tech was not really offering anything new; rather it was adding a futuristic veneer to the status quo.

It would be easy to dismiss all four futuramas as mere marketing, a form of promise making that no one should take seriously. But in investment circles, in engineering research, and in policy forums, the futuramas' essential premises have been governing principles. They take car dependency as a given, not as an option. They cast technology not as a means of offering us choices but as the "solution" that will make car dependency work. They have not only forecast implausible futures but also reflected and protected the status quos of their eras.

In the United States in the 1930s, the social groups with the greatest influence on the future of American surface transportation, including urban mobility, subscribed to the principles for which all four futuramas have stood. Ostensibly, all promised congestion relief and safety. Autonorama has also promised a sustainability that is somehow consistent with practically unlimited driving. Since the 1970s, sustainability has been and remains primarily an effort to make each car cleaner, even as the total number of cars, and miles of car travel, proliferate, thereby offsetting the gains. In state departments of transportation the officially favored paths to safety, efficiency, and sustainability have been no more realistic than any of the four futuramas; they have merely been much less imaginative. Autonorama's claims are based on new sensors, machine learning, computer processing, and wireless networking. But none of the technological innovations overcome the contradictions embedded in the drive-everywhere city—contradictions that make all four visions strangely alike.

To relieve congestion by eliminating delays to drivers no matter the cost is only to invite more driving. For those in the business of selling driving, this result was not a bug but a feature.[29] By diminishing the time cost of travel, delay reduction also promotes dispersion of destinations, which in turn negates much of the benefit. As site developers, businesses, and residences respond to the assumption that long-distance driving is less burdensome, their location decisions are less constrained by distances. These effects keep people in vehicles longer and at higher speeds, exposing them to more total hazard even as engineering innovations reduce particular risks; they also divert people from safer modes of travel.

Automation reduces some kinds of risk while introducing others. In gauging the safety benefits of autonomy, promoters of driverless cars routinely commit an elementary error in arithmetic: they subtract all the crash-causing deficiencies that human drivers are susceptible to, but fail to add all those that their robotic substitutes are susceptible to. Autonomous vehicles are allegedly "smart," and certainly are relative to an empty conventional car. But with a human driver of average competence at the wheel, a conventional car is still vastly smarter. For all our failings, humans are extraordinarily good at reading real-world environments, at distinguishing obstacles, and at anticipating hazards. So far, to work in real environments, cars in full automated riving mode have looked relatively smart in part because they have been confined to highly dumbed-down environments, such as limited-access highways or the suburban roads of Phoenix, where the cognitive demands on human drivers are light. An ordinary bicyclist on a busy bike lane, or an typical pedestrian on a crowded sidewalk, performs feats of information processing and motor coordination that developers of automated driving systems can only dream of. For many years to come, engineers will have no means of engineering out the false negatives that can lead autonomous vehicles to kill without engineering in so many false positives that no one would pay money to ride in one. In a busy urban setting, an AV with near-zero false negatives would necessarily travel at very low average speeds, and would brake far more frequently than a human driver of average driving competence.

The more successful engineers are at developing AV systems that actually do relieve congestion and increase speed safely, the more total driving will grow. This effect has already been proved through seven decades of efforts to relieve congestion and to make speed safe for conventional cars. This effect, in turn, will tend to negate any sustainability gains that AVs might have to offer. It's taken decades to get the share of the US grid that is powered by renewable energy sources up to about 15 to 20 percent. If the grid would have to charge the vehicles of a US population that depended upon electric AVs, it's not clear how this fraction could grow as it must. Hence in next-generation, high-tech car dependency, the carbon footprint of road vehicles would remain unsustainably high.

Zero crashes, zero emissions, zero congestion

The reckless promise making, revived by impressive technological innovation, continues unabated. One third of the way into the twenty-year forecast of *2030 Xing!* General Motors issued its 2017 Sustainability Report.

Although none of the goals promised in the film was anywhere remotely close to fulfillment, the promises remained undiminished in their extravagance. The contents of the report are true to its title: *Zero Crashes, Zero Emissions, Zero Congestion.* In the pages within, GM CEO Mary Barra reiterates: "Our vision" is of "a future with zero crashes, zero emissions, and zero congestion."[30]

In 2017 this vision, superficially new, was in fact eighty years old. Shell's 1937 City of Tomorrow, in which tomorrow meant 1960, was also to be a clean place where drivers drove safely, never slowing below 50 miles per hour until they arrived at their destinations. True to Charles Kettering's precept, such promises still keep the consumer dissatisfied, perpetuating transport consumerism of not only vehicles but the elusive car-dependent city that effortlessly accommodates all drivers' demands. The problem in consumerist promise making is not to fulfill the promises but to keep the promises ever new, ever credible. To this end, promoters of all four futuramas have been eager invokers of science, today especially under the preferred heading of "data."

The pursuit of the utopian city where car dependency works faultlessly, including the high-tech version that forever lies twenty years hence, is not merely unrealistically ambitious. It is also destructive. Those pursuing an ever-receding horizon inevitably degrade other (less expensive and more practical) possibilities. A city optimized for drivers keeps not only drivers dissatisfied but everyone else too. Wherever fast driving is ubiquitous, and by whatever technology the choice is enabled, other choices decline or vanish.

Driving then ceases to be a choice at all; it becomes a systemic obligation. Destinations grow ever farther apart; walking, cycling, transit, and other means of mobility become ever less practical once fast driving dominates. For all its burdens on public budgets, car dependency is redefined as normal, while the carless or those who cannot drive are officially classed as unfortunates: the "transit dependent."[31] In such places, car ownership is "liberating" only because the environment is so hostile that no one can meet everyday needs without one. It is a private remedy for a state-imposed disability. Owning a car becomes an obligation whether the owner can afford it or not. It is the price of citizenship and the prerequisite for a job. Having no car may prevent employment, but buying, fueling, insuring, garaging, and maintaining a car may preclude accumulating any savings.

The next Oxycontin

Automated vehicles' near-term possibilities have been grossly exaggerated, much as opioids' were. With AVs, we are now in a position much like the one we were in in the 1990s, when Purdue Pharma and other companies oversold new opioid formulations. The problem then was not merely that these companies exaggerated their products' benefits. Opioids, though sometimes necessary, could also be profoundly dangerous.

AVs are, too, and in similar ways. Promoters of both have promised utopian benefits in return for crossing thresholds beyond which there is no easy return; thereafter, ever more will be needed. What begins as a benefit soon becomes a new baseline; dependency follows. As automated driving makes long-distance commutes more tolerable, it affects location decisions, making long-distance driving necessary. The difference is that while it's too late to avert the opioid epidemic, we can still prevent the automated vehicle (AV) catastrophe.[32]

The opioid epidemic was a preventable disaster. Its underlying cause was an effort to convert real social needs into opportunities to market products that could not really solve the problems, but would sell much better if they could be credibly presented as solutions. DDT was sold as the modern way to save crops, forests, and gardens from hungry insects. Filtered cigarettes, and "low tar" and low nicotine brands, were sold as ways to make smoking safe. We've forgotten it now, but even plastic soda bottles were introduced in the 1970s as the environmentally friendly alternative to glass and aluminum.[33] In these cases, including the novel opioid formulations of the 1990s, general acceptance of these products as solutions was a short-term business success but a long-term social failure.

In all cases, including AVs, the supposed remedies were distractions from better alternatives, and reversing course was (or remains) extremely difficult. Enterprises with a business interest in the products sponsored or publicized research that predictably yielded results favorable to the businesses concerned. The Tobacco Industry Research Committee, established in 1954, was a notorious example; decades later, it has analogues in the AV sector.[34]

In all cases, businesses and trade associations also sponsored journalism that favored their agendas. Reputable publications have published items from AV businesses as if they were articles; the disclosures that they are paid content are often easy to miss. For example, a 2019 article in *MIT Technology Review* begins: "Autonomous vehicles are here, and they're here to stay." The author was listed as MIT Technology Review Insights, though readers could also find the detached and rather cryptic clause "in association with Intel." Only weeks or months later did editors label the article "Sponsored Content: Produced in association with Intel."[35]

Have we learned to be vigilant? Like all the earlier innovations, AVs are business opportunities that have been pitched as deliverance from grave afflictions—this time, road casualties, carbon dioxide emissions, and traffic congestion. The question before us is whether we will continue to permit them to distract us from proven alternatives that are far simpler, far less expensive ways to deliver what AVs can only promise.

Just a few years ago, we heard predictions from reputable sources that no one would need a driver's license in 2020.[36] Among those experts who are not in some way part of the business, however, many see almost no chance that AVs can be common in the next decade or two. In some locations, AVs with trained safety drivers have already been carrying passengers, but of course, passengers have been getting the same service from paid human drivers of motor vehicles for well over a century. Automated railway trains, still with a human operator in supervision, have been in service for more than fifty years.[37] Beyond strictly controlled fixed routes, there is no discernible way yet toward a future in which no such drivers are necessary in passenger vehicles on roads. And until safety drivers are unnecessary, driverless cars won't really be driverless.

But the worst news about AVs is not that they can't deliver on their promises. In two ways, AVs are not just disappointments by their own standards but actual threats. First, to the extent that they are indeed developed and deployed—that is, to some fraction of the extent that their promoters promise—AVs are likely to worsen the very aspects of passenger transportation they are supposed to improve. Second, AVs are an attractive but expensive distraction from things we can do today at far less cost that yield affordable, sustainable, equitable, healthful, and efficient mobility. Much as elaborate but ineffectual cigarette filters were an attempt to perpetuate cigarette smoking when it was clear that smoking itself was the problem, AVs are, more than anything else, an attempt to perpetuate car dependency when car dependency itself is the problem.

Just as we were promised that AVs would make driver's licenses unnecessary before eleven-year-olds would be old enough to drive, we also used to hear about AVs preventing nearly all collisions.[38] This promise, too, has

recently proved untenable, though it persists in more qualified terms. We are still assured that AVs are "safer than a
human driver."[39] To achieve this far more modest goal, an
AV requires sensors, hardware, and software that together
typically cost more than the car they equip, plus a human
driver (a safety driver or an operator). There's no clear path
ahead toward a destination in which an AV costs less than
twice what a conventional car costs, and needs no paid
safety driver on public roads.

Nevertheless, General Motors still commits itself to that
unspecific future of zero crashes, zero emissions, zero congestion.[40] If deployed, however, AVs would tend to worsen
health, increase total carbon dioxide emissions and other
environmental threats, and worsen traffic congestion. They
would also tend to exacerbate social inequities and even
impair actual human mobility.

AVs can have none of these effects if they are never
widely deployed. Yet even if AVs as road vehicles remain
confined to narrowly specialized uses only, the mere
development effort, including the extravagant promises, remains hazardous. The more seriously doctors in
the 1990s pursued the kind of pain relief that Purdue
Pharma and other pharmaceutical companies sold, the
graver was the threat to the long-term well-being of their
patients. Similarly, the more seriously we pursue a future
in which AVs are supposed to solve all our personal transportation problems—while they perpetuate the underlying condition of car dependency—the harder it will be to
actually solve them by the proven means we already have

at our disposal. In short, AVs threaten to perpetuate and exacerbate car dependency and all its associated costs in terms of sustainability, affordability, public health, social equity, and spatial efficiency.

Safety

Zero crashes is the first of GM's three zeros, and AVs promoters' favorite selling point is safety. Yet passenger vehicles that can approximate zero crashes already exist. They're called trains.[41] Trains are expensive to build and maintain, but so are AVs and the systems they depend upon. But it's much less clear that AVs that are not on rails will ever come anywhere remotely close to zero crashes, or indeed that they can even improve upon the shocking status quo: about thirty-seven thousand fatalities a year in the United States. AV manufacturers' challenge would be hard enough if they could have, as their sole goal, to make vehicles that are safe. But their actual challenge is far more difficult. They must make safe vehicles that passengers will pay to ride in—a vehicle that will not stop every time it detects something with a 1 percent chance of being a hazard, and a vehicle that isn't so thoroughly equipped with hardware that few could afford to ride in it.

The zero-crashes promises depend upon a persistent obfuscation. We are told what AVs theoretically *can* do; this is then equated with what they actually *will* do. Together, lidar, radar, and cameras can detect objects and respond (steer, brake) much faster than a human being.

This fact is then used to justify claims that AVs will be "safer than a human driver."[42] But the very sensitivity of AVs' sensors means that the vehicle detects far more than it can or should respond to. It either must, with perfect accuracy, distinguish those objects for which it must brake or steer from all others, or it must brake or steer so often that frustrated passengers will choose another way to go.

As a matter of business necessity, AVs must be programmed to take chances. In a messy real world, AVs cannot have 100 percent confidence, or even just always err on the side of caution. There can be no market for vehicles that often make unexpected sharp turns or that hard-brake every few seconds or minutes. While AV companies assert their commitment to safety first, if, in calculating the trade-off between safety and convenience, one company favors caution more than its competitors, its competitors will have the better passenger experience to offer.

Such calculations have already been made, and they were a factor in the death of Elaine Herzberg, the woman killed by a self-driving Uber in Tempe, Arizona, in 2018. The vehicle detected Herzberg 5.6 seconds before it struck her, but it did not automatically brake, because it was programmed to limit false positives (unnecessary braking).[43] AV developers will not ignore the lesson that cost Elaine Herzberg her life, but neither can they escape the dilemma that will keep AVs hazardous: an AV that never crashes would have to be too cautious for practical or profitable use.

Automation short of full autonomy can mitigate this problem by keeping the human driver's attention and judgment in play. Lane keeping, adaptive cruise control, and various alerts can all help. But such systems interact with human drivers in ways that can limit or even negate their benefit. AV promoters like to invoke science, but they do so selectively. They seldom bring up risk compensation, an effect characterized in 1975 by economist Sam Peltzman. Peltzman contended that drivers responded to safety measures by converting them from safety improvements into convenience benefits.[44] He considered seat belts in particular, because they had recently been mandated as standard equipment, but similar effects apply to median strips, shoulders, and guardrails. A sleepy driver may be tempted to keep driving, rather than pull over and rest, confident of the protection that such safety features afford.

In Peltzman's own later summation, he "argued that because seat belts reduce the likelihood that drivers are harmed if they crash, they encourage more reckless driving." The 1975 paper was controversial, and Peltzman later agreed that it was a "primitive piece of work," but risk compensation has since been generally accepted as a well-documented fact. As Peltzman explains: "My critics don't quarrel with the basic theory of an offsetting response. There is a continuing debate about the magnitude of this response in specific cases."[45]

High-tech safety systems in cars can induce risk compensation. It is typically an unconscious effect, but some drivers have even shown off their own conscious risk compensation responses to automated driving. Tesla's Autopilot feature engages adaptive cruise control and lane-keeping systems, but its very name might have been devised by a researcher who wanted a way to stimulate a risk compensation effect in study subjects, because it suggests that it takes care of everything for the driver. Some attention-seeking Tesla drivers have posted videos of themselves sleeping or otherwise disengaged from driving; other Tesla "drivers" have been recorded on video, fast asleep, from neighboring cars. Autopilot has been implicated in deadly crashes that have killed twenty people.[46]

The subject tends to devolve into binary terms: automation saves lives, or automation kills. In fact the propositions are related: safety features save lives better when risk compensation effects are taken seriously and mitigated. By this standard, naming a safety feature Autopilot doesn't help. Safety features are often worthwhile, and risk compensation effects seldom negate a safety feature's entire benefit. Peltzman maintains: "I never say you shouldn't wear a seat belt. People have taken me to be anti-seat belt. That's ridiculous. It's a complete misunderstanding of what I was trying to do."[47] But promoters of automated driving systems often ignore risk compensation effects, thereby exaggerating the safety benefits of automated driving systems.

Wherever high-tech safety systems are the subject, safety is routinely equated with vehicle occupants' safety. If we care about people both in and out of vehicles, then every safety effort should begin with the question, "Safety for whom?" Even the best safety systems in cars are biased in favor of the vehicle's occupants, at the expense of others outside the vehicles. Every measure to make driving safe for drivers and their passengers is really an effort to make fast driving safe. When vehicle safety features induce drivers to be less attentive or to drive faster, they can also mean new dangers for pedestrians and cyclists.[48] But even low-tech and no-tech ways to make fast driving safe impose hazards and other burdens on others. Wide urban arterial routes invite fast driving and deter everything else, in part because they imperil anyone who tries to negotiate the vicinity outside of a car.[49]

Driving would not be particularly dangerous if cars traveled at a walker's pace. This fact explains why the first automatic car safety feature was the speed governor, which limits a vehicle's maximum speed to a given setting. Local proposals to require speed governors on all motor vehicles were not unusual a century ago; in 1923 a petition for an ordinance requiring speed governors set at 25 miles per hour on all vehicles in Cincinnati attracted forty-two thousand signatures. The point was not vehicle occupants' safety but the safety of everyone else.[50] Speed governors' bias against vehicle occupants should help us see the bias of most safety features today against everyone else—including the countless people classified by researchers, policy makers, and tech promoters as "drivers" who, in the absence of good choices, are drivers only by necessity rather than preference. In the late 1960s, desperately needed reforms, beginning with seat belts in all cars, made driving safer for drivers. Since then, the implicit message of predominant road safety expertise has been that if people crossing four busy traffic lanes to get to a bus stop, or riding a bike along the narrow shoulder of an urban arterial, want priority safety consideration, they should buy a car; if they want safety for their children, they should drive them to every destination.

Commenting in 1953 on RCA's miniature electronic highway, the one that television pioneer Vladimir Zworykin set up on a basement floor in Princeton, New Jersey, *Time* magazine reported that some feared "that Zworykin may be increasing the very hazard he is trying to diminish," because already, the state-of-the-art divided highway "demands too little" to keep drivers alert. "If the highway itself does their driving for them, they may fall even deeper into drivers' coma." Even with full automation, in the event of "some irregularity—an electronic failure or a blown front tire," the combination of speed and a trance-like state would leave drivers too little time to react.[51] By then, "highway hypnosis" had been in the road safety lexicon for at least seventeen years; in 1936 a reporter diagnosed it among drivers on New Jersey's newest motor routes. By his definition, "the driver, anaesthetized by smooth, speedy riding on broad, level stretches of concrete pavement, enters a comatose state."[52] The term caught on after the war, especially when an article about it, written by a psychologist, was published in *Parade*, a popular Sunday newspaper insert.[53] Road safety experts concurred: the less drivers had to do, the less capable they were of responding promptly to an unexpected hazard.[54]

Highway hypnosis is a consequence of the fact the people are poor at paying attention to nothing. An airline passenger with twenty minutes to get to the next terminal to catch a connecting flight—at O'Hare Airport on a weekday afternoon—will negotiate chaotic pedestrian traffic with an agility that makes the latest inanimate autonomous systems seem hopelessly incompetent. But give a driver nothing to pay attention to, and this prodigious capacity dissolves. Though human incapacity to pay attention to nothing has been well documented for more than seventy years, promoters of automated driving systems still tend to discount it, and sometimes to proceed as if it doesn't exist.

During World War II, the British depended on the attention of radar operators, whose tedious but vital task it was to watch radar readings on cathode ray tubes. Some radar installations were committed to detecting enemy submarines. At stake were the lives of crewmen among ships at sea, and the ships' cargoes that the people of Britain depended upon. It was the lookout's job to notice the extremely rare and subtle indication on the screen that a submarine had reflected a transmitted radio wave back to the receiver. When radar operators noticed a submarine, they alerted the Royal Air Force; pilots could then try to locate the submarine to attack it. But if radar operators failed to notice the anomaly on the radar screen indicating a submarine, a ship and its crew might be lost. It was a collaborative effort between machine and human, and both were essential to success.

Even under such life-and-death circumstances, however, radar personnel's performance was often unreliable. The RAF turned to a psychologist, Norman Mackworth. In an experimental setup simulating a radar lookout's job, he timed RAF cadets as they waited attentively for a distinct but rarely occurring anomaly in the rotation of the second hand of a special clock. The white clock face had no numbers and no minute or hour hand, and the lone, black second hand normally took 100 seconds (instead of 60) to complete a rotation. Every second, the hand advanced one distinct step—except on rare, apparently random occasions, when it advanced two steps. It was the study subjects' task to notice these rare events, and record them.

Mackworth found that the cadets' performance began strong but deteriorated with time. In the first half hour, the average cadet had missed 16 percent of the anomalous second-hand movements; in the second half hour, the average was 26 percent. The remedy was clear: don't trust humans, no matter how diligent and conscientious, to pay attention to nothing. They cannot do so reliably for more than a half hour.[55] Mackworth published his results in 1948, but seven decades later, people designing high-tech systems that depend upon sustained human vigilance still have not given them their due. Driving a conventional car, of course, demands vigilance, too, but humans sustain their attention far better when they have things to pay attention to, and when their attention is constantly needed.

In 2018, seventy years after Mackworth's study was published, Uber was operating self-driving vehicles on the streets and roads of Tempe, Arizona. Though the cars were programmed to limit safety maneuvers that passengers would find unpleasant, all of them were supervised by safety drivers who were to be ready to intervene at any moment. Such, at least, was the proposition. In fact, the safety driver's task, whenever the car was in autonomous mode, was to pay attention to nothing.

Such work was hard enough in the 1940s, when Mackworth conducted his study. His RAF cadets were closely supervised, however, with nothing else to do. After hours of uneventful driving, in a car that was in autonomous mode and performing faultlessly, a safety driver's temptation to look at a phone—and eventually to stare at it—was high. It is no surprise, then, that eventually a safety driver, driving the same route for the seventy-third time, was watching a program on her phone as her car traveled unsupervised at 45 miles per hour.[56] She had ceded her part in the machine-human collaboration that was supposed to keep the system safe. It was an entirely predictable event.

After Herzberg's death, tech companies and automakers showed growing interest in bypassing the intermediate stage (where driver and automated systems collaborate) to "full autonomy" (where the automation is so good that human supervision is unnecessary). But the leap has proved daunting, and automated driving systems that share responsibilities with human drivers are still a practical limit. With automated driving systems, the car takes care of the boring tasks (staying in the lane, maintaining speed, decelerating as a vehicle ahead is neared), while the human driver is ready to take over should the need ever arise. And it may never arise—meaning that the driver, for perhaps hours at a stretch, is expected to pay attention to nothing.

Alerts can help, but a driver who needs alerts is no longer contributing to the human-machine collaboration. Risk compensation tells us that while alerts may begin as a clear safety gain, drivers are likely to grow dependent on them, letting them become an unconscious excuse to pay less attention. Automated driving systems have saved lives. Given what we know about extreme inattention among some drivers who were killed while their Tesla's Autopilot was engaged, we can safely conclude that they have cost lives as well. According to an automation optimist: "At present, there are insufficient data to comment on whether Tesla's current Autopilot, or other types of (partially) automated driving systems, are safe or unsafe compared to manual driving."[57]

It is, again, not a binary problem. Automated systems work best when they promote human-machine collaboration—admittedly no easy task. Too often, however, they deter it, for example, by requiring drivers to pay attention to nothing, or by inducing overconfidence (as the name Autopilot surely does). When the predictable crashes ensue, companies have been disposed to blame "human error," and regulators have sometimes agreed.[58] But to design a system that assigns humans responsibilities that defy ordinary cognitive performance limits, and then blame "human error" when the human does not fulfill them, is to blame an individual for traits common to the species. In such cases, tech companies might be tempted to resort to blaming "species error" instead—but this would be to blame themselves, since the species is rather well known, and sound system design must accept its attributes as givens. Drivers and their cars (automated or not) are not two distinct systems operating in parallel. Drivers make their judgments as human components with human cognitive traits within a system that includes the vehicle, making the isolation of human error always difficult and often impossible.

Promoters of fully automated cars often promise that they will be safer because they will follow all rules of the road scrupulously, and strictly comply with speed limits. According to one authority writing in 2020: "Automated vehicles will obey speed limits, stay within the lane lines," and "stop at stop signs and red signals."[59] Another forecast anticipates a pedestrian's daydream: "Because autonomous vehicles will be risk-averse," people on foot may "be able to behave with impunity." Therefore AVs "may facilitate a shift toward pedestrian-oriented urban neighborhoods," though "autonomous vehicle adoption may be hampered by their strategic disadvantage that slows them down in urban traffic."[60]

But it's too soon to know, and the assumption is unjustified. We have seen pedestrians lose their advantages before. When automobiles first proliferated on American streets a century ago, their drivers had to yield to pedestrians everywhere they encountered them. Speed limits were very low, and the law was on the pedestrian's side. The consequence was not that driving was permanently deterred and pedestrians prevailed but that enterprises with a business interest in a future for cars in cities organized to influence laws, norms, and engineering standards in their favor. If AVs proliferate, means will be found to deter pedestrians who would slow them down. An offending pedestrian might be subjected to obnoxious sounds, or even to facial recognition systems.

Drivers who find scrupulously observant AVs frustratingly slow will prefer their own cars, and resist policy efforts to restrict conventional cars in favor of AVs that strictly follow every rule. Promoters of AVs will then have to apply their vehicles' prodigious computational power to working out just how far beyond the limits of the traffic rules they can go without penalty. Just as machine learning programs can learn to help AVs distinguish a plastic bag from a more serious obstacle, they can learn where, when, and by how much a speed limit may be exceeded with impunity. Competitive pressures will also give companies reason to program cars that tactically exceed speed limits.

Circa 2006, Volkswagen engineers programmed VW diesel models for the US market to determine when they were being subjected to state emissions tests, and to temporarily run the engine more cleanly to pass inspection. This cheat was illegal, but programming a car to moderately exceed the speed limit may not be—after all, a state that takes a strict regulatory position would be inviting other states to attract business by taking a laxer position. Machine learning can enable AVs to optimize rule breaking; programs, applying a cost-benefit analysis better than any human driver can, may learn just how much they may exceed a speed limit and just which rules violations are worth committing. States that demand code that ensures unwavering compliance with all rules are less likely to have scrupulously compliant AVs than no AVs at all. A reliable AV that costs far more than a conventional car but that is also much slower will have a limited market.

Much as AV developers must compete to offer passengers a convenient ride, states compete to attract the businesses engaged in developing AVs. And just as a tech company that puts safety first risks losing customers, a state that puts safety first risks losing tech companies. The consequence is an incentive to compromise safety standards so as to attract business. In December 2016, after California refused to permit Uber to operate self-driving cars on public roads, Arizona's governor, Doug Ducey, issued a press release: "Arizona welcomes Uber self-driving cars with open arms and wide open roads. While California puts the brakes on innovation and change with more bureaucracy and more regulation, Arizona is paving the way for new technology and new businesses. . . . California may not want you, but we do."[61] The cost of welcoming Uber was permitting Uber to take chances with the lives of Arizona's residents. Despite Herzberg's death, the incentive persists.

Hence the safety performance that AVs theoretically can deliver does not tell us what they actually will deliver. But even the theoretical benefit is in doubt. In typical accounts of theoretical safety performance, all the human faults that machines do not commit (particularly fatigue, inattention, intoxication, and recklessness) are subtracted, but numerous machine faults that humans do not commit are not added in.[62] Computers are subject to unexpected processing delays. Objects human drivers easily identify may be much harder for AVs. Humans are and will remain far better at estimating other humans' intentions.

Aging hardware, exposed to varying heat, cold, and humidity, may err. To work, sensors must be exposed enough to be vulnerable. Programming judgments can have undesirable consequences: for example, in the car that killed Elaine Herzberg, every time the system reclassified the object it was detecting, it recalculated its trajectory anew, beginning each recalculation by assuming the object was static. The procedure was a factor in Herzberg's death because the program reclassified her several times.[63] Particular programming deficiencies would come and go, but deficiencies in general would persist. The ubiquitous assertions to the effect that AVs don't drink, get drowsy, check their phones, or become impulsive omit these and other machine vulnerabilities.

The complexity of crash prevention is compounded by the devilish problem of combining AVs and conventional cars. Unless AVs are to be confined to a few reserved routes forever, they would have to mix with human-driven vehicles for many years. Legislators who care about reelection will not support proposals to ban conventional cars in order to smooth the transition. Manufacturers can begin by installing vehicle-to-vehicle communications systems in all cars, including conventional cars, so that conventional cars and AVs interact better. But such systems will be expensive, and meanwhile, millions of cars without such systems would remain on the road for decades.

Health, emissions, congestion, and social equity

But is zero crashes even the right goal? Cars are a public health matter both because of the injuries and deaths that crashes cause, and because they are a primary factor in sedentary living, a major contributor to cardiovascular disease, obesity, and diabetes.[64] Where street patterns are optimized for driving, they deter walking, with consequences for health.[65] Car emissions also cause or worsen asthma and other health conditions, and distribute the health hazards inequitably.[66] If, eventually, all cars are electric vehicles, the power demand may compel retaining electric power plants that burn fossil fuels, which may have health implications of their own.[67]

In the most optimistic accounts of the AV future, collisions per vehicle mile of travel (VMT) will fall. But as horrific as the road death toll is, sedentary living is a far greater contributor to premature death. AV developers promise "seamless mobility"; that is, passengers would have door-to-door service on demand. And since passengers could use their travel time for work, play, or sleep, they may be willing to travel much farther. This in turn means that distances between destinations would grow, as decision makers adjusted to a world in which distance matters less. Hence total time sitting in vehicles would likely go up, both because car users would spend more time in vehicles, and because those who had not been car users might turn to cars as growing distances make alternatives to driving even less practical. The result would be an increase in sedentary living, and a consequent exacerbation of the health toll of sedentary living.

Declining risk per mile traveled may be offset by rising total vehicle miles of travel. Indeed, this tendency is attractive to automakers. In a 2015 report, the consultancy KPMG promised automakers that "consumers want one trillion miles of more mobility," and that AVs could meet the demand.[68] At the current US road fatality rate of 1.1 deaths per 100 million VMT, that would mean 11,000 more road deaths.[69] If AVs were, say, twice as safe as conventional cars (a very optimistic estimate), the result would mean five or six thousand additional deaths each year. Fortunately, the overall content of the KPMG report gives us ample reason to doubt the validity of its conclusions. Yet even its aspirations are troubling. And because passengers would generate data as they traveled in AVs, and the data would be collected and monetized,[70] tech companies would seek ways to keep passengers in cars longer, for the same reason that they found ways to keep people on their phones longer. Conventional cars have already contributed to disastrous public health trends. "Seamless mobility," growing distances between destinations, and in-car media may accelerate the disaster.

Because safety is AV promoters' favorite selling point, it warrants as much attention here as carbon dioxide emissions, congestion effects, and social equity together. Turning to emissions: AV developers favor electric vehicles, which have no tailpipes and hence zero tailpipe emissions. They depend on electric power grids, which in the United States are now at about 15 to 20 percent renewables. If the total extent of driving stayed constant, a switch to electric-drive vehicles would reduce total emissions. The picture gets a little better when the greater energy efficiency of electric vehicles is taken into account; we can also hope that the share of renewables in the grid will grow.

But the AV future that we are presented with is a future of much greater total driving. AV developers themselves celebrate the freed-up time that vehicle occupants would enjoy in an AV. A falling time cost of travel means more reason for longer commutes, longer journeys, and more remote locations for businesses and residences. Even without AVs, car-centric transportation planning, in the pursuit of less delay for drivers, has driven destinations ever farther apart.[71] Hence in AV promoters' brightest scenarios, demand on the grid would rise prodigiously, both as the passenger vehicle fleet becomes electric, and as people drive more. Such a surge might stop or even reverse the trend in the share of the grid that is generated by renewables. In turn, this means that the total emissions picture might be little better, or even worse, than the status quo today. But electric power includes other environmental implications, particularly those having to do with the sourcing and the disposal of the metals that batteries require. In both cases, however, the people most affected may be too distant and out of sight to command the attention they deserve. This would, of course, be a case of history repeating itself. The sourcing of fuel for conventional automobiles, exposure to the pollutants they emit, and disposal of worn-out automobiles have all disproportionately burdened people who don't drive.

AVs would tend to relieve congestion in several ways. They could space themselves more closely together in fast traffic, reduce variability in speeds, and automatically select optimum routes, making more efficient use of exiting street capacity. They could depart from congested areas to find parking. As taxis or as microtransit ("mobility as a service"), they would induce some car owners to go carless, so that more use could be made of fewer cars.[72] But all these effects are counteracted by others that would tend to worsen congestion.

Efficiency gains can have surprising effects. As the efficiency of a device improves, it will make better use of the time, energy, or other resources it requires. At the same time, however, the devices become more advantageous to use and are therefore used more. A faster internet connection saves you time whenever you go online, but it also makes going online more rewarding and less frustrating, so you're likely to spend more time online, not less. The effect has been well established since 1865, when the

English polymath Stanley Jevons investigated the problem of how long Britain's coal reserves could be expected to last. By conventional wisdom, the forecast was good. Though steam engines for railways, steamships, factories, and other work were consuming a lot of coal, their efficiencies were improving steadily, and as they improved, total coal consumption per year would surely fall. Jevons, however, showed that while efficiency improvements in steam engines reduced coal consumed per unit work, they collectively increased total coal consumption as steam engines grew more profitable to use. In the uses they already had, they were used more; meanwhile entirely new uses became profitable. The consequence, Jevons explained, is that efficiency gains in the use of a resource tend to increase total consumption, not diminish it.[73]

Interstate highways were sold on grounds of traffic safety and national defense, but above all as congestion relief. But because they made driving more efficient for each driver, they stimulated enormous increases in total driving, negating their purported benefit to the point that before the network was completed in the 1990s, the promoters of Futurama 3 were claiming that congestion was costing $100 billion a year. This claim was a favorite justification for a new smart highways program that was supposed to cost even more than the interstates. As Jevons could have told them 130 years earlier, however, the efficiency improvements they promised would have accelerated the driving growth trend, diminishing or negating the congestion relief they sold.

In cities, Uber and Lyft tend to exacerbate congestion for some of the same reasons that AVs would.[74] The necessity of parking a conventional car often compels drivers to leave it blocks from their destination, typically in a less congested area. But with an Uber, a Lyft, or an AV, passengers summon a car to a location of their choosing, and they take it to or near the door of their destination. At busier destinations, traffic-choking drop-off and pickup lines would form. Long "car lines" at schools already exist because the school children don't park. AVs would have a similar effect on their adult passengers. A century of experience with conventional cars teaches us how urban form will respond to these pressures. Cars (conventional and AV) set a low density limit, to which they offer their own solution: low-density sprawl accessible by car only. AVs, however, would multiply the effect by letting their occupants do as they please with their time. This trend in turn would increase the total energy requirements of passenger transportation.

Although GM's triple promise is silent about social equity, fully autonomous vehicles may someday let people who cannot safely drive a car enjoy cars' benefits without depending upon someone else to drive. It's difficult to see how this can be achieved, however, since anything less than full autonomy would be of little use, and there's no clear path to affordable, safe, and practical full autonomy, except on certain dedicated routes. Nevertheless this possibility clearly warrants investigation, provided more promising possibilities are not neglected.

In other respects, however, AVs appear to be far more likely to worsen transportation inequities. "Shared" (rented) AVs may be a means for some to forgo car ownership, but AVs are so expensive that even just riding in one will have to be pricey. Costs for essential equipment (lidar, batteries) are falling, but from such high starting points that the cost of a riding in a small driverless vehicle will have to be closer to cab fare than to bus fare. The long-term economics look better for larger autonomous buses, but conventional buses are still way ahead, and they, too, can serve populations that cannot drive.

Manufacturers appear to be content to develop AVs that will be unaffordable to many people—and perhaps even to most. But this does not mean that those who can afford AVs will have a new option while those who cannot will at least have what they have now. Widely deployed, AVs would tend to make all other means of mobility harder, at least by accelerating the tendency for destinations to grow farther apart. By speeding travel for drivers, conventional cars promoted a geographic diffusion that degraded bus service and often made walking or cycling impractical. Such trends made car ownership less a convenience than a necessity, even among people who could barely afford the many expenses involved. AVs may be introduced merely as options for those who choose to pay for them, but they will tend to reshape environments in ways that would soon make them practical necessities. In such a case, AVs would worsen already gross social inequities in transportation. The conventional car exacerbated class divides in transport; AVs would perpetuate this effect.

Given its implausibilities, Autonorama may appear to be a failure. But such an assessment would be like judging salesmanship by the product. Decades ago, when I spent a week in sales school ahead of a very brief career in door-to-door selling, I learned that success in sales does not begin with a good product but rather with a skill for telling an attractive story in which the product is the protagonist. The story begins in the present, where a hardship burdens the customer, but it unfolds in a future in which the product vanquishes the hardship. If this future is strategically timed, the seller will be gone when the product fails to fulfill its heroic role. The consequent credibility gap will deter further sales, but memories fade. In time, old products can be repackaged as new solutions, and old stories can be rewritten with new characters. The product does not have to work as promised—indeed one product's disappointments become the next seller's opportunity. The next product needs only a seller, a skillful storyteller whose confident enthusiasm inspires credibility. By this standard, all four futuramas have been successes, and among them Autonorama has been second to none.

CHAPTER 5

Data Don't Drive

*Technology is too important to be left to
the technology companies.*[1]
— Jack Stilgoe

In December 2020, BMW and Amazon Web Services
announced their intention to "team up to accelerate
data-driven innovation in the automotive industry."[1]
Though definitions of *data driven* have been vague,
inconsistent, and scarce, the term is a consistent favorite among proponents of AVs. Now often associated
with *big data*, a term that began to emerge in 2010,
data driven is much older and has proved more durable. Though *big data* continues strong, its frequency of
use has ebbed; meanwhile *data driven* continues its long
acceleration. If big data is a sprinter, data driven has
been a marathon runner.

Every futurama has had means of shielding its visions from criticism and of marginalizing other visions. As fanciful as they have been, futuramas have flown the flag of science and walled themselves with invocations of science. Visions of the future depend upon human values and cannot be assessed apart from values—but values invite debate. Science, however, can claim an authority that disqualifies others. Limited access to expertise, resources, and data can concentrate scientific authority, giving it political power. When researchers are hired and put to work in the service of an interest group's agenda, their message may have little to do with science, but it may retain science's authority anyway—at least for a time. And as credibility erodes, hired science can adapt to restore it. After the credibility gap that followed from the unkept promise of smart highways in the 1990s, promoters of high-tech car dependency found new ways to hoard scientific authority and use it to shield their vision from criticism. Rather suddenly, their agendas were "data driven."

Only data-driven solutions count

"Data driven" has proved versatile and adaptable. The computer programmers who introduced the term in the 1970s would not have recognized its typical uses since the 1990s. To programmers, a data-driven program was one that responds to the data it processes. This obscure technical term got its breakout opportunity in the 1990s, through the vehicle of total quality management (TQM). As a management fashion, TQM was in decline by 1995,[2] but its redefinition of *data driven* has been its enduring legacy.

In TQM, decision-making was to be determined not by reasoning, experience, or intuition, but by data. Popularizers of TQM celebrated data-driven decision-making, known among insiders as DDDM. TQM promised that "data driven analysis . . . counteracts political influence."[3] Its advocates welcomed the associations of *data driven* with technology, but were indifferent to its technical definition. For example, in 1992 and 1993, CareerTrack, a company that offered public and private business seminars, hosted numerous seminars introducing ambitious business people to TQM in dozens of US and Canadian cities. At all of them, according to CareerTrack's billing, audiences learned that "only data-driven solutions count."[4] TQM celebrated "data-driven decision making" (DDDM), and though the TQM fashion is over, DDDM is still exalted in business circles.[5]

The doctrine embeds a flawed assumption. Data cannot "drive" or make judgments; data can only guide them. Even in a data-driven program, the program's responses to data are ultimately human determined. Sound judgments are data guided, not data driven. Someone must decide which data matter and which do not; no such judgment can be data driven. Someone must interpret the data. A ship's compass guides the navigator; it does not and cannot drive the ship or choose the destination. Data can tell people which efforts are serving their goals and which are not, but the goals are chosen first, and by people. In a dark place, a flashlight guides but does not drive its holder. Terabytes or petabytes of data can transform the guidance that data analytics have to offer, but humans must still determine what to do with the results. A searchlight is far more illuminating than a lighted match, but even a searchlight only guides.

But TQM's promoters, such as CareerTrack, could not have settled for insisting merely on data-guided judgments. No one needs to pay for a seminar to tell them that data matter; there would have been nothing novel in it. In 1893, exactly one hundred years before CareerTrack's seminar speakers were celebrating data-driven solutions, F. W. Taylor was beginning a career advising executives that extensive, precise measurements would revolutionize their businesses.[6] Such guidance was far too familiar to qualify TQM as the management breakthrough its advocates purported it to be.

In its loose terminology, CareerTrack was not betraying TQM's pioneers. According to a researcher who was himself a TQM practitioner for twenty years, TQM itself was never "data driven"; the management gurus who inspired it "relied heavily upon personal experience and anecdotal evidence."[7] TQM's advocates elevated *data driven*, despite its essential flaw, to a new cardinal virtue—a virtue more often asserted than measured. The effective manager is data driven. Long after TQM's decline, "data-driven leadership" remains idolized.[8]

After their technical successes in the 2007 DARPA Urban Challenge, promoters of autonomous vehicles soon celebrated themselves and their products as "data driven." AV enthusiasts assigned a surprising new purpose to the word: it characterized AVs as not merely feasible but inevitable, even irresistible. Media relayed the claims. "Autonomous vehicles are coming, whether we like it or not," announced *The Car Connection* in 2012.[9] "There is no doubt that self-driving cars are coming," reported *The Economist* in 2012.[10] The *Wall Street Journal* and *Time* concurred.[11] "The data-driven car is coming—whether you like it or not," explained *InformationWeek* in 2014.[12] Data drive, not people.

These forecasts of inevitability, as if human judgments were unnecessary or worse, reflected a growing confidence in what DDDM could do in the age of big data. In 2008 Chris Anderson, the editor in chief of *Wired*, wrote an editorial for the magazine proposing that big data substantially removed humans as the intermediaries between problems and answers. "This is a world where massive amounts of data and applied mathematics replace every other tool that might be brought to bear," Anderson wrote. "Out with every theory of human behavior. . . . With enough data, the numbers speak for themselves."[13] The future indeed could and should be data driven, and not merely data guided. Data itself would disintermediate human judgment. What Anderson proposed, according to two commenters, was not merely that data-driven decision-making is apolitical but that big data analytics "depoliticizes data."[14]

Anderson's enthusiasm was widely shared. Soon researchers

from first-class universities, publishing their work in peer-reviewed journals of research, accepted *data driven* despite the promotional baggage it carried from its TQM days. Many of them kept to the modifier's original, narrow, technical sense, for programs that respond to data in human-determined ways. But even when researchers' usage was careful, the term acquired a credibility that invited exploitation by those who claimed their corporate agendas were data driven. As the word proliferated in published research articles, AV promoters insisted not only that certain programs were data driven in a strict, technical sense, but their companies, products, and solutions were also somehow "data driven."

Coinciding closely with the proliferation of the term in research, management books promised to make their readers "data-driven leaders." In 2008, Thomas C. Redman published *Data-Driven: Profiting from Your Most Important Business Asset*, though *data driven* appears nowhere in the text of the book.[15] The trend soon accelerated: A 2014 book promised to teach *Data-Driven Leadership*.[16] More remarkably, a 2016 book claimed *Data Driven Leaders Always Win*, a thesis that itself defies data-guided evaluation.[17] Taking the opposite extreme, another book on data-driven leadership promised specifics: *Use Real Numbers to Improve Your Business by 352%*.[18] The persistence of the trend suggests that *data driven* sells books[19]; it also appears to sell AV enthusiasm.

A little scrutiny indicates that what these guides really advise is quite predictable: data-guided profit seeking. It should come as no surprise that for-profit companies (unlike computer programs) are never data driven but

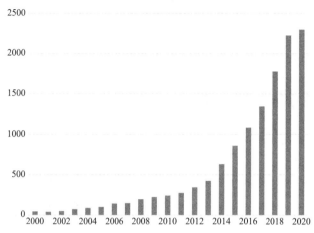

"Data driven" in the titles of research articles in the Web of Science Database, 2000–2020. (Data: Web of Science)

rather profit driven; data matter (or not) only according to whether they serve this purpose. But this rather obvious fact has not prevented companies from claiming that their "mobility solutions" are superior because they are "data driven."[20] More troublingly, news media have generally accepted and amplified such claims.

Because data monetization obscures the distinction between a data-driven company and a profit-driven company, data driven may appear to be an apt descriptor for a profit-seeking company. Since data can be monetized, data seeking by a for-profit enterprise *is* profit seeking. But this fact makes the distinction more important, not less. Because data are not all equally monetizable, a profit-driven company that monetizes data will favor some data over others; it will also want more data overall. Hence a "data-driven mobility" company will be less interested in mobility than in data, and then only certain kinds of data. Such a company will favor more trips, not fewer, and more time spent in vehicles, not less. Profit seeking induces companies to offer their customers a good product—but if a mobility company's paying customers are data brokers and the product is data, then data collection, not mobility, comes first.

Jack Stilgoe has aptly observed that "this mismatch" leads "companies to obfuscate the real nature of the exchange."[21] Such a company will be more interested in promoting transport consumerism than in serving mobility needs. Transport consumerism will tend to better serve the affluent passenger, whose data are of more value. Other passengers, far from being merely neglected, will tend to be disserved, because mobility systems are networks subject to network effects. The twentieth century should have taught us that accommodation of expensive transport does not merely neglect affordable mobility; it actively degrades it. Similarly, it should have taught us what Charles Kettering already understood in 1929: that transport consumerism is uninterested in satisfying consumers' mobility needs; it wants to promote consumption by "keeping the consumer dissatisfied."

Transport-driven data collection

To a truly "data-driven mobility" company, mobility is not the point. It is in the business of transport-driven data collection through transport consumerism. Though the vocabulary is new, the mischievousness of data is clearly not. In the twentieth century, motordom used data to show—purportedly—that hazards attributed to motorists were in fact due to the pedestrians their vehicles struck, that congestion caused by motor vehicles was best relieved by accommodating more motor vehicles, and that a circumstantial decision to drive in the absence of any decent alternative was the expression of an absolute preference to drive. Data that served the interests of the predominant interest groups prevailed. Other data, no less important to the people getting around, were neglected. Ruth Oldenziel has documented such "vanishing tricks," whereby less profitable mobility modes and practices disappeared from purportedly objective engineering reports.[22] In the 1971 classic *Autokind vs. Mankind*, illustrator Richard D. Hedman captured such legerdemain in a cartoon that is as apt today as it was fifty years ago.[23]

Digital data collection, however, has imparted a new degree of distortion to the mobility landscape, by making transport a means of collecting monetizable data. Some data companies have made this point themselves, as emphatically as any of their critics would have done. In 2006, a consultant named Clive Humby told a conference of advertisers: "Data is the new oil."[24] By then, Humby had already proved that he could extract crude data streams from customers and refine them into a profitable resource.[25] In transport, data extraction entails getting people into vehicles more often, and for longer periods.

"Data is the new oil" soon proliferated in tech and

investment circles. The possibilities of data collection in transport were most memorably expressed by Brian Krzanich, the CEO of Intel Corporation. Courting partners in the automobile business, Krzanich delivered a keynote address at the AutoMobility Conference of the 2016 Los Angeles Auto Show, promising industry that AVs equipped with Intel hardware would generate lucrative data for them.[26] Krzanich repeated the appeal in a corporate press release. For the title of his speech, he used Humby's dictum: "Data Is the New Oil."[27] This time the promise was that AVs would serve as prodigious collectors of monetizable data. Krzanich explained: "Every autonomous car will generate the data equivalent of almost 3,000 people"—so much data that carmakers would have to partner with Intel to process it all. Intel could help companies collect "data that tracks how many people are in the car, music preferences of each passenger, or even what stores or brands passengers prefer and, when you are near them, tees up sale items." Krzanich pledged that, with partners in the automobile industry, Intel would "accelerate automated driving" to take advantage of this "opportunity." He announced that Intel was "targeting more than $250 million of additional new investments over the next two years to make fully autonomous driving a reality." He closed with a direct appeal: "Let Intel be your trusted partner as the world moves toward fully automated driving." The endeavor, he promised, would "improve safety, mobility and efficiency," but above all, it would "create value from data."[28] In Krzanich's vision, data is the new oil and the vehicle occupant is the oil well.

Krzanich's candor reveals the importance of identifying what really "drives" an enterprise. An AV manufacturer or fleet operator may call itself a "mobility company," but if it seeks maximum collection of monetizable data, it may degrade actual mobility both for its customers and for others. Manufacturers of mobile phones and their data-collecting clients have learned how to turn a communications device into a data-collection device, sometimes in ways that are debilitating to the device's owner.[29] Companies engaged in the "attention economy" value attention over practical utility to the point that mobile device addiction is now a perennial contender for formal classification as a mental health condition.

AV promoters have promised that AVs will be the "ultimate mobile device." If such devices join the attention economy, we may anticipate efforts to induce compulsive use of them as well. If Krzanich is right and an hour in an AV generates three thousand times the data of an hour on a phone, the incentives will be powerful. If AV manufacturers and fleet operators find ways to promote excessive vehicle use to generate more data, the costs in terms of sustainability, equity, safety, health, and practical mobility itself may be comparable to those incurred by the advent of conventional car dependency. Rather than "self-driving mobility," the effects might better be termed "self-driving data generation." In discussions of the security of user data from illicit, third-party access, we should wonder if the licit second party is any more trustworthy.

In the "car data monetization arena"

It is not easy to imagine what compulsive AV use would look like, but the same might have been said twenty years ago about phones, the addictive properties of which were largely unforeseen. As Krzanich was preparing to deliver his remarks at the 2016 LA Auto Show, he had access to a new report from McKinsey & Company that presented industry insiders' review of the possibilities. By their own account, AVs are less a means of improving mobility than of overcoming the greatest single constraint on personal data collection besides sleep: the attentional demands of driving.

"How would the car infotainment change, once fully autonomous vehicles are on the market and drivers/riders have the freedom to devote themselves to other tasks?" the report asks. "How much more content and how many more movies and virtual-reality videogames could be sold if drivers could enjoy them while riding in their autonomous vehicles?" The consultancy estimated that "full autonomy might be the main enabler for certain use cases, such as offering virtual-reality movies or games to drivers/riders." If tech companies and automakers make the most of the "car data monetization arena," they could develop a world market worth "up to USD 450–750 billion by 2030."[30]

To do this, AV developers must make car occupancy "social and fun." They can offer passengers "a social and interactive experience," like social media on wheels. "With in-car screens and augmented reality as the interface, this type of data also has the potential to support interactive games between drivers." To these companies, the attraction of AVs is uninterrupted access to the passenger's attention through digital "fun"—and "what is fun for drivers can be quite lucrative for the players who control car data's social space." Besides automakers and AV tech companies, these "players" could include "suppliers, gaming software houses, and telcos," plus "the social media giants, who could gain more in-car access to their users."[31] In 2017 anyone hoping to cash in on the data monetization bonanza in autonomous vehicles could get a readable guide to the subject.[32] While automakers were telling the public that AVs are for safe, sustainable, and efficient mobility, tech companies were telling automakers that AVs are their opportunity to get in on the growing monetizable data market.

Such trends are not driven by data. They are driven by *monetized* data—in a word, money. "The difference between the *almost right* word and the *right* word," Mark Twain explained, "is really a large matter—'tis the difference between the lightning-bug and the lightning."[33] When *data* is used where *monetized* (or *monetizable*) *data* is intended, the conflation treats vast realms of real data—including data of vital importance to people—as nonexistent. It is this kind of fallacy that can make a parking lot an obviously superior use for a half acre of urban land than a playground, or a golf course better than a wetland, or a high-end condominium better than a low-rent apartment building. In all such evaluations, public policy is implicated, and in public policy, more than material profitability is at stake. Sound public policy considers profitability, but it also considers other values. Good policy is data guided, and recognizes value in data that data monetizers neglect.

Data are not and never can be equal. One person's shade tree is another's obstacle. Both responses are data, but neither datum can tell us what to do (if anything) with the tree. Someone must choose, either directly or through an algorithm, and the choice may be data guided, but it will not be data driven. Information is like money. Whose pocket is it in? What's the exchange rate? When the information indicates a conflict, who is prioritized?

The champions of "data-driven decision making" claim the mantle of rationalism, asserting that their methods are the only alternative to "gut instinct."[34] They might have something to learn, therefore, from Isaac Newton, whose work is esteemed among rationalists. Newton demonstrated that while any object may have acceleration, acceleration alone will not determine which of two objects will prevail in a collision. An object's force—its drive—is due not only to its acceleration but also its mass. By analogy, all data that people care about have acceleration. But data's force, their drive, is due to the mass behind them. Data don't drive; power does. Excluding human judgment is not to depoliticize data. Data that people care about are inherently political—because people care about them.

Motordom's history in the United States confirms what the historical record more generally demonstrates:

agendas, not data, drive history. An agenda is the product of a social group's interests, ideas, and values; a group's agenda reflects what its members judge to be profitable, true, or right. Because all three constituents of an agenda vary by group, no one agenda suits all, and agendas cannot be reduced to interchangeable quantities. Agendas determine which data matter and which do not; they also determine how much data matter, and in what way. Because agendas are diverse, there is no objectifying or depoliticizing data, and efforts to do so are likely to be efforts at agenda advancement. In the beginning is the agenda; the data follow.

Perpetuating car dependency the smart way

Futuramas have sold not just cars but also fast, safe, congestion-free driving. These were not promises anyone could fulfill, but in keeping the consumer dissatisfied, they were true to Charles Kettering's precept. Always just over an ever-receding horizon lay the high-speed, delay-free, drive-everywhere city. Highway engineers and policymakers tirelessly pursued it, routing expressways through cities and recommitting urban real estate to car storage. The harder they strove to accommodate all driving, the more they deterred all alternatives to driving, and the more they made driving a practical necessity for everyone, whether they could afford it or not. The futuramas sold motor utopia; the never-finished product was car dependency.

Twentieth-century highway engineers designed roads to prevent collisions, with considerable success. Highway design, together with new vehicle safety standards, diminished the risk of each mile traveled. Above all, highway engineering was a relentless effort to reduce vehicular "delay" due to traffic congestion, at breathtaking cost. Yet despite the declining road risk per mile, total casualties—including about thirty-seven thousand deaths each year—have remained so high that AV promoters cite them as the primary justification for their high-tech ambitions. And that they have remained so high was an entirely predictable effect of the effort to relieve "delay" (delay to motor vehicles) at any cost. Every such effort promoted growing dependency on the most hazardous mode of transport. Car dependency is consumerism's greatest achievement. The business enterprises that benefit from it naturally strive to perpetuate it. Autonorama is the latest version of this effort.

For credibility, each new iteration of the old promises must make an impression of novelty. Vocabulary is a means of evoking novelty; a new name can give an old idea a state-of-the-art appearance. Systems can be called *solutions*, renting can be called *sharing*, and transport can be called *mobility*. About twenty years ago, social scientists began to limit their use of the words *transport* and *transportation* in favor of the word *mobility*.[35] They had good reasons. Transport and transportation bore connotations of people and goods in motorized vehicles. In surface transportation, this meant particularly cars, trucks, buses, and trains. The word was also associated with certain quantifiable values: in transport, high speed is better—even if growing distances negate much of the benefit. Transport tended to be treated as an economic transaction measured in time, dollars, and deliveries. But social scientists wanted a means to look at transport, especially passenger transport, without bringing all this baggage along.

So with increasing frequency, they spoke of "mobility." Freed from the connotations of transport, they could consider mobility in all its variety: driving certainly, but also walking purposefully, strolling, cycling, propelling a wheelchair, crossing a street. They included the qualitative experiences associated with mobility, such as listening to music in the car, waiting at the bus stop, conversation, or finding privacy through an opened book. What they found is that the expression *passenger transportation*, at least as it has typically been used, misses as much as it captures, and thereby distorts.

A person in a vast exurb with ample transportation in the form of an expensive personal automobile may feel more isolated—physically and socially—than a person with no more than an old bicycle who lives where coffee may be had at the next corner, and where the bus stops every twenty minutes. The resident of the exurb may have more transportation, and certainly travels much more in terms of distance, but she also has poor choices. Her car will not be an additional choice but the only practical choice. The person with a bicycle in a cycling-friendly district may have greater mobility, in the sense that she can meet her needs locally, easily, cheaply, and sometimes enjoyably, across much shorter distances. Above all, when the time spent in travel is regarded not as a total loss but a qualitative experience, walking and cycling tend to look much more like worthy modes of mobility, even if studies of transportation often neglect them.

Even during Futurama 3, the promoters of transport consumerism through high-tech car dependency had perceived the advantages of the term *mobility* over *transportation*.[36] The coalition that became IVHS America and, later, ITS America, began as Mobility 2000. Still, during Futurama 3, *transportation* remained the predominant byword in the industry. Insiders called their industry automated transportation systems (ATS). As Futurama 4 emerged in the early 2000s, however, *mobility* soon became the word of choice. Strangest of all, some are promising a high-tech future of "autonomous mobility," when the mode that best suits this term is walking.[37] People are "pedestrians by design," and walking is autonomous mobility.[38] Walking, however, generates no monetizable data. Paradoxically, therefore, to a data-driven mobility company, walking does not count as mobility.

Like their 1950s counterparts, the covers of industry reports, in depicting urban mobility, tend to conspicuously stress vehicular transport on highways. Autonorama is not interested in modes of mobility demonstrating that small can be beautiful, or that less can be more. They want the benefits of the word *mobility*, with all its humane connotations. They want transport and transportation, but without their unflattering associations, so they renamed them. A real embrace of mobility as a supplement to transport would mean walking away from car dependency as the dominant model in passenger transportation. Car dependency, however, is simply far too lucrative to abandon. Consequently, the tech and auto sectors abuse the mobility label, treating it as a stylish new outfit with which to dress up the old-fashioned words that better suit their actual enterprises.

The examples are abundant, but perhaps the best comes from KPMG's 2015 report to the auto industry—the one that promises that "consumers want one trillion miles of more mobility."[39] Whatever this means (if anything at all), it can't mean that human beings want real *mobility*, such as neighborhoods in which they can walk to a shop. Many do—though this is not a promise a tech company or an automaker can use to sell products. A 2019 report from Allison+Partners takes the reinvention of the word *mobility* a step further. In the press release, the consultancy announced that the report "uncovers a shift from car culture to mobility culture," but reassures readers that in this purported "mobility culture," cars will remain ubiquitous and predominant, and car dependency will persist.[40]

Those who would not be deceived must insist that we use terms carefully. If the AV sales force closes the deal, people may get far more transportation, but at an incalculable cost to their mobility. If mobility becomes just a more fashionable synonym for transportation, we can expect true mobility to suffer.

Industry reports from tech companies and automakers about the future of mobility in cities occasionally depict pedestrians, cyclists, and transit riders in the periphery. Most, however, like these two, feature high-speed, energy-intensive vehicular transport. (a. Canalys, "The Road to Autonomous Vehicles," 2018; b. Future Agenda, "The Future of Autonomous Vehicles," 2019)

PAVE

It was 2010 when *2030 Xing!* presented a vision of ubiquitous, fully autonomous vehicles seamlessly moving millions of residents door to door. By 2018, more than a third of the way to 2030, the closest anyone could get to experiencing the vision on actual roads was to summon an Uber with trained safety driver who could put the vehicle in self-driving mode under constant human supervision. In that year, such an Uber struck and killed Elaine Herzberg. Predictably, the AV promoters argued that the media made too much of this and a handful of other deaths associated with automated vehicles; after all, conventional cars kill about a hundred people a day in the United States alone. But Herzberg's death was worthy of all the attention it received, because it was grounds to question assumptions that AV promoters had too often taken for granted. Could AVs ever be the safe, affordable, and inclusive mode of transportation that their developers promised? By 2018 the question was overdue.

Even before Herzberg's death, American drivers' confidence in AVs was low. In 2016 the American Automobile Association found that 75 percent of drivers "would be afraid to allow an autonomous vehicle to drive itself with them in it."[41] By January 2018, the distrust had diminished: 63 percent reported they would fear riding in an AV.[42] But after deaths linked to automated vehicles, including the one that killed Herzberg, confidence fell. In May 2018, AAA found that 73 percent of drivers surveyed "would be afraid to ride in a fully self-driving vehicle."[43]

Where consumer demand rules, the conclusion might have been that AVs are a dead end and not worth pursuing. But consumer demand has little to do with enthusiasm for AVs among tech companies and automakers. Indeed, the ubiquitous disruption notion reduced consumer demand to a distraction. Competing for investors and corporate partners, companies remained committed to an AV future they still routinely called inevitable. From this perspective, consumers' distrust was an anxiety to be relieved among a population too ill-informed to judge. The need, therefore, was to educate consumers.

History was repeating itself, or at least rhyming. In 1996 ITS America, the smart highway industry coalition, found that people outside the industry were uninterested in what it was selling. ITS America's conclusion was not that it had something to learn about what the public really wanted but rather that it would have to "educate the public" through a "national awareness campaign."[44] Twenty-two years later, AV promoters, facing a similar disappointment, reached the same conclusion. According to one: "The biggest hurdles to widespread adoption of automated vehicles are Joe and Jane Consumer."[45]

In January 2019, at the annual Consumer Electronics Show (CES) in Las Vegas, companies in the AV sector launched a trade association to undertake this educational mission.[46] They called it PAVE: Partners for Automated Vehicle Education. According to its first press release, PAVE's mission was (and is) "to inform the public and policymakers about the potential and the reality of advanced vehicle technologies and self-driving vehicles," and "what's possible in the future—including the benefits for safety, mobility and sustainability."[47] From the start, PAVE was torn between a stated commitment to agenda-free education and its members' commitments to a future of ubiquitous AVs. Above all, given its members' agendas, PAVE could not afford to learn from or listen to the public it set out to "educate."[48]

DDT, cigarette smoking, and the opioid epidemic can have some redeeming value if they are recognized as costly practical lessons. Any major social need will be an opportunity to sell products. While some of these products may help, all will be represented as solutions, the benefits of all will be exaggerated, and their undesirable effects will be denied, discounted, or ignored. Companies will sponsor and publicize the research that's useful to their agendas, while other research, lacking such support, will be overlooked. Companies will present press releases and even write journalistic articles for media to promote their products. They will blur the line between public relations and research, and the line between marketing and journalism. While AVs may be useful components of future mobility systems, they are not in themselves the solutions their promoters claim they are. High-tech car dependency is still car dependency, an affliction so lucrative to some that they will invest vast resources in efforts to save it. Let us not be fooled.

Escape from Futurama

*Future historians may well be amazed by
our distorted sense of proportion.*
—Rachel Carson, *Silent Spring*

A bucket is a useful tool, but at lunchtime it's no substitute for a soupspoon. The twentieth-century effort to rebuild cities around automobiles failed because like buckets, cars are useful tools that can't serve all needs well. The pursuit of the drive-everywhere city served no one well—not even drivers. The consequences of the attempt were destructive, expensive, wasteful, inequitable, unhealthful, and unsustainable.

The pursuit of high-tech driving will not make car dependency work. Instead it will make it harder to develop the things that actually do work. In the name of aspirations of dubious feasibility tomorrow, it diverts resources, research effort, policy attention, and money from tasks that can make a difference today. The pursuit of high-tech driving is not really innovative; it is a leftover from the mid-twentieth century, when public policy in the United States prioritized the automobile over all other modes. Car dependency doesn't work, and the fault is not in the technology. A car is a transport tool, not a mobility panacea. Like other tools, it is well suited to some jobs and unsuited to many others.

Fortunately, we don't have to continue to try to make the car what it inherently is not: an affordable and energy-efficient mode of transport that is well suited to every personal transport need. If a wrench makes a poor nail driver, the solution is not to develop a high-tech wrench but to choose a hammer for driving nails. For urban mobility, we already have the tools we need.

Most reports on the future of urban mobility—particularly the showy ones that get the most attention—reflect the corporate agendas of their sponsors. They depict futures of high-tech car dependency, assuring us that we can solve all our problems if we buy enough sensors, software, and processing power. An exception was a 2020 study conducted for Germany's Federal Foreign Office, called *Transport for under Two Degrees*.[1] To determine what a sustainable transport future would look like, one consistent with less than 2 degrees C of global warming, the researchers surveyed 346 transport experts worldwide, following up with in-depth interviews. They wanted to know what it would take to adjust world transport to carbon neutrality, or as close to it as possible. The conclusions were not exactly heartening; getting to net zero greenhouse gas emissions will of course be extremely difficult at best. Yet in one respect, the report was very encouraging. We don't have to wait for high-tech miracle cures, it suggested. We can start right now. We already have what we need.

For urban mobility, the findings were captured succinctly in a *Forbes* headline by Carlton Reid: "Bicycles and Buses Will Be Future's Dominant Modes of Urban Mobility, Predict 346 Transport Experts."[2] This was hardly the techno-futurism that four generations of futuramas had led us to expect—but neither was the study a rejection of high technology. It will take the best that technology has to offer to make public transportation convenient, efficient, clean, and affordable enough to serve the needs the report recommends for it. The report recast technology from the solver of our problems to a source of tools—high tech, low tech, and no tech—that we can use to manage our problems better. Its prescription is to turn our attention from the daunting task of trying to make car dependency work, to things we already know how to do—and can learn to do better.

We don't know what people prefer

The biggest obstacle in the path toward a more sustainable mobility future is not technology but public policies, laws, and engineering standards that prioritize driving at the expense of everything else.[3] These in turn are inherited historical legacies that influence current patterns, supporting unfounded notions about what people prefer. These notions are sustained in part by selective and misleading versions of history that have been prepared for us by the people who sell car dependency.[4]

At the National Museum of American History in Washington, DC, visitors can learn why American cities lost their once-ubiquitous electric streetcars. "Americans chose another alternative—the automobile," a sign on a wall reads. Today most commuters "prefer to drive alone in their cars from their homes to their workplaces."[5] The sign paradoxically interprets the loss of choices as a choice, and driving in the absence of good choices as a preference to drive. Of course, millions resorted to driving, reluctantly, when they lost all practical alternatives. Given their circumstances, an economist has concluded that "most American workers probably would have shifted to commuting by automobile even if they hated driving."[6] Millions of others, however, struggled to get by without a car in a world redesigned around the implicit assumption that every adult has one—or should.[7] The sign treats "Americans" as a distinct category, when Americans are obviously diverse in their mobility needs, their budgets, their practices, and their preferences.[8] In so doing, it delegitimizes the needs and the preferences of millions.

The museum, which is part of the Smithsonian Institution, is taxpayer supported and free to the public; in 2019 it attracted 2.8 million visitors.[9] Its big transportation exhibit, where the sign about disappearing streetcars is found, is called *America on the Move*. It's in the General

Motors Hall of Transportation, established in 2003 by a $10 million gift from GM; the American Automobile Association contributed $5 million.[10] The sign's claims about history would have us believe that motordom's prodigious and relentless efforts to win policy priority for cars were a wasted effort, because all they had to do was let the popular preference prevail.[11] But motordom never trusted popular preferences so much, and as a result, it's harder to know how people would like to get around. We can't know what Americans prefer, because most have poor choices.

Since the 1930s, US transportation policy—local, state, and national—has prioritized the least efficient mode at the expense of all the others. In the 1920s, the companies that make and sell cars, and those that build roads, lobbied hard to redefine traffic and transportation problems in ways that favor driving. Roadbuilders strove to achieve—in their words—"a radical revision of our conception of what a city street is for."[12] Pedestrian safety, once defined as the responsibility of drivers, was redefined to prioritize drivers. Traffic congestion, once taken to be a symptom of excessive reliance on cars to move people, was redefined as a problem of inadequate streets. Street railways, once justified as spatially efficient passenger vehicles, were faulted as obstructers of automobiles. Collisions between motor vehicles, once attributed to excessive speed, were reattributed to inadequate roads. Strangest of all, the delay that motorists once caused one another by choosing to drive was redefined as a public responsibility to be relieved only through new road capacity, which in turn gradually changed driving from a choice among alternatives to a practical necessity.[13]

The consequent car dependency that afflicts us is the primary cause of all the symptoms that AVs are supposed to relieve: the crashes, the pollution, and the congestion. The AV sales force promises to make car dependency safer, more sustainable, and more spatially efficient. In a similar promise decades ago, tobacco companies promised to make cigarette smoking safer, first by adding filters of ever-increasing elaborateness, then by offering "low-tar" and low-nicotine brands. In retrospect, this strategy was a short-term business success but a long-term public health disaster. It duped smokers into delaying the only step that made sense: to quit smoking. Automated driving systems that promise more than convenience or niche applications—that promise to bring crashes, emissions, and congestion to an end—are similar dead ends. Just as tobacco companies once extended smoking addiction by claiming they offered safe cigarettes, companies today are promising safe, sustainable, and efficient cars that really only extend car dependency.

Car dependency, however, is not a necessity. Far from it. At least in cities, almost all the alternatives to driving or riding in a car are simpler to implement, less expensive to accommodate, safer, more sustainable, more spatially efficient, and more socially equitable. In a world that has been rebuilt for drivers, alternatives to driving can appear to be difficult to offer. But accommodating all would-be drivers and all their demands is actually harder, though we've routinized this expensive priority so successfully that we hardly notice it anymore. Walkability, cycle routes, and basic transit are so much less expensive that even if we diverted only 10 percent of the funds now going to building, maintaining, and policing roads to these means of mobility, we could start to see beneficial trends in a year or two that AVs, at their best, could not begin to deliver for at least another decade.

Far too often, policy makers commit the same error as the sign in the museum. They observe that people overwhelmingly choose to drive and then conclude that they have an absolute preference to drive. In 1993 a Federal Highway Administration report made the conflation strikingly obvious: "Statistics show that Americans prefer their automobiles to all other forms of transportation. Only in rare cases do alternative modes of transportation carry more than a small percentage of all trips."[14] Circumstantial behavior was equated with essential preference. In Denver's 2008 Strategic Transportation Plan, readers learn that "55% of Americans would prefer to drive less and walk more"; three pages later, the document claims that "our behavior illustrates a continued preference to drive."[15] The report proposes an inconsistency between reported and actual preferences, while committing the error of equating circumstantial practices with essential preferences.

In a 2019 report for transit agencies, KPMG makes the same error: citing data indicating circumstantial practices, it concludes that "the private car remains . . . the preferred mode of choice."[16] By the same illogic, one might serve limp, old carrots at a buffet table and conclude from the resulting disinterest in them that no one likes carrots. We know from ample experience that where walking, cycling, and transit are well accommodated and prioritized, and can serve practical daily needs, people walk, cycle, and take transit.

In the absence of choice, choosing to drive is not a preference to drive. A city where the alternatives to driving are so poor that nearly everyone reluctantly resorts to driving will look just like a city where nearly everyone has an unconditional preference to drive. Though the two cities look the same, they are profoundly different: the one city is oppressive and wasteful while the other is merely extravagant by popular choice. To tell the difference would take more than a study of mode usage, and even more than a survey of reported mode preferences. Only a historical study can reveal if a car-dependent environment is more the consequence of a mass demand for cars than its cause. Of course, both factors have been in interactive play wherever cars prevail. Conventional wisdom, however, is historically naïve, and has heavily favored accounts of car dependency that attribute it to mass demand for cars. The explanation is typically taken as self-evident—so much so that no historical inquiry is deemed necessary. Such shortcuts in reasoning excuse proposals to perpetuate car dependency, including proposals for AV-dependent cities.

Implicit in much of the promotion of AVs is a presumption that as we pursue a high-tech future, we have little or nothing to learn from the past. The vacuum left by historical naïveté does not go unfilled. Sucked into the void are various misleading commonplaces, above all that America is a "car culture": a society in which cars were welcomed and favored because they suited predominant values. The notion is about half true; like most half truths, it is also misleading. It was nurtured, developed, refined, and propagated by the first, the most persistent, and the most audible historians of the automobile in American society: automobile manufacturers.

The histories of the car that we grew up with were told for us by motordom. Their versions of history captured the real enthusiasm for cars, calling it "America's love affair with the automobile."[17] But they selectively omitted persistent resistance, especially in cities, to car domination. The resistance was ubiquitous, stubborn, and enduring. Left out of motordom's account, however, it has also been forgotten. The omission enables and protects assumptions that car domination is the popular will, and therefore that efforts to make mobility sustainable, affordable, healthful, and equitable must accept it as a given. Fairer and less partial historical accounts, however—accounts that recover pasts that were selectively omitted from history—will demonstrate that car dependency was not the product of mass preferences. The discovery can free us from far-fetched efforts to apply technology to perpetuate car dependency at any cost.[18]

Perhaps the greatest threat of AVs is that they take car dependency as a given. Since car dependency is a fact of life (the implicit reasoning runs), how do we make it safer, more sustainable, and more efficient? Such a framing makes no more sense than treating cigarette smoking as a constant. Car dependency is no more a given than cigarette addiction. Indeed, the news is better for cars. In the case of cigarette addiction, quitting entirely was the only remedy. But we do not have to totally abandon cars.

Cars, even conventional cars, can be one of many useful devices in a diverse variety of mobility tools. The threat is *car dependency*, where there are no good choices, where even the poor must drive or ride in cars, and where urban form reshapes itself around cars so completely that nothing else works. Urban form reshaped itself around street railways and was reshaped again around cars. When we reset our priorities again—this time around the most healthful, sustainable, affordable, and spatially efficient modes—urban form will adapt yet again.

We have good examples

We don't have to speculate about what we can do now, at relatively low cost and with technology we already have, to make urban mobility much more sustainable, efficient, healthful, and equitable. Among US cities, New York and San Francisco in particular have set examples worth emulating.[19] The National Association of City Transportation Officials has developed standards and guides that are helping American cities improve real mobility, not merely move more cars faster.[20]

But the United States has much to learn from other countries too. As New York City's transportation commissioner from 2007 to 2013, Janette Sadik-Khan made her city a model for the country in its promotion of walkability, cycling, and public transportation. In turn, Sadik-Khan credits her success in part to "stealing good ideas" from other countries.[21] For example, in the 1970s, Bogotá, Colombia, introduced a mobility innovation that is inexpensive, sustainable, inclusive, and popular—and since 2000, it has spread to numerous cities on multiple continents. An early convert to Bogotá's innovation was New York.

The idea is called *ciclovía* (bikeway). Every Sunday and holiday, numerous major streets are closed to vehicles, to be taken over by humans on bikes, on foot, on skateboards and scooters. In 1995 ciclovía was barely surviving on just eight miles of streets. That's when the new head of the city's recreation department, Gil Peñalosa, made a cause of ciclovía; he got more support when his brother Enrique was elected mayor in 1998. By the early 2000s, Bogotá had seventy miles of ciclovía routes—many of them major traffic arteries—all closed to motor vehicles every Sunday from seven o'clock in the morning until two in the afternoon. They proved immensely popular.[22]

In August 2008, Janette Sadik-Khan introduced ciclovías to New York City, calling them Summer Streets: 6.9 miles of Manhattan streets were temporary car-free public parks on three Saturdays that month.[23] The gamble paid off, and New York continued to experiment with ways to make the city more inviting to pedestrians, cyclists, and transit riders.

Though officially an effort to promote recreation, ciclovías were also weekly proof that people can enjoy streets and navigate them without driving—if the streets prioritize them. Business owners who associated dense motor traffic with commerce discovered new markets from people on foot and on bikes. Many people who learned to bike on Sundays had a new chance to become cyclists on weekdays. In the early 2000s, ciclovías attracted worldwide attention and have since been adopted, by various names, in numerous cities worldwide.[24] By themselves, they can't relieve car dependency. But they are an inexpensive first step that can help a city's residents—and its policy makers—question the assumptions that perpetuate car dependency.

Another lesson from Bogotá is the value of temporary, easily reversible experiments. Skeptics can be reassured that if a temporary experiment fails, the idea will be abandoned. Sadik-Khan recalls that Gil Peñalosa told her how he persuaded Bogotá to expand ciclovías in the 1990s. He made an agreement with the city: if it would permit him just one Sunday when he could do what he wished— such as adding more ciclovía mileage—he would back off if the results were disappointing. His proposal was easy to accept. When the results exceeded expectations, the experiment also made it easier for the city to retain and expand ciclovías.[25]

Opposition to congestion pricing has consistently

dropped following implementation, making temporary trial periods advantageous to its proponents. For example, before Stockholm implemented congestion pricing in 2006, the idea faced the opposition of 80 percent of residents. It got its chance when the city introduced the system on a temporary basis, with the promise that the charges would cease if residents disapproved after a seven-month trial. During the experiment, rush-hour motor vehicle traffic in the city traffic dropped 20 percent. The city center was both more pleasant and more efficient. When the trial ended, the charges were lifted and the traffic jams returned. In a referendum held soon thereafter, a slight majority approved the congestion pricing, and Stockholm has had it ever since.[26] In 2009 Janette Sadik-Khan, with Mayor Michael Bloomberg's support, closed some traffic lanes in an effort to turn Times Square from a site where pedestrians and motor vehicles converged in a tense, perpetual standoff into a place primarily for people on foot or seated in chairs, conversing, eating, or taking in the sights and the sounds. The project had its chance because it was presented as temporary and reversible. Once it was in place, it won ample support, and has been retained.[27]

As Bogotá's mayor from 1998 to 2001, Enrique Peñalosa earned a reputation for making the city a place where people could get around without a car. This helped him win a second term as mayor, from 2016 to 2019. Peñalosa put his guiding principle in urban mobility this way: "An advanced city is not one where even the poor can get around by car, but one where even the rich use public transportation."[28] Under Mayor Peñalosa, Bogotá became much more hospitable to pedestrians and cyclists, and with better bus service too.

Like Sadik-Khan, he was on the lookout for good ideas from other cities. He admired a bus system in Curitiba, Brazil, called RIT (Rede Integrada de Transporte, or Integrated Transportation Network). Since 1974 RIT has operated long, articulated buses: vehicles in three segments that can bend where the segments join. Patrons pay in advance; doors along the length of the high-capacity bus permit rapid boarding and alighting. The buses run along dedicated routes, like trains, so they aren't delayed by traffic jams. Patrons can depend on faster and more reliable service than ordinary buses offer. Inspired by Curitiba's example, Mayor Peñalosa helped Bogotá introduce TransMilenio in 2000. Like RIT, TransMilenio is a bus rapid transit (BRT) system, on which buses follow a dedicated lane so that other traffic does not obstruct them.[29] In the 2000s, BRT has proliferated worldwide; Sadik-Khan, an early convert, made sure New York introduced a version of BRT it calls Select Bus Service.[30]

Peñalosa was eager to learn from international examples, but he was selective about them. In a 2011 interview, he said: "Latin America should look more to Amsterdam than to Miami."[31] This is the kind of wisdom that can guide us toward a better mobility future, and Peñalosa chose his foreign example well. The Netherlands has proved that much more sustainable, healthful, efficient, and inclusive mobility systems are possible with the technology we have now. Dutch people have choices, including driving, but the other ways of getting around are so attractive that the Dutch drive much less than Americans. For transportation on roads and rails, an average American's carbon footprint is about 2.5 times that of the average resident of the Netherlands.[32] The country also consistently ranks high on indices of national well-being.[33]

The Netherlands is the most engineered country on earth—26 percent of its land area lies below sea level and requires constant engineering to remain inhabitable. But the Dutch draw as needed from the whole sociotechnical spectrum of tools, including everything from zero tech to state-of-the-art high tech; there is no disdain for low tech that works. The result is that travel in the Netherlands without a car can be much more convenient than comparable travel in the United States with a car—including an automated car. The public transport network integrates bicycles, such that travelers may ride their own bike to the railway station, ride a safe electric vehicle (a train) to the station in the destination city, then take a public transport bike almost to the door of the building they're traveling to. Those who prefer not to bike can take convenient buses and trams.

Bicycle routes are safe, continuous, and ample; they serve cities, suburbs, and intercity travel. The bicycle traffic on them is far less expensive to accommodate than the equivalent motor traffic would be; it's also more sustainable, safer, and more healthful. On some city streets, cyclists and drivers share the pavement, but with priority for cyclists. Electric bicycles have made bicycling practical for more people, over longer distances, and in more areas, including the country's hilly east and southeast. In the Netherlands, one quarter of all trips taken are taken by bicycle; in the city of Utrecht, half of all commuting trips are by bike.[34] The system is not cheap, but at the national level, it is cheaper than supplying ever greater road capacity to maintain car dependency (including high-tech car dependency), and at the personal level, it spares those who prefer not to own a car from the expense of having to own one anyway.

There has been persistent skepticism about the value of the Dutch example for North America. The United States is too big, the objections go, or Americans are more attached to their cars. Or presumably the Dutch government always favored cycling, or the Dutch people had a unique history of resistance to car domination. At most, such objections merely demonstrate that the example is not perfect—but no example is. They also don't bear close scrutiny. New Jersey is about half the size of the Netherlands, and with comparable population density, topography, climate, and per capita GDP. Its mobility deficiencies relative to the Netherlands are due to none of these factors. What matters day to day is not the size of the country but the distances between destinations, and in the United States, the official response to distance has been to make fast driving possible and safe, at almost any cost. Over time, this priority has had the quite predictable effect of gradually lowering densities and increasing distances, which tends to make driving the only practical choice. The correction, then, is to begin to make density attractive again; this shortens distances, making high-speed driving less necessary.[35]

The other supposed differences don't stand up to examination either. Like Americans, Dutch people who can afford cars generally buy one. About three-quarters of Dutch households own a car, and their drivers are generally quite attached to them.[36] Using data from fifty million drivers, Waze (a navigation app owned by Google) rated the Netherlands as the best country in the world to drive in.[37] The Dutch just don't have to drive their cars for everything they need. In the Netherlands, the fact that millions like to drive does not become an excuse to prioritize cars everywhere, for all purposes. The Dutch government did not always favor cycling as a major transport mode; in the 1960s and 1970s, it strove to accommodate drivers' demands even at the expense of everyone else. It took years of mass pressure from people demanding safer and more inviting streets to compel the government to shift its priorities.[38]

Finally, the Dutch resistance to car domination in the 1960s, '70s and '80s does not make the experience in the Netherlands categorically different from the experience in the United States. In the United States, in numerous cities large and small, and in many suburbs, too, car domination was persistently resisted right through the apogee of "car culture" in the 1950s to 1970s. Just as in the Netherlands, in places where fast driving made walking unsafe, and deprived children of the safe use of their local streets, people protested.

In particular, mothers organized local protests demanding stop signs and whatever else might make their streets useful for anything besides driving. Women were often left isolated in single-car homes where the husband did most of the driving, while public transportation systems cut back service; for them, a car-dependent society offered poorer mobility choices and endangered their children. The American traffic protests even resembled those in the Netherlands: volunteers blocked streets, picketed intersections, and carried signs, attracting local press attention. The differences were that the American protests began earlier, achieved only local successes, and were forgotten.[39]

By the 1980s and 1990s, the prevailing answer to their grievance was the two-car family, the minivan, and the parental shuttle service for children. American bicyclists also strove persistently for a place in the city streets of motor-age America.[40] Their efforts call into question easy stereotypes about a monolithic car culture. The scarcity of pedestrian and cycling advocates in books, museum exhibits, and films about the history of the car in the United States is no coincidence; the predominant national historian of the automobile has been and still is motordom.[41]

The endless spiral

In *Silent Spring*, writing of the absurd and destructive pursuit of an environment devoid of agricultural pests, Rachel Carson observed: "Future historians may well be amazed by our distorted sense of proportion."[42] The same might well be said of the absurd and destructive pursuit of the car-dependent city.

Indeed, when Carson wrote these words, Jane Jacobs had recently offered a similar assessment in her influential book *The Death and Life of Great American Cities.* Superficially, the writers' subjects were quite different: for Carson, gardens, farms, and forests; for Jacobs, cities, streets, and neighborhoods. More fundamentally, however, the subjects were much alike. Both wrote of ecosystems, in which complex webs of interdependencies make interventions to master or control particular nodes of the web invitations to trouble. Both warned that people who promise utopian perfection, whether in agriculture or in human geography, meddle with powers beyond their control. Much like Carson wrote of chemical companies and the eager users of their pesticides, Jacobs wrote of the city planners who strove to control urban ecosystems without appreciating the interdependencies they were disrupting. "As in all Utopias," Jacobs wrote, "the right to have plans of any significance belonged only to the planners in charge." They impose on the city "the dishonest mask of pretended order, achieved by ignoring or suppressing the real order that is struggling to exist and to be served."[43]

In cases like these, technological innovation has been misrepresented as the solution to a problem—whether the problem is crop loss, urban disorder, delay to drivers, traffic crashes, or emissions. In such cases, specific problems are attacked in isolation from the web of interdependencies in which they are inextricably embedded, destabilizing essential balances. Ever more toxic compounds, as Carson explained, could not durably solve farmers' or gardeners' problems, and the attempt had disastrous effects. Invasive urban renewal projects, explained Jacobs, cannot subject the urban organism to expert control. Similarly, ever more advanced automobiles do not solve the problems of car dependency, and the attempt to use them for this purpose has disastrous effects too.

In their complexity, the ecosystems on which agriculture depends and the cities that transport systems serve have much in common. As Carson noted, high-tech innovation in chemical pesticides is no deliverance; it leads instead to an "endless spiral," a "process of escalation . . . in which ever more toxic materials must be found."[44] In car-dependent transport, the endless spiral is equally predictable. Beginning in the 1930s, US cities, responding like ecosystems to policies that attacked driver delay and the hazards of driving, succumbed to an "endless spiral" that imposed car dependency on nearly all, without curing the afflictions of congestion or crashes. As Carson explained, ecosystems resist mastery and afflict those who seek it with unexpected problems. In ecosystems, including gardens and cities, most problems can be managed but not eliminated; a balance between competing goods may be more desirable than the triumph of one good over the others; a zeal for perfection may do more harm than good.

These cautions ought to make us impatient of Autonorama's habitual abuse of the word *ecosystem*. When automakers and tech companies speak of the "mobility ecosystem"—as they often do—they are misusing both words, and we must not be taken in.[45] They don't mean mobility but only what can be sold, as transport services, as mobile entertainment, or as data—and the difference matters. And by *ecosystem*, they merely mean the constellations of companies competing and collaborating to score the big deals with corporate partners, elected officials, investors, and clients.[46] The enterprises engaged in the farming of corn, wheat, or soybeans are not an ecosystem; they are a cluster of agricultural businesses that depend on a natural ecosystem they can work with but not control. In the same way, vehicle manufacturers, tech companies, and transport apps and services are not a mobility ecosystem, or even an autonomous vehicle ecosystem; they are businesses that depend on a human ecosystem they can work with but not control. In both cases, the harder the businesses strive to control the real ecosystems, and compete to maximize short-term profits from them, the greater harm they will do to them.

The mobility ecosystem of autonomous vehicle developers does not care about the real mobility ecosystem, which includes people who pay little or no money for their mobility and from whom little or no data can be collected. In the real mobility ecosystem, such people are vital to the system's health; in the AV mobility ecosystem, their existence is generally unnoticed, except as impediments.[47] As components of the real mobility ecosystem, people who are not spending money or generating monetizable data cannot be excluded, marginalized, or controlled without damage to the system as a whole, because an ecosystem—including a city—is a web of interdependencies.

In *Silent Spring*, Carson diagnosed the error behind the reckless use of pesticides: a failure to appreciate the web of interdependencies in the ecosystems that the poisons disrupt. "The history of life on earth has been a history of interaction between living things and their surroundings," she wrote. "In nature, nothing exists alone."[48] In this statement, Carson was expressing the position of the inventor of the word *ecosystem*, the ecologist Arthur Tansley. In 1935 Tansley objected to the word's application to distinct subsets of an ecosystem as if they were separate from it.[49] We can be confident, then, that he would object to corporate "ecosystems" that exclude many of the people who are implicated in them.

It would be interesting to ask Jacobs and Carson to comment on the so-called disruptive innovation that is so widely celebrated as an inevitable and beneficial force. Both writers' most famous books are masterly studies of the subject, though they've been ignored by the business gurus who prescribe disruption wherever they go. Jacobs and Carson warned us that disruption is hazardous at best; better to seek a flawed equilibrium than to disrupt it in the hope of a better result. Humans cannot control ecosystems, natural or urban, they warned; when they try, they trigger effects beyond their control. Then the ecosystems become the disruptors. About once a generation, nature reminds us that technology does not govern our destiny. We have been overdue for a reminder. Since the 1990s, it's been fashionable to call technology a source of disruption, but on the disruption scale, the pandemic of 2020–21 put technology in its place.

Both Jacobs and Carson also offer us a more encouraging version of human-induced disruption, however. Their books disrupted the status quo in their respective fields. The environmental and urbanist values that they spoke for, against the tenor of their time, found and mobilized receptive audiences, thereby promoting constructive change. Even the institutions they criticized have had to offer them tokens of respect. As the news about the climate emergency has worsened, we are confronted by new versions of the kinds of contradictions they examined. People demanding responses to the climate emergency that actually promote sustainability instead of just invoking it; people calling for cities that are inclusive, affordable, and healthful; people seeking ways to limit the disruptions of consumerism so as to avert the greater disruptions that they can trigger, can learn from their disruptive example.

Technology is not the problem

Predictions that automated driving will make car dependency work have been failing for sixty years. Numerous innovations have offered important safety and efficiency benefits, but nothing has come close to solving the problems that make ubiquitous driving hazardous, spatially inefficient, unsustainable, and inequitable. When the predictions fail, the usual explanation has been that the technology was not ready—with the implication that someday, inevitably, it will be ready. In a 2016 book, *Driverless*, the authors take the position that driverless cars are coming. To their credit, they commit extensive attention to twentieth-century efforts to automate driving; most treatments of the subject are comparatively indifferent to the past. The authors therefore had to justify their optimism about autonomous vehicles in light of decades of failures. To explain the failure of the automated highways of Futurama 3, they offered the predictable reason: "the information technology of the day wasn't mature enough."[50]

To readers of *Silent Spring*, this reason may have a familiar ring. Rachel Carson reviewed the struggle of pesticide manufacturers and their customers to find the right chemical agent, and the right concentration for application, to solve the problems of insect pests. Impressive results could be achieved, but solutions were elusive. Without ever damning all uses of poisons for gardening, agriculture, or forestry, Carson showed that the problem was not the particular chemical agent or the particular application. The problem was the notion that harvest losses to insects are a problem to be solved. Chemical companies were authoritatively telling their customers that their insect problems could be solved, and the customers liked what they heard. Carson cautioned them that in some endeavors, a search for solutions is doomed. Failure at solving the insect problem does not mean that a more potent chemical agent is needed, or that a stronger concentration is required. Failure in this struggle is the normal consequence of striving to solve a problem in a realm that defies solutions. It is getting the problem wrong.

Rachel Carson was not the first to observe that in ecosystems, the pursuit of solutions initiates a cycle of perpetual overconsumption that solves nothing. When Charles Kettering, in 1929, advised his colleagues in business to "keep the consumer dissatisfied," he based this recommendation on the same observation. Kettering appreciated that if you can convince people that a solution is possible—that a state of perfect satisfaction is possible—you can persuade them to buy whatever it takes to get there. Though this idea has only recently been called (and criticized as) solutionism,[51] both Kettering and Carson articulated it long ago, if in quite different ways. The promise must be presented credibly, and kept always in sight but just out of reach. As a means of practical transport, autonomous vehicles have been a failure. But as a means of keeping a treadmill of misplaced consumption turning, they have been an extraordinary success.

Technology can solve no human problem for us, but humans with technology *can* solve problems for ourselves. Generalized, Rachel Carson's warning is about what goes wrong when this distinction is lost. A caution about the absence of technological solutions, however, is no counsel of despair—quite the opposite. It means that we can finally step off the treadmill of misplaced enthusiasm, overspending, and consequent disappointment. It means that we can save a lot of wasted effort and money, and recommit some of it to measures—technological and social—that solve nothing, but improve balance, offer choices, and promote community health.

When futuristic "solutions" displace practical sufficiency

In a recent history of the promotion of automated vehicles, Jameson Wetmore observes that automakers and tech companies are "seeking to shape our expectations, goals, and values surrounding the technology. They are telling us what automated vehicles will look like, how they will be integrated into society, what problems they will solve, and how our lives will change." He cautions us: "If we as citizens, consumers, or the general public would like to entertain other possibilities, we need to consider and reflect on alternative ideas."[52]

AVs are just different enough from conventional cars to be presentable as a means of escape from the traffic spiral, much as DDT appeared to be the means of escape from the low-intensity pesticide spiral that preceded its introduction. But if DDT was no such escape, neither are AVs—and for much the same reasons. In complex systems, such as natural and urban ecosystems, dense interdependencies are such that no element of the system may be isolated and "solved" without innumerable effects on other elements; these effects, in turn, tend to counteract the attempted solution. When such solutions fail, the lack is not in the technology; it is in the misframing of the task as a problem to be solved, or as an enemy to be defeated. "The chemical war is never won," wrote Carson, "and all life is caught in its violent crossfire."[53]

Especially in a car-dependent city, a war on congestion is also never won, and for much the same reason—though the urban destruction in any such effort will be great. Short-term success in such a war invites more traffic and ever-greater needs to drive. Success in a war on traffic hazards invites greater speeds and other offsetting effects. Success in promoting zero-emissions vehicles adds load to power grids, delaying efforts to achieve so much as 50 percent power from renewables. All three wars can cause vast incidental casualties, for example to the public health (particularly because of sedentary living), and to social equity and sustainability (as low-cost and less resource-intensive mobility possibilities are degraded). Wars on elements of complex systems generally solve nothing; rather their effects on other elements of the system cause new problems. Applied to complex systems, high-tech innovations never just solve problems—they change problems, disrupting balances and introducing new problems. In cities that ultimately became car dependent, conventional cars and the roads that served them were presented as ways to "get from A to B," as if A and B were fixed constants. But they also changed A and B, and all the other destinations. Yet wherever Autonorama is on display, including in versions that published as academic research, these effects are scarce or absent.

Such systemic effects are not news. In chapter 15 of *Silent Spring*, called "Nature Fights Back," Carson explained ecosystems' uncontrollable responses to efforts to control them. By then, Jane Jacobs had already pointed out much the same thing for cities. The final chapter of *The Death and Life of Great American Cities* is called "The Kind of Problem a City Is." In it, Jacobs observed that cities are "problems in organized complexity, like the life sciences." Innumerable elements "are all varying simultaneously *and in subtly interconnected ways*." Jacobs's book is an attack on would-be urban problem solvers who, from an "Olympian view," treat the city "as a collection of separate file drawers." Jacobs compared the "vandalism of nature" that Carson was investigating with its equivalent in cities, concluding that "the two responses are connected."[54]

But Autonorama is no failure. An enterprise's success and failure must be judged by its goal. Like Charles Kettering, the promoters of AVs are not interested in transport sufficiency. Sufficiency, though conducive to contentment, sustainability, and stability, is not a winning business model. Therefore they promise future transport perfection. The promise cannot be kept, but keeping it is not the point. To Carson, the "endless spiral" of escalation was a destructive absurdity, but to those selling products that propel the escalation, it's good business.

In this effort, promoters of (automated) car dependency have misrepresented their systems as solutions that are smart and data driven. They are none of these things.

So-called "smart" systems are only smarter than well-conceived conventional systems if, in the calculations of smartness, the human components of conventional systems are excluded. Such exclusion is as ubiquitous as it is improper. Indeed smart systems are in important respects dumber, because instead of applying the extraordinary intelligence of the human user, they must largely suppress it. Neither can any data, as data, drive anything; at best, data guide. Data, however, can be monetized, and money does indeed drive. But transport systems that are driven by monetized data will forgo sustainability, public health, and social equity for the sake of data generation and collection.

Futurama, including Autonorama, persistently misrepresents tools as solutions. As solutions, technology purportedly solves our problems for us. But technologies are tools, and tools only equip us to solve our problems ourselves. In Autonorama this confusion is compounded by the characterization of some technology as smart, as intelligent, and even as autonomous, and therefore as more worthy of human users' trust than human judgment. But whatever simulation of smarts, intelligence, or autonomy that technology achieves was developed and applied by humans, whose human interests, biases, and ambitions influenced their design decisions and are encoded in the smart systems they make.

When a smart car behaves as if the user experience is worth protecting even at some risk to the safety of other street users, as the Uber that killed Elaine Herzberg did, it is behaving like a human driver, not like a flawless super-human entity. Its behavior is as much the responsibility of human beings as the behavior of any conventional car. A fully automated car is not actually smart, intelligent, or autonomous. It is the mindless extension of the humans who wrote the program that governs its decisions. In turn the programmers' job is to ensure that the car behaves as its corporate owners want it to behave. If it's worth it to them to take chances so as to offer passengers a better user experience than a more cautious competitor, they will ensure that the car takes such chances. Indeed, if they want a successful business, they will have to take them.

Above all, AVs are no solution to mobility problems. Car dependency is consumerism's greatest triumph; promoters of automated driving are less interested in human mobility than in preserving car dependency. AVs may be useful minor supplements to diversified mobility systems. But much as filtered and "low tar" cigarettes were a dangerous detour that extended cigarette smoking for decades, AVs are a dangerous distraction from the means we already have before us to secure more sustainable, less expensive, more healthful, and more equitable urban mobility.

Sustainability, health, and social equity demand innovation, but we have been sold a defective version of innovation that cannot be trusted to deliver such goods. Innovation, once a synonym of improvisation, has been reduced to high-tech novelty. For eighty years, such technofuturism has been a dangerous distraction. As a kind of truncated innovation, it rules out of serious consideration many of the tools and techniques we need to devise a more sustainable future. It miscasts humans as complications instead of assets. It mistakes the simple for the obsolete.

In urban mobility, most high-tech innovation has been committed, ironically, to perpetuating the unsustainable car dependency we inherited from the twentieth century. In her remarks to the 2019 Automated Vehicles Symposium, Nicole Nason, the Federal Highway Administrator, justified USDOT support of AVs in part as a means of offering travelers choice. "I want to reaffirm the Department's position regarding the freedom of the open road. We want to protect the freedom of all Americans to make mobility choices that best serve their needs."[55] But the irony of all efforts to accommodate drivers' needs is that, because of systemic effects, they have the effect of degrading all other choices until, for millions, there is no choice. The car is a practical necessity, as important to first-class citizenship as the right to vote.

Real urban mobility innovation will require not autonomous vehicles but autonomous people: travelers with choices. This in turn will necessitate reinventing or rediscovering innovation. A complete innovation palette will include high tech, zero tech, and everything between. Such full-spectrum innovation will take advantage of the intelligence of the humans in the mobility system instead of striving to engineer it out. It will learn from history instead of disdaining it. It is time to try it seriously. When we rescue innovation from the technofuturists and recover the tools they excluded, we will find that, with full-spectrum innovation, we can do more today, at far less cost, than what they promise to deliver at unlimited expense at an ever-receding future date.

Beyond the iCitizen

Data-collection techniques, like other technologies, are tools. We need the right tool for the job, and we need to choose the right job. To begin well, we must recognize that once data are put to work for any social purpose, all data are political.

The most vocal proponents of data's depoliticizing possibilities are those in the best position to select, evaluate, and act upon it. Conversely, others in less advantageous positions tend to admit data's political character. Particularly in the public sphere, where transportation largely resides, data-driven depoliticization can resemble marginalization or exclusion. The fitting response, therefore, is deliberate inclusion.

For such a program there are valuable precedents. Second to none is Jane Jacobs, whose *Death and Life of Great American Cities* is a demand to value data that the data monopolizers had ignored. The book is a denunciation of such hoarding of data and their significance. "Sidewalk width," for example, "is invariably sacrificed . . . partly because city sidewalks are conventionally considered to be purely space for pedestrian travel and access to buildings, and go unrecognized and unrespected as the uniquely vital and irreplaceable organs of city safety, public life and child rearing that they are." Jacobs condemned the kind of data reductionism by which "citizens . . . could be dealt with intellectually like grains of sand, or electrons or billiard balls." Of the visions of conventional city planners and their "planning pseudoscience," Jacobs wrote: "As in all Utopias, the right to have plans of any significance belonged only to the planners in charge."[56] The same might be said of the data-driven visions issuing from the tech companies and automakers of the twenty-first century.

Besides transport, education and healthcare have been sectors subject to data-driven excesses, sometimes to the detriment of the people whom professionals in these fields are committed to serving, even when the data are not monetizable. Data-driven decision-making won influential adherents in both fields. Physicians and educators have offered cautions about the effects and proposed constructive responses from which we can learn. Like Jack Stilgoe, who noted that promises of data-driven, transformative change typically yield "more of the same," Alfie Kohn has argued that data-driven education innovations, represented as reforms, typically "focus on fixing the kid so he or she can better adapt to the system rather than asking inconvenient questions about the system itself." Like Jane Jacobs, Kohn finds a disconnect between the data interpreters and the data sources: "An individual's enthusiasm about the employment of 'data' in education is directly proportional to his or her distance from actual students." "The best teachers," he

argues, "tend to recoil from earnest talk about the benefits of 'data-driven instruction.'"[57]

Also like Jacobs, Dr. Abraham Verghese has cautioned
that professionals, with an appropriate interest in objec-
tivity, may entirely miss the experience of the humans
they care for. In 2011 Verghese, a professor at Stanford
Medical School with an ample appreciation of the value
of medical technology, wrote an op-ed for the *New York
Times* called "Treat the Patient, Not the CT Scan." "Medical technology can blind doctors to the needs of the
sick," he warned. The physician's attention, absorbed in
test results and other disembodied data, may not engage
directly with the patient. "This computer record creates
what I call an iPatient—and this iPatient threatens to
become the real focus of our attention, while the real
patient in the bed often feels neglected, a mere place-
holder for the virtual record."[58] The ubiquity of disembodied data in matters of transport planning should have
us asking: "What for these realms is the equivalent of the
iPatient? How do we include and empower the real person behind the iCitizen?"

Data that matter cannot be depoliticized. Neither can
public services such as transportation be left to companies driven by monetizable data, because of the mismatch
between what such companies purport to sell (transport)
and what they actually sell, at least in large part (monetizable data).[59] Professionalization of planning is not enough,
both because of the inherently political character of data
that matter, and because professional standards inevitably

reflect, to some extent, the agendas of the most influential interest groups.

But there is another possibility: the deliberate and inclusive politicization of transport planning. In 1965 Paul Davidoff published a manifesto for such an approach, calling it "Advocacy and Pluralism in Planning." As if contesting data-driven decision-making before the term existed, Davidoff contended that no such objective calculations are possible, because "values are inescapable elements of any rational decision-making process." Data therefore cannot drive sound decisions, as "the right course of action is always a matter of choice, never of fact."[60] Davidoff proposed "advocacy planning" instead: an inclusive planning in which expert planners' clients are diverse public constituencies, many of them historically excluded.

Such an approach may evoke visions of procedural stalemate or NIMBYism, but these afflictions are often the symptoms of the distrust that exclusion induces and that only inclusion can relieve. Where trust has been earned, and where outsiders find themselves invited inside, inclusive planning procedures have been substantial if imperfect successes. Examples include the Netherlands, where the "polder model" constructively engages constituencies that are generally excluded elsewhere, and more recently Taiwan's brand of "digital democracy," which helped the country set a world record in the success of its response to the 2020–21 pandemic.[61]

Unlike data-driven decision-making, which is a flawed analogy with computer programming, Taiwan's digital governance has borrowed more successfully from the programming model. For example, Taiwan's national government uses digital tools to open policy forums to all who have access to the web. Instead of relegating citizens to passive and largely unwitting objects of data collection, the government turns the tables and invites citizens to tell it, and the general public, what they prefer, what they oppose, what they propose. Of course, these preferences and proposals are not all feasible or mutually consistent, but at its best the data generation can yield a rough consensus that is closer to optimum than any exclusionary process can produce. The term *rough consensus* is borrowed from programming; programmers working collaboratively have found that they have a better chance of producing excellent code if they settle for rough consensus, instead of unanimity, and then revise the result in another round. Unlike Autonorama or other utopias, rough consensus does not promise perfection, but it can and does deliver improvement. In so doing, it also earns the trust it needs to work.

Techniques of this kind correct a destructive error. Data collected passively, from subjects who don't even know which of their data are collected and for what purpose, tell us little about what people want, and are subject to interpretations that their sources might dispute—if they had the chance. Data collected passively from car drivers can be and are used to measure supposed demand for road capacity for cars; data that may someday be generated and collected from AVs, as Intel's Krzanich forecast it, would be "more of the same." But if they were asked, some of these motorists would report that they would walk if zoning ordinances did not keep residences and workplaces far apart, that they would bike if they felt safe doing so, or that they would ride transit if the schedules were better. In Taiwan, citizens don't have to hope that the data collectors will derive these interpretations from the data they generate, or that the authorities will survey them. They present the data themselves, and not just to the data collectors, but to each other. They can see others' preferences directly and thereby form constituencies of their own, with agendas of their own.

If 10 percent of the public resources that have gone into high-tech driving had instead gone into real mobility—practical opportunities to walk, to bike, or to ride a bus, a streetcar, or a train, we might have good mobility choices that would serve the mobility needs that the promoters of high-tech driving merely promise to meet, and at extraordinary expense.

We have choices

In Autonorama, technology chooses for us. It's become a cliché: like it or not, autonomous vehicles are coming, and sooner than you think. What we want is unimportant, because technology drives history, and technology, we are told, has chosen autonomous vehicles. Satisfying needs has never been the point: Charles Kettering's advice was to keep the consumer dissatisfied; Clayton Christensen's was not to get too close to the customer. In Autonorama, if the public isn't interested, then the public doesn't understand and must be educated.

When Autonorama admits that there are in fact choices, it frames the choices for us, in a strange binary: we may have status quo car dependency, or we may have high-tech car dependency. Even framed this way, the choice is nowhere near as obvious as the high-tech driving sales force would have us believe. As they tell it, however, the promoters of autonomous vehicles recognize the failure of car dependency—it's too dangerous, too inefficient, and unsustainable. But as the only alternative, they propose high-tech car dependency. They present it to us as perfection—as not just an improvement in safety, efficiency, and sustainability but the solution that will finally deliver us from our afflictions. For this supposed perfection of tomorrow, we are asked to commit vast resources in the form of money, applied research, and expert attention today. We are asked to believe, on scant evidence but plenty of fanfare, that the next generation of technology will finally deliver car dependency that works.

Our actual situation is vastly better than this. Citizens, as consumers, as travelers, and as voters, have choices now, and at a very low cost we can quickly expand our range of choices. Autonorama asks us to limit our choices, whether to none ("like it or not . . ."), or to a binary alternative (status quo car dependency or high-tech car dependency). In response, we must insist on the whole vast menu. We must reject the situation as it has been framed for us, and frame it for ourselves. Where we hear that we have no choice, we must insist on choice. Where we hear that technology determines what we will do, we must reply that we choose what we will do, and then choose the technology we need for the job. Where we hear that our practices prove that we prefer to drive, we must explain that our practices are responses to a status quo that gives us no good choices. Wherever alternatives to driving have been attractive possibilities, people have taken advantage of them, to the benefit of not just the individual but also the community.

Despite these advantages, the critics of car dependency face daunting rhetorical obstacles. We can be caricatured as people who want to deprive others of choices. A critic of car dependency can expect to be misrepresented as an opponent of cars. A carpenter who prefers to drive nails with a hammer is not an opponent of wrenches but a person who appreciates what a wrench is for—and what it is not for. A critic of car dependency is likely to agree that there are many jobs for which a car is the right tool. Especially in cities, however, a car makes a poor all-purpose tool, as the per-person energy requirements of any car-dependent city will attest. The wasteful and destructive reconstruction necessary to retrofit an older city to car dependency is evidence of how unsuited cars are to be all-purpose transportation for everyone, everywhere. Critics of car dependency are the advocates of using the right tool for the transport job at hand.

It will help us to use the right tool for the job if we

stop subsidizing the wrong tool so lavishly. Though public transportation is frequently condemned as a prodi-
gal waster of public subsidies, it cannot begin to compete for this title with automobility. Even in congested
areas, drivers seldom pay for the expensive road capacity
they use. Their gasoline taxes cover only a fraction of the
expense, and the payment is disconnected from the value
of the road capacity used. "Highways do not—and except
for brief periods in our nation's history—never have paid
for themselves through the taxes that highway advocates
call 'user fees,'" the Public Interest Research Group has
reported.[62] When tolling operations were expensive to
operate and intrusive obstacles to driving, their limited
use was understandable. Today, however, expanding toll-
free road capacity in response to congestion is like a big-
box department store charging by the pound, and con-
tinually ordering more high-end electronics to keep its
shelves stocked. It makes no sense.

There is even good reason to allocate a share of road
toll revenues to fund alternatives to driving. If the AV
promoters were serious about wanting to reduce casualties, increase efficiencies, relieve congestion, and improve
sustainability, they would agree. Especially as we face
the climate emergency, there is a public benefit to all in
transportation trends away from driving passenger cars
(low tech or high tech, gasoline or electric) and in favor
of more efficient modes. Drivers who continue to drive
benefit in terms of congestion relief, community health,
and sustainability when other drivers choose other modes

of surface transportation. Moreover, many drivers, given the choice, would want a share of their toll to fund means of transport they might prefer. Despite the constant celebration of data, departments of transportation have collected little in the way of information that can tell us what the millions who drive not by preference but by practical compulsion would prefer if they had the choice. The remedy is to let people generate data that reflect their preferences. If reluctant drivers could designate a share of their toll for their mode of preference, they could hope to get the choices they now lack.

This book is not an entry into the debate about whether the automated driving revolution is good or bad, or whether it will yield (as a perennial question would have it) a transport "heaven" or a transport "hell." It is a plea to stop asking such questions. We are not passive subjects hoping that technology will deliver us from our misfortunes. We are people with tools—old and new, low tech and high tech—and our tools give us choices. Let us choose.

The question, then, is what future do we want, and how do we use the tools we have now to get it? We may find that we need new tools—technology we don't yet have—but let us choose the future tech we need and commit it to our purposes. The question is not "What does the high-tech future have in store for us?" or even "How do we get the high-tech future we want?" Let's ask what future we want and need, and then talk about the technology we need to get it. We err when we frame our task as adapting to new technology. We do better when we adapt tech to our purposes. If we can agree that our mobility purposes include, in debatable proportions, sustainability, affordability, efficiency, inclusivity, equity, and health, we can at last take best advantage of what technology has to offer us.

Acknowledgments

Almost a decade ago, when people first asked me what history has to tell us about the future of autonomous vehicles, they began me down a path that led—quite unexpectedly—to this book. The book's existence is, for better or for worse, due to them.

It was Marty Wachs, a historian whose work I had admired since grad school, who first pressed me to apply my historical work to the problem of the future of mobility. That was in 2014, and since then, the conversations have never stopped. I owe much to many people who offered their ideas, and who asked me for mine. They include Carol Atkinson-Palombo, Laurence Aurbach, Emily Badger, Clayton Banks, Louis Beaumier, Jeff Becker, Catherine Cox Blair, Andy Boenau, Garnette Cadogan, Jeff Cherry, Matt Cox, Matthew Crawford, Tom Dansie, Hans-Liudger Dienel, Ger Duijzings, Eric Dumbaugh, Johnathon Ehsani,

Mike Enskat, Tomás Errázuriz, Mike Esbester, Larrie Ferreiro, Sally Flocks, Mathieu Flonneau, Norman Garrick, Noah Goodall, Sarah Goodyear, Doug Gordon, Tom Graham, Vince Graham, Art Guzzetti, Rick Hall, Pat Jones, Wes Kumfer, Jane Lappin, Per Lundin, Wesley Marshall, Jeffrey Michael, Andrew Mondschein, Massimo Moraglio, Aaron Naparstek, Bob Noland, José Peralta, Olatunji Oboi Reed, Carlton Reid, Erik Sabina, Andrew Salzberg, Laura Sandt, Frank Schipper, Angie Schmitt, Michael Schwarz, Sarah Seo, Greg Shill, Steven Shladover, Shail Shrestha, Jessie Singer, Stefanie Sohm, Jack Stilgoe, Joseph Stromberg, Pieter van Wesemael, Jameson Wetmore, Paul Steely White, Octavio Zegarra Lazarte, and David Zipper. The questions that they asked me compelled me to look for answers, and ultimately to write this book. Their conversation, plus conversations with others who are named in the paragraphs that follow, informed and improved my work. If this book has merits, most are due to them.

A profound influence on my thinking about sustainable urban mobility has been my experience in the Netherlands during five visits there. The first two, in 2009 and 2012, were funded by Rijkswaterstaat, the Ministry of Infrastructure and Water Management. Three more, in 2018–19, were funded by the Royal Netherlands Academy of Sciences (KNAW). My months in the Netherlands confirmed for me what common sense had already suggested: that much more sustainable, efficient, inclusive, and healthful mobility is already feasible, and can also be more practical, more convenient, and more pleasurable than car dependency. I am profoundly grateful to the funding agencies, and to the people who made these opportunities possible: Professor Gijs Mom and Professor Ruth Oldenziel, both of the Technical University of Eindhoven.

To Ruth Oldenziel I also owe my inclusion in an international network of scholars in the history of sustainable urban mobility. Through getting to know its members, reading and listening to their work, and conversing with them, I gained the practical equivalent of a graduate degree in mobility studies. Because every member of this group was important to me intellectually and personally, I hesitate to name any subset of them. Nevertheless I owe Colin Pooley, Tiina Mannistö-Funk, and Martin Emanuel a special acknowledgment. At Colin Pooley's invitation, we collaborated on a special issue of *Urban History*, each of us contributing one article. In any more sustainable future, walking must be a major everyday mode of practical mobility; working with these three colleagues and with all the others in the network that Ruth assembled reassured me that in this personal conviction, I have excellent company.

Cycling, too, must be a common, everyday mode of practical mobility. In this aspect of the matter, Ruth Oldenziel has again been a profoundly important influence. As a contributor to and editor of the superb Cycling Cities series (published by the Foundation for the History of Technology in Eindhoven), together with other experts in cycling history, Ruth has been a source of invaluable expertise and guidance.

In my consideration of bicycling, my experience in 2018 at World Bicycle Forum in Lima, Peru, was energizing. For this opportunity, I am forever indebted to José Peralta and Octavio Zegarra Lazarte. In Lima I participated in my first two (and still my only two) Critical Mass cycling events, and enjoyed a Sunday ciclovía. Joining the cycling advocates there and participating in these events helped me appreciate what more sustainable, inclusive, and healthful mobility looks like, and how committed people are promoting it. The events also led to my remote collaboration with Shail Shrestha, organizer of the 2020 World Bicycle Forum and of Kathmandu Cycle City 2020. In his steadfast advocacy, Shail has been an example to me and countless others.

A constant source of inspiration has been the advocates of commonsense mobility who have given me the chance to get acquainted with them and their work. Their extraordinary commitment has deepened my own. They include Laurence Brown, Noah Budnick, Vince Caristo, Anna Dragovich, Sally Flocks, Oliver Gaskell, Sarah Goodyear, Doug Gordon, Corinne Kisner, Gosia Kung, Jill Locantore, Aaron Naparstek, Fionnuala Quinn, Olatunji Oboi Reed, Angie Schmitt, Jessie Singer, and Paul Steely White, though I've been fortunate to meet many others as well, and to get acquainted with still more remotely. Among these esteemed people, I must single out Sally Flocks, the founder and former CEO of PEDS in Atlanta. Sally has been an inspiration to me both for her recent advocacy in behalf of walkability in Georgia, and also as a subject of some of the historical documentation I have studied about her pioneering early work with PEDS in the 1990s.

As a success in the tech sector and a prominent community advocate, Clayton Banks of Silicon Harlem has done me the honor of giving my criticisms of some approaches to technology a hearing, including me in his programs, and extending to me the opportunity to meet some of the many extraordinary people in his enormous circle of associates. By giving me a chance, he made me strive to do better. Similarly Pat Jones, CEO of the International Bridge, Tunnel, and Turnpike Association, has repeatedly challenged me to show the relevance of my historical work to audiences engaged in transportation problems today. Anyone who invites me to speak to people who are in the transportation business has guts; I can only hope that the gamble was worth it. I am indebted to Pat for taking a chance on me.

Over the years, some of these people have been mentors to me, and for this I owe them everything. They include Carol Atkinson-Palombo, Clayton Banks, Eric Dumbaugh, Sally Flocks, Norman Garrick, and Jameson Wetmore. Then there are those whose mentorship, generosity, and wisdom have been of decisive and enduring importance—to my work, to my career, and to me personally: Brian Balogh, W. Bernard Carlson, Gijs Mom, and Ruth Oldenziel. My good fortune in meeting these four scholars, and in somehow gaining their confidence, is beyond measure.

Friends have helped me to have the grounding I need

to get jobs like this one done, despite the demands and inevitable vicissitudes of everyday life and work. Many have been important to me, but I must name at least Kim Forde-Mazrui, Walt Heinecke, and Bill Keene.

I have been extremely fortunate to work with Heather Boyer of Island Press. I was impressed from the beginning by her recognition of what I hoped this book would be. She then confirmed this impression in all the editorial work that followed. The extensive practical help, especially in seeking permissions for the images, was invaluable, though I am most grateful for the thoughtful care that she brought to her reading of the manuscript. I am grateful as well to Sharis Simonian and all the others at Island Press who have assisted in all aspects of its publication.

My greatest debts, of course, are to my family, whose patience, support, and love sustain me. Among family members, both Greta Dershimer and Elaine Page have been sources of moral and practical help. My sons Will and Paul have given me a greater sense of purpose, in part by personalizing the future for me. Will also gave me some excellent editorial suggestions, and Paul's perceptive design sense influenced the book's cover design for the better.

Above all, I owe this book to Deborah. In accepting the risk that comes with marrying a grad student studying history, she inspired me to strive to ensure that it was a risk worth taking. She offered me excellent editorial suggestions as well, but above all, it has been her patience, her trust, and her love that have made everything else possible.

About the Author

University of Virginia School of Engineering and Applied Science

Peter Norton is a historian and an observer of cities, streets, and people. He is an associate professor of history in the Department of Engineering and Society at the University of Virginia. He is the author of *Fighting Traffic: The Dawn of the Motor Age in the American City* (MIT Press). He is a member of the University of Virginia's Center for Transportation Studies, and has been a visiting faculty member of the Technical University of Eindhoven in the Netherlands. Norton is an advocate of commonsense mobility and a frequent speaker on urban mobility's past, present, and future. He lives with his family in Charlottesville, Virginia.

Notes

Introduction: Not If but When

Epigraph. Arthur C. Clarke, letter to the editor, *Science* 159, no. 3812 (January 19, 1968): 255.

1. Thompson Products, "Want to Build a Car That Drives Itself?" (advertisement), *Fortune*, August 1958, 195. Months after this ad appeared, Thompson Products changed its name to TRW.

2. The blurb was written by Dr. Gary Schuster, who is identified as "former Dean of Sciences, Provost, and Interim President of Georgia Tech"; it is on the back of Rutt Bridges, *Our Driverless Future: Heaven or Hell?* (Understanding Disruption, Inc., 2018).

3. Joseph Hummer, *Driverless America: What Will Happen When Most of Us Choose Automated Vehicles* (Warrendale, PA: SAE International, 2020), 93.

4. US Department of Transportation, "Remarks as Prepared for Delivery by US Department of Transportation Secretary Elaine L. Chao," Autonomous Vehicle Symposium, San Francisco, July 10, 2018.

5. Akshay Anand, in Bill Vlasic and Mike Isaac, "G.M. to Buy Cruise in Push for Self-Driving Cars," *New York Times*, March 12, 2016, B2.

6. For an excellent start, see Jack Stilgoe, *Who's Driving Innovation? New Technologies and the Collaborative State* (London: Palgrave Macmillan, 2020).

7. US Department of Transportation, "Remarks by Chao."

8. For this opportunity, I am grateful to Laura Sandt of the Highway Safety Research Center, University of North Carolina, and to Jane Lappin, of the Toyota Research Institute. I am also grateful to Steven Shladover of the University of California, Berkeley, who chaired the panel.

9. PRWeb, "Resort in Orlando, Florida, Goes Green," news release, June 21, 2008, www.prweb.com/releases/2008/06/prweb1040494.htm.

10. Federal Highway Administration, "As Prepared Remarks for Federal Highway Administrator, Nicole R. Nason, Automated Vehicles Symposium 2019, Orlando, FL," July 17, 2019, cms8.fhwa.dot.gov/newsroom/prepared-remarks-federal -highway-administrator-nicole-r-nason-automated-vehicles -symposium.

11. US Department of Transportation, "U.S. Secretary of Transportation Announces Automated Driving System Demonstration Grant Winners," September 18, 2019, cms7.dot. gov/briefing-room/us-secretary-transportation-announc-es-automated-driving-system-demonstration-grant.

12. Such failed promises are very common; examples follow. "Nissan today announced that the company will be ready with multiple commercially viable Autonomous Drive vehicles by 2020." *Nissan News*, "Nissan Announces Unprecedented Autonomous Drive Benchmarks," news release, August 27, 2013, usa.nissannews.com/en-US/releases/nissan-announces -unprecedented-autonomous-drive-benchmarks.

Chris Urmson (then director of self-driving cars for Google) made these remarks at a TED conference: "My oldest son is eleven, and that means in four and a half years he's going to be able to get his driver's license. My team and I are committed to making sure that doesn't happen" (because autonomous vehicles will make driver's licenses unnecessary). Urmson, "How a Driverless Car Sees the Road," TED Vancouver, March 17, 2015, www.ted.com/talks /chris_urmson_how_a_driverless_car_sees_the_road/transcript.

Tim Adams quotes BMW's Michael Aeberhard: "We think sometime after 2020 we will be ready for the first highly automated function, which means that the driver will be actually able to do something other than monitor the system." Adams, "Self-Driving Cars: From 2020 You Will Become a Permanent Backseat Driver," *Guardian* (US edition), September 13, 2015, www.theguardian.com/technology/2015 /sep/13/self-driving-cars-bmw-google-2020-driving.

Danielle Muoio, "10 Companies Making a Bold Bet That They'll Have Self-Driving Cars on the Road by 2020," *Business Insider*, October 12, 2015, www.businessinsider. com/google-apple-tesla-race-to-develop-self-driving-cars -by-2020-2015-10.

Jay Ramey, "The Ultimate Self-Driving Machines Will Take Over in 2021," *Autoweek*, July 7, 2016, www.autoweek. com/news/a1849501/ultimate-self-driving-machines-will -take-over-2021.

Georgina Prodhan quotes BMW's senior vice president for autonomous driving, Elmar Frickenstein: "We are on the way to deliver a car in 2021 with Level 3, 4 and 5." Prodhan, "BMW Says Self-Driving Car to Be Level 5 Capable by 2021," *Automotive News*, March 16, 2017, www. autonews.com/article/20170316/MOBILITY/170319877 /bmw-says-self-driving-car-to-be-level-5-capable-by-2021.

13. Alexandra Sage, "Nimble Tech Firms Must Adapt as Promised Self-Driving Revolution Hits Speed Bumps," Reuters, September 23, 2019, www.reuters.com/article/us-autos -autonomous-phantom-focus/nimble-tech-firms-must-adapt -as-promised-self-driving-revolution-hits-speed-bumps -idUSKBN1W81AE. See Stilgoe, *Who's Driving Innovation?*, 8.

14. For self-driving vehicles, the claim "not if but when" prolif-erated in 2014, following its use in two publications: Doug Newcomb, "2013: Year of the Autonomous Car," *PC Magazine*, December 26, 2013; IHS Automotive, *Emerging Technologies: Autonomous Cars—Not If, but When* (London: IHS, January 2014).

15. Charles Duhigg, "Did Uber Steal Google's Intellectual Property?," *New Yorker*, October 22, 2018.

16. Months after the 1958 ad (Thompson Products, "Want to Build," 195) appeared, Thompson Products changed its name to TRW (later TRW Automotive). In 2015 TRW Automotive was acquired by ZF Friedrichshafen; it is now ZF TRW Automotive Holdings Corp. ZF denied permission to include an image of this ad in this book.

On the long history of selling automated driving in the United States, see Sven Beiker, "History and Status of Automated Driving in the United States," in *Road Vehicle Automation*, ed. Gereon Meyer and Sven Beiker (Cham, Switzerland: Springer, 2014), 61–70; Fabian Kröger, "Automated Driving in Its Social, Historical and Cultural Contexts," in *Autonomous Driving: Technical, Legal and Social Aspects*, ed. Markus Maurer et al. (Berlin: Springer, 2016), 41–68; and Jameson M. Wetmore, "Reflecting on the Dream of Automated Vehicles: Visions of Hands-Free Driving over the Past 80 Years," *Technikgeschichte* 87 (2020): 69–94.

17. ZF Press Center, "Level 2+ and Level 4: At CES, ZF Highlights Progression toward Automated Driving," news release, January 22, 2020, press.zf.com/press/en/releases/release_14145.html. See ZF advertisement in *Autonomous Vehicles Technology*, January 2020, 3. (ZF also ran this ad in 2019.) ZF denied permission to include an image of this advertisement in this book.

18. Thompson Products, "Want to Build," 195.

19. Charles Kettering, "Keep the Consumer Dissatisfied," *Nation's Business* 17, no. 1 (January 1929): 30–31, 79.

20. General Motors, *2017 Sustainability Report: Zero Crashes. Zero Emissions. Zero Congestion*, www.gmsustainability.com/_pdf /resources-and-downloads/GM_2017_Executive_Summary .pdf.

21. Jameson M. Wetmore, "Driving the Dream: The History and Motivations behind Sixty Years of Automated Highway Systems in America," *Automotive History Review* (Summer 2003): 4–19; Wetmore, "Reflecting on the Dream," 70. Wetmore had been making this observation since the late 1990s.

22. Clarke, letter to the editor, 255.

23. Jameson Wetmore has observed: "Twenty years is the perfect timeframe for a prediction. It seems close enough that it will happen in many of our lifetimes, and therefore it is worth working toward. At the same time, it is far enough away that the person, company, or government making the prediction probably won't be held responsible if time passes and the promises aren't met." Wetmore, "Reflecting on the Dream," 70.

24. Stilgoe, *Who's Driving Innovation?*, 48.

25. Stilgoe, 58.

1. Futurama 1: New Horizons

Epigraph. General Motors Corporation, Research Laboratories Division, Technical Data Department, *Research Looks to New Horizons* (Detroit: GM, 1939), 32.

1. For substantiation of this and the following paragraph, see Norton, *Fighting Traffic: The Dawn of the Motor Age in the American City* (Cambridge, MA: MIT Press, 2008).

2. Charles F. Kettering, "Keep the Consumer Dissatisfied," *Nation's Business* 17, no. 1 (January 1929): 30–31, 79 (79).

3. Delay reduction for motorists, with consequent road design favoring high speed for motorists to the neglect of other values, was an official value by 1932; by 1941 it was a governing principle recognized as such in the leading textbook of traffic engineering. Committee on Traffic and Public Safety,

Limited Ways: A Plan for the Greater Chicago Traffic Area Committee on Traffic and Public Safety, vol. 2, *Limited Ways for the Greater Chicago Traffic Area* (Chicago: Committee, 1932), 30; Maxwell Halsey, *Traffic Accidents and Congestion* (New York: John Wiley, 1941).

4. Norton, "Four Paradigms: Traffic Safety in the Twentieth-Century United States," *Technology and Culture* 56, no. 2 (April 2015): 319–34.

5. Miller McClintock, "The Fool-Proof Highway of the Future," *Safety Engineering* 68, no. 1 (July 1934): 22.

6. "Unfit for Modern Motor Traffic," *Fortune* 14, no. 2 (August 1936): 85–92, 94, 96, 99; "Four Frictions," *Time* 28 (August 3, 1936): 41–43. The quoted statement is from *Fortune*; McClintock made a very similar statement to *Time*.

7. Hal Foust, "Elevated Roads Will Increase Car Ownership," *Chicago Tribune*, November 6, 1938, part 5, 13.

8. Foust, 13.

9. J. C. Furnas, "—And Sudden Death," *Reader's Digest* 27 (August 1935), 21–26.

10. Peter Norton, "History as Motordom's Tool of Agenda Legitimation: Twentieth-Century U.S. Mobility Trajectories," in *A U-Turn to the Future: Sustainable Urban Mobility Since 1850*, ed. Martin Emanuel, Frank Schipper, and Ruth Oldenziel (New York: Berghahn, 2020), 67–90.

11. Norman Bel Geddes, *Horizons* (Boston: Little, Brown, 1932), 244, 246–47.

12. Roland Marchand, "The Designers Go to the Fair II: Norman Bel Geddes, the General Motors 'Futurama,' and the Visit to the Factory Transformed," *Design Issues* 8, no. 2 (Spring 1992): 22–40.

13. Miller McClintock, "'Of Things to Come'" (address, Detroit, June 1, 1937), in *New Horizons in Planning, 1937* (Chicago: American Society of Planning Officials, 1937), 34–38.

14. McClintock, 35.

15. McClintock, 34–36.

16. McClintock, 36–38.

17. "Auto Show Draws Capacity Crowds; Features 'City of Tomorrow' Display," *Wisconsin Jewish Chronicle*, November 19, 1937.

18. Shell Union Oil Corporation, "Motorists of 1960 Will Loaf Along at 50—Right through Town," *Life* 3, no. 15 (October 11, 1937): 81. In 1937 Shell ran several variations on these advertisements, all depicting the model of the city of 1960; see *Life*, July 12, 1937, *Saturday Evening Post*, September 18, 1937, and *Life*, November 1, 1937.

19. E. W. Murtfeldt, "Highways of the Future," *Popular Science* 132, no. 5 (May 1938): 27–29, 118–19.

20. Charles M. Upham, "What about Tomorrow's Highways?," *Pacific Road Builder and Engineering Review* 50, no. 2 (February 1939): 25.

21. Murray D. Van Wagoner, "Superhighways Ahead," in *Proceedings: Thirty-sixth Annual Convention, San Francisco, March 7–10, 1939*, American Road Builders' Association (Washington, DC: ARBA, 1939), 12–20.

22. Van Wagoner, 12, 17, 20.

23. Van Wagoner, 6–17.

24. Charles M. Upham, "A Proposed National Highway System," in *Proceedings: Thirty-sixth Annual Convention, San Francisco, March 7–10, 1939*, American Road Builders' Association (Washington, DC: ARBA, 1939), 101–105 (101).

25. Upham, 101.

26. E. W. Moeller, "The Need for Continued Public Interest in Highway Development," in *Proceedings: Thirty-sixth Annual Convention, San Francisco, March 7–10, 1939*, American Road Builders' Association (Washington, DC: ARBA, 1939), 421–27 (423).

27. Van Wagoner, "Superhighways Ahead," 16–18.

28. L. I. Hewes, "Some Highway Problems of Today," American Road Builders' Association, *Proceedings: Thirty-sixth Annual Convention, San Francisco, March 7–10, 1939* (Washington, DC: ARBA, 1939), 21–31 (25).

29. Hewes, 31.

30. Committee on Elevated Highways, "Report of the Committee on Elevated Highways," in *Proceedings: Thirty-sixth Annual Convention, San Francisco, March 7–10, 1939*, American Road Builders' Association (Washington, DC: ARBA, 1939), 281–97 (297).

31. Moeller, "Continued Public Interest," 422.

32. Moeller, 421.

33. Moeller, 421–24.

34. "Exposition to Portray City of 1999," *National Safety News* 39 (January 1939): 74.

35. "Exhibit Shows S.F. of 1999," *Oakland Tribune*, February 15, 1939.

36. Arthur Pound, *The Turning Wheel: The Story of General Motors through Twenty-Five Years, 1908–1933* (Garden City, NY: Doubleday, Doran, 1934), 44.

37. General Motors Corporation, Research Laboratories Division, Technical Data Department, *Research Looks to New Horizons* (Detroit: GM, 1939), 8, 32.

38. General Motors Corporation, Department of Public Relations, *New Horizons of Industry through Research* (New York: GM, 1939).

39. Alfred P. Sloan, "An Invitation to General Motors Dealers" (New York: GM, June 14, 1939), 10–11.

40. General Motors Corporation, *Futurama* (1940), n.p.

41. "Keynote," editorial, *Michigan Technic* 58, no. 1 (October 1939): 16.

42. Paul Garrett, "Survey of World's Fair Exhibit," December 15, 1939, quoted in Marchand, "Designers Go to the Fair," 22–40 (35).

43. General Motors, *Futurama*.

44. General Motors.

45. General Motors.

46. Jam Handy and General Motors Corporation, *To New Horizons* (1940).

47. Handy and General Motors.

48. Handy and General Motors.

49. Lippmann, "A Day at the World's Fair," *Washington Post*, June 6, 1939, 9.

2. Futurama 2: Magic Highway, USA

Epigraph. Zworykin, in John Lear, "A Car That Drives Itself," *Collier's*, August 7, 1953, 82–87 (82).

1. General Motors Corporation, *Key to the Future* (1956), produced and directed by Michael Kidd.

2. General Motors, *Key to the Future*.

3. General Motors Corporation, *Design for Dreaming* (1956), MPO Productions, directed by William Beaudine.

4. US Chamber of Commerce, *People, Products and Progress 1975* (1955).

5. US Chamber of Commerce, *People, Products and Progress*.

6. Walt Disney Productions, *Disneyland*, episode: "Magic Highway, U.S.A" (1958), produced and directed by Ward Kimball, written by Larry Clemmons, cartoon story by Charles Downs and John Dunn, first broadcast May 14, 1958, on ABC.

7. "Magic Highway, U.S.A."

8. "Magic Highway, U.S.A."

9. Alistair Cooke, "Univac's' Hour: Triumph of Electronic

Brain," *Manchester Guardian*, November 6, 1952, 1; Serge Fliegers, "Will Machines Replace the Human Brain?," *American Mercury* 76, no. 349 (January 1953): 53–61.

10. George W. Gibson, "Why Don't We Have Crash-Proof Highways," *Mechanix Illustrated*, June 1953, 58–60, 184.

11. John Lear, "A Car That Drives Itself," *Collier's*, August 7, 1953, 82–87.

12. Lear, 82–87.

13. "Driving without Drivers?," *Time*, August 3, 1953, 50–51.

14. US Congress, House, National Highway Program, 84th Congress, 1st Session, 1955, House Document No. 93, in *The Eisenhower Administration, 1953–1961: A Documentary History*, vol. 1, ed. Robert L. Branyan and Lawrence H. Larsen (New York: Random House, 1971), 538.

15. Eisenhower, "Remarks at the Dedication of the Hiawatha Bridge," Red Wing, Minn., October 18, 1960, in *Public Papers of the Presidents of the United States: Dwight D. Eisenhower*, vol. 8 (Washington, DC: National Archives and Records Service, 1961): 780–81 (781); Eisenhower, "Address in Philadelphia at a Rally of the Nixon for President Committee of Pennsylvania," October 28, 1960, 815.

16. James Cope, in U.S. House of Representatives, Committee on Public Works, Subcommittee on Roads, National Highway Study, June 30, 1953, 385–436 (414–15, 417).

    In the 1950s, the assertion "We pay for good roads whether we have them or not" was popular among road advocates. They sometimes attributed it to Thomas H. MacDonald, who led the federal Bureau of Public Roads from 1919 to 1953. In 1923 MacDonald wrote: "For the use of the principal highways is so extensive that the people pay for adequate highways whether they have them or not, and they pay less if they have them than if they do not." MacDonald, "Basic Principles of Highway Management and Finance," *Highway Topics* 1, no. 4 (October 1923): 5–8, 24–25 (5).

17. Peter Norton, "Infrastructure: Streets, Roads, and Highways," in *Oxford Research Encyclopedia of American History* (New York: Oxford University Press, 2016), americanhistory.oxfordre.com; Norton, "Eisenhower and the Interstate System," in *Crucible: The President's First Year*, ed. Michael Nelson, Jeffrey L. Chidester, and Stefanie Georgakis Abbott (Charlottesville: University of Virginia Press, 2018), 149–54; Mark Rose, *Interstate: Express Highway Politics 1941–1989*, rev. ed. (Knoxville: University of Tennessee Press, 1990).

18. "Highway of the Future," *Electronic Age* (RCA) 17, no. 1 (January 1958): 12–14; Vladimir K. Zworykin and Leslie E. Flory, "Electronic Control of Motor Vehicles on the Highway," *Proceedings of the 37th Annual Meeting of the Highway Research Board* (1958): 436–51.

19. Science Service, "No-Hands Driving Not So Far Ahead," *Chattanooga Daily Times*, February 28, 1958, 25.

20. "Highway of the Future," 12–14; Zworykin and Flory, "Electronic Control."

21. "Highway of the Future."

22. UP, "Safety on Highways of Future Gets Boost from Lincoln Demonstration," *Holdrege Daily Citizen*, October 11, 1957, 1.

23. Science Service, "No-Hands Driving," 25.

24. "G.M. Test Car Guided by a Magnetic Path," *New York Times*, February 14, 1958, 37; UP, "GM Demonstrates Self-Guided Car but It's Got Bugs," *Wisconsin State Journal* (Madison), February 15, 1958, sec. 1, 5; "Electric Cable Steers Auto Automatically," *Science News Letter*, March 1, 1958, 134; "Electronic Guidance Tried Out," *St. Louis Post-Dispatch*, April 20, 1958, part 6, 7F–8F; General Motors Corporation, *The Future Is Our Assignment: A Glimpse behind the Scenes at the General Motors Research Laboratories* (Detroit: GMC, 1959), 41.

25. Frank Henry, "Automobiles That Drive Themselves," *Baltimore Sun*, July 5, 1959. A1.

26. Kenyon Kilbon, "Tomorrow's Thruway Is Here Today!," *Electronic Age* 19, no. 3 (Autumn 1960): 26–29.

27. Kilbon, 26–29.

28. Joseph C. Ingraham, "Electronic Roads Called Practical," *New York Times*, June 6, 1960, 31.

29. Commonwealth of Pennsylvania, "Science Promises a Future Free of Traffic Accidents," advertisement, *Pittsburgh Post-Gazette*, July 30, 1961, sec. 4, 3.

30. RCA, "How RCA Transistors Will Run Your 'Electronic' Car of Tomorrow," advertisement, *Fortune* 70, no. 6 (December 1964): 42.

31. *Futurama II* ride narration from GM *Futurama II Souvenir Book*; narration written by Edward Reveaux and spoken by Alexander Scourby. An amateur audio recording of the *Futurama II* ride was recorded by Ray Dasher. All are available online, thanks to Bill Young, at www.nywf64 .com.

32. General Motors Corporation, *Metro-Mobility* (Detroit: GMC, 1965?), Hagley Museum and Library.

33. GM, *Metro-Mobility*.

34. Ford Motor Company, *Magic Skyway*, Allegro Film Productions, 1965, www.youtube.com/watch?v=12EEFo-qUrlE; Ford Motor Company News Bureau, "'Space City Part of Ford's 'Magic Skyway,'" news release, n.d., via Bill Cotter, WorldsFairPhotos.com; Ford Motor Company, "Ride Walt Disney's Magic Skyway," brochure, 1964, The Henry Ford; Richard Barrett, "Take Walt Disney's Magic Skyway to New Adventure at the Ford Wonder Rotunda," *Ford Times* 57, no. 5 (May 1964), Bill Young at www .nywf64.com.

35. "Preparations Made for 'Magic Skyway,'" *Los Angeles Times*, February 28, 1965, sec. I, 15.

36. Steve Mannheim, *Walt Disney and the Quest for Community* (London: Routledge, 2002), 36.

3. Futurama 3: From CenterCore to Demo '97

Epigraph. Elizabeth Pennisi, "Auto(-matic) Commute: Technology Revolutionizes the Ride to Work," *Science News* 141, no. 12 (March 21, 1992): 184–85, 187 (184).

1. National Automated Highway System Consortium, *Automated Highway System (AHS): System Objectives and Characteristics* (Troy, MI: November 3, 1995), 19–27; Potential Contributions of Intelligent Vehicle / Highway Systems (IVHS) to Reducing Transportation's Greenhouse Gas Production," *Transportation Research Part A: Policy and Practice* 27, no. 3 (May 1993): 207–16.

2. Jameson M. Wetmore, "Reflecting on the Dream of Automated Vehicles: Visions of Hands-Free Driving over the Past 80 Years," *Technikgeschichte* 87 (2020): 69–94 (85).

3. Jack Raymond, "Kennedy Defense Study Finds No Evidence of a 'Missile Gap,'" *New York Times*, February 7, 1961, 1, 21.

4. "The 'Credibility Gap,'" *Guardian*, April 5, 1961, 6.

5. Murrey Marder, "Greater Skepticism Greets Administration Declarations," *Washington Post*, December 5, 1965, A21.

6. Rachel Carson, *Silent Spring* (Boston: Houghton Mifflin, 1962), 13; US Public Health Service, *Smoking and Health: Report of the Advisory Committee to the Surgeon General of the Public Health Service* (Washington, DC: US Government Printing Office, 1964); Ralph Nader, *Unsafe at Any Speed: The Designed-In Dangers of the American Automobile* (New York: Grossman, 1965); Helen Leavitt, *Superhighway—Superhoax* (Garden City, NY: Doubleday, 1970).

7. *2001: A Space Odyssey*, directed by Stanley Kubrick (Metro-Goldwyn-Mayer, 1968); E. F. Schumacher, *Small Is Beautiful: A Study of Economics as If People Mattered* (London: Blond and Briggs, 1973).

8. Eisenhower, "Text of the Address by President Eisenhower," news release, January 17, 1961, 3, www.eisenhowerlibrary.gov/sites/default/files/research/online-documents/farewell-address/1961-01-17-press-release.pdf.

9. Alfred L. Malabre Jr., "Head-On Collision with the Super-highway Complex," *Wall Street Journal*, June 11, 1970, 16.

10. Robert Poole, *Earthrise: How Man First Saw the Earth* (New Haven: Yale University Press, 2008).

11. Jules Bergman, science editorial, *ABC Evening News*, aired December 4, 1970, on ABC, www.youtube.com /watch?v=9uTg0UyQIdc&t=1211s.

12. Sam Gennawey, *Walt Disney and the Promise of Progress City* (Orlando: Theme Park Press, 2014).

13. Steve Mannheim, *Walt Disney and the Quest for Community* (London: Routledge, 2002), 17.

14. Mannheim, *Quest for Community*, 25–26.

15. Victor Gruen, paper presented at the National Citizens Planning Conference of the American Planning and Civic Association, Little Rock, June 1957, in *American Planning and Civic Annual* (Washington, DC: APCA, 1957), 18. See Gruen, "Who Is to Save Our Cities?," *Ekistics* 18, no. 105 (August 1964): 116–18.

16. M. Jeffrey Hardwick, *Mall Maker: Victor Gruen, Architect of an American Dream* (Philadelphia: University of Pennsylvania Press, 2004).

17. Victor Gruen, *The Heart of Our Cities—The Urban Crisis: Diagnosis and Cure* (New York: Simon and Schuster, 1964), 245.

18. Marvin Davis and Herbert Ryan designed the model. Marty Sklar, "Model History," n.d., The Original E.P.C.O.T. (theoriginalepcot/progress-city-model/model-overview).

19. The untitled, twenty-five-minute Florida Project film is available online; for example, at www.youtube.com/watch?v=UEm -09B0px8 (ImageWorks / RetroWDW).

20. Florida Project film.

21. *Epcot Center Guide Book* (Eastman Kodak and Walt Disney World, 1986).

22. A transcript of the narration, with scene descriptions and still

photographs, is available at Walt Dated World, waltdated world.com/index.htm, a website administered since 2001 by Mouseketeer Alison. In the following paragraphs, Walt Dated World provided the source material for quoted statements and for some scene descriptions. World of Motion's narrator was Gary Owens, a radio personality and voice actor best known for playing a straight-man announcer on the television program *Laugh-In*.

23. Dan Lavanga, "Lasers Pierce the Realm of Art," *Cornell Engineer* 51, no. 2 (1985): 10–12 (10).

24. Automotive News, "Auto Industry Works to Clear Congestion," *Times-Advocate* (Escondido), October 28, 1988, E11.

25. Moshe Ben-Akiva et al., "The Case for Smart Highways," *Technology Review*, July 1992, 39–47 (40).

26. General Motors Corporation, *Metro-Mobility* (Detroit: GMC, 1965?), Hagley Museum and Library.

27. Lyle Saxton, "Mobility 2000 and the Roots of IVHS," *IVHS Review* (Spring 1993), 11–26; Texas Transportation Institute, *Mobility 2000: Proceedings of a National Workshop on IVHS*, College Station, TX, March 19–21, 1990; Richard Whelan, *Smart Highways, Smart Cars* (Norwood, MA: Artech House, 1995), 44–45.

28. Michael G. Sheldrick, "Driving while Automated," *Scientific American* 263, vol. 1 (July 1990): 86, 88 (88).

29. General Motors, *Metro-Mobility.*

30. James Costantino, "The IVHS Strategic Plan for the United States," *Transportation Quarterly* 46, no. 4 (October 1992): 481; Moshe Ben-Akiva et al., "Smart Highways," 41.

31. "Statement of General Motors Corporation before the House Science, Space, and Technology Subcommittee on Transportation, Aviation and Materials," presented by William M. Spreitzer, GM Research Laboratories, Washington, June 7, 1989; US House of Representatives, Committee on Science, Space, and Technology, Subcommittee on Transportation,

Aviation, and Materials, testimony of William Spreitzer, June 7, 1989, 121–29.

32. An early example is Harold Walsh, "Road Program Investment Seen Tripling Original Goal," *Los Angeles Times*, January 23, 1957, 22.

33. In a late concession to the trend, in 2015 the Consumer Electronics Association renamed itself the Consumer Technology Association. Google Books Ngram Viewer, books. google.com/ngrams.

34. "Statement of General Motors Corporation," 1989; Testimony of William Spreitzer, 1989.

35. Scott Lund, "Intelligent Vehicle/Highway Systems in the U.S.: In Need of a Vision," SAE Transactions 100, section 6: *Journal of Passenger Cars* (1991): 1258–79 (1260).

36. Agnew, in Marshall Schuon, "Gridlock: When You Have It Too Good," *New York Times*, July 2, 1989, sec. 8, 4.

37. "Intelligent Vehicle-Highway Systems: A Smart Choice for the Future" (Federal Highway Administration, 1990), video, 12 min.

38. "Intelligent Vehicle-Highway Systems."

39. Lamm, in *Transportation Infrastructure: Panelists' Remarks at New Directions in Surface Transportation Seminar*, US General Accounting Office (Washington, DC: GAO, December 1989): 8–21 (20).

40. House of Representatives, Committee on Public Works and Transportation, Investigations and Oversight Subcommittee, Statement of Rodney E. Slater, Federal Highway Administrator, US Department of Transportation, "Intelligent Vehicle-Highway Systems," July 21, 1994, 13.

41. Ronald K. Jurgen, "Smart Cars and Highways Go Global," *IEEE Spectrum* 28, no. 5 (May 1991): 26–36 (35).

42. General Motors Research Laboratories, "GMR DAIR System: Highway Communications for Safety," *Projects* PR-154

(June 1966), GM Heritage Center, gmheritagecenter.com; E. A. Hanysz et al., "DAIR: A New Concept in Highway Communications for Added Safety and Driving Convenience," *IEEE Transactions on Vehicular Technology* 16, no. 1 (October 1967): 33–45.

43. Dan A. Rosen, Frank J. Mammano, and Rinaldo Favout, "An Electronic Route-Guidance System for Highway Vehicles," *IEEE Transactions on Vehicular Technology* 19, no. 1 (February 1970): 143–52.

44. Phoebe Hoban, "Directional Signals: Road Maps Get Computerized," *New York* 18, no. 27 (July 15, 1985), 14, 16.

45. Hoban, "Directional Signals," 16.

46. John Holusha, "Testing 'Smart' Roads to Avoid Traffic Jams," *New York Times*, October 19, 1988, D10.

47. Jill Walker, "Car Computer Put to a Test in Heavy Los Angeles Traffic," *Washington Post*, June 27, 1990, H1–H2.

48. Richard Whelan, *Smart Highways*, 18–21; Paul Whitworth, *Public Acceptance and User Response to ATIS Products and Services: The Role of Operational Tests in Understanding User Response to ATIS* (Washington, DC: US Department of Transportation, December 1993), Appendix E: Pathfinder, A19–A24 (A24).

49. Bill Siriu, "On-Board Navigation Systems for Your Car," *Popular Electronics* 10, no. 1 (January 1993): 39–42, 92; Paul Whitworth, *Public Acceptance*, Appendix F: TravTek, A25–A29; Richard Whelan, *Smart Highways*, 21–28; Ashley Auer, Shelley Feese, and Stephen Lockwood (Booz Allen Hamilton), *History of Intelligent Transportation Systems* (Washington, DC: US Department of Transportation, May 2016), 33; Jack Keebler, "'Smart Highways' Help Cars Navigate in Test," *Marion Star*, April 20, 1993, 3A.

50. Marshall Schuon, "In Florida, Testing Road to the Future," *New York Times*, April 5, 1992, sec. 8, 16.

51. Steve Ditlea, "Navigation Systems on Board," *Popular Science* 246, no. 3 (March 1995): 88.

52. Vernon M. Church, "Technology Takes the Toll," *Popular Science* 240, no. 3 (March 1992): 78–80; John C. Vincent, "Smart Systems for Smart Roads," *Military Engineer* 84, no. 553 (November–December 1992): 43–45.

53. Richard Ernsberger Jr. and William Underhill, "Toll Booths without Coins," *Newsweek*, July 8, 1991, 41; Glenn Rifkin, "Electronic Toll-Taking Is Being Put to the Test," *New York Times*, September 9, 1992, D1, D4; Vincent, "Smart Systems for Smart Roads," 44–45; Doug Ferguson, "PikePass Spreads to Other States Based on State Success," *Oklahoman* (Oklahoma City), June 6, 1993, sec. A, 16.

54. National Highway Users Conference, *Highway Transportation Re-makes America* (Washington, DC: NHUC, 1939).

55. Stephen C. Fehr, "Charging More Tolls Studied as a Solution to Traffic Woes," *Washington Post*, June 26, 1994, B1–B2.

56. Transportation Research Board, National Research Council, *Curbing Gridlock: Peak-Period Fees to Relieve Traffic Congestion*, vol. 1: Committee Report and Recommendations, special report 242 (Washington, DC: National Academy Press, 1994); Fehr, "Charging More Tolls."

57. Any toll on a busy turnpike is a crude version of congestion pricing in that the payment tends to mitigate congestion. More versatile congestion pricing predates electronic toll collection; Singapore introduced a system based on special license plates in 1975. In 1998 Singapore became the first city to use electronic toll collection to automate congestion pricing. Over the following decade, London, Stockholm, and Milan introduced automated congestion pricing. In 2017 variable congestion pricing was introduced on express lanes of Interstate 66 near Washington; see Aarian Marshall, "Virginia's $40 Toll Road Better Be the Future of Driving," *Wired*, December 9, 2017. On the new congestion charging plan for New York City, see Regional Plan Association, *Congestion Pricing in NYC: Getting It Right* (New York: RPA, September 2019).

58. John Burgess, "Videotapes Show 'Smart' Bombs in Action," *Washington Post*, January 19, 1991, A17, A22; John T. Correll, "The Emergence of Smart Bombs," *Air Force Magazine*, March 2010, 60–64.

59. Marcia D. Lowe, "Smart Car 54, Where Are You?," *Washington Post*, December 12, 1993, C5.

60. Richard Whelan, *Smart Highways*, 43.

61. Moshe Ben-Akiva, et al., "The Case for Smart Highways," *Technology Review*, July 1992, 39–47 (45); Calvin Sims, "Smart Cars May Change How Americans Travel," *Austin American-Statesman*, May 9, 1994, C1, C4 (C4); Elizabeth Pennisi, "Auto(-matic) Commute," 184–85, 187 (184).

62. Ashley Auer, Shelley Feese, and Stephen Lockwood (Booz Allen Hamilton), *Intelligent Transportation Systems*, 14.

63. E. Scott Reckard, "Automated Cars to Cost $350 billion," *Sun* (San Bernardino County), January 4, 1992, B8.

64. "Automated Cars and Roads? No problem. Got $350 billion?," *Ukiah Daily Journal*, January 17, 1992, 10.

65. IVHS America, *Strategic Plan for Intelligent Vehicle-Highway Systems in the United States* (Washington, DC: IVHS America, May 20, 1992).

66. James Costantino, "IVHS Strategic Plan," 481–90 (489).

67. Elizabeth Pennisi, "Auto(-matic) Commute," 184.

68. Crain News Service, "Flagging Defense Contractors Turning to 'Smart' Highways," *Cincinnati Enquirer*, May 8, 1993, E3.

69. US House of Representatives, Committee on Public Works and Transportation, Intelligent Vehicle-Highway Systems (IVHS), testimony of Lawrence Dahms, June 29, 1994, 6. See Kathleen Day, "The Highway of the Future: Defense Contractors Use Existing Technology to Become Road Warriors," *Washington Post*, March 14, 1994, Washington Business sec. 1, 14.

70. Sims, "How Americans Travel," C1, C4 (C4); Rockwell International, "Rockwell Battles Gridlock with Military Technology," advertisement, *Wall Street Journal*, March 22, 1993, A15.

71. Lockheed, "To You, It's a Satellite. To Us, It's Systems Integration," advertisement, *New York Times*, July 21, 1993, A17.

72. Intermodal Surface Transportation Efficiency Act (1991), section 6054(b).

73. "G.M. Wins U.S. Competition for Automated Car System," *Wall Street Journal*, October 7, 1994, B6.

74. "Demo '97: Proving AHS Works," *Public Roads* 61, no. 1 (July–August 1997): 31.

75. James H. Rillings, "Automated Highways," *Scientific American* 277, no. 4 (October 1997): 53.

76. Al Rothenberg, "Guided Missiles: Experiments in No-Hands Driving and Navigation Guidance Are on the Road to Reality," *Chicago Tribune*, sec. 12, 1, 5.

77. NAHSC, *National Automated Highway System Consortium Technical Feasibility Demonstration Summary Report* (Troy, MI: NAHSC, February 1998), 99.

78. Rillings, "Automated Highways," 53–55.

79. "Demo '97: Proving AHS Works," *Public Roads* 61, no. 1 (July–August 1997): 30–34.

80. ITS America, "Super Smart Transportation," *Fortune*, March 31, 1997, 47–53.

81. James Costantino, "Overcoming an Identity Crisis: The Intelligent Transportation Industry and ITS America's National Awareness Campaign," *Public Roads* 61, no. 1 (July–August 1997), 27–29, including quoted statement by ITS America's treasurer, Dick Braun (27).

82. Carr in Costantino, "Overcoming an Identity Crisis," 28.

83. Costantino, "Overcoming an Identity Crisis," 29.

84. US Department of Transportation, Research and Innovative Technology Administration, *Intelligent Transportation Systems Benefits, Costs, Deployment, and Lessons Learned Desk Reference: 2011 Update* (Washington, DC: USDOT, 2011), 7–8.

85. "Statement of General Motors Corporation before the House Science, Space, and Technology Subcommittee on Transportation, Aviation and Materials," presented by William M. Spreitzer, GM Research Laboratories, Washington, June 7, 1989; US House of Representatives, Committee on Science, Space, and Technology, Subcommittee on Transportation, Aviation, and Materials, testimony of William Spreitzer, June 7, 1989, 121–29.

86. Jameson Wetmore, who attended Demo '97, noted that NAHSC was too cautious to make official forecasts. Wetmore reports that among themselves, however, many insiders "estimated it would be 20 to 30 years until there is a substantial automated highway network." Wetmore, "Driving the Dream. The History and Motivations Behind Sixty Years of Automated Highway Systems in America," *Automotive History Review* (Summer 2003), 4–19.

87. *Star Wars*, directed by George Lucas (Lucasfilm, 20th Century Fox, 1977); *Tron*, directed by Steven Lisberger and Donald Kushner (Walt Disney Productions, 1982); *Back to the Future Part II*, directed by Robert Zemeckis and Bob Gale (Amblin Entertainment, Universal Pictures, 1989).

88. *North County Times* (Escondido), August 7–10, 1997.

89. NAHSC, *Technical Feasibility Demonstration*; Rillings, "Automated Highways," 80–85.

90. Matt Nauman, "Cars of Tomorrow Hit the Automated Highway," *Chicago Tribune*, August 31, 1997, sec. 12, 1.

91. "Demo '97: Where the Research Meets the Road," (NAHSC, 1997), video, 10 min., www.youtube.com/watch?v=C9G6 JRUmg_A.

92. "ITS America's President to Depart" and "NAHSC Changes

Program Manager," in *Public Roads* 61, no. 4 (January–February 1998): 54.

93. Wetmore, "Reflecting on the Dream," 86.

94. Lowe, "Smart Car 54," *Washington Post*, December 12, 1993, C5.

95. Adrian K. Lund and Brian O'Neill, *IVHS: Can It Deliver on Safety?* (Arlington: Insurance Institute for Highway Safety, July 1994).

96. Bryan Gruley, "Analysts Post Caution Sign on High-Tech Highway Plans," *Detroit News and Free Press*, August 7, 1994, D1–D2.

   Asked in 2021 if he could recall Costantino's "unprintable" word, Gruley replied that he had forgotten—but added: "I'd bet a thousand bucks the guy said 'bullshit;'" email message to author, February 9, 2021.

97. Pennisi, "Auto(-matic) Commute," 184.

98. US Government Accountability Office, *Highway Congestion: Intelligent Transportation Systems' Promise for Managing Congestion Falls Short, and DOT Could Better Facilitate Their Strategic Use* (Washington, DC: GAO, September 2005).

99. Conference participants stressed that even high-tech cars would need high-tech roads. National Automated Highway System Consortium, *Summary Report of the Cooperative and Autonomous Workshop 27 and 28 April 1998, Washington, D.C.* (Washington, DC: NAHSC, 1998), 4.

100. Lund, "Intelligent Vehicle/Highway," 1276.

4. Futurama 4: Autonorama

Epigraph. *2030 Xing!* (film), by SAIC and General Motors, directed by Kuang Sheng, 2010, www.productionhub.com/video/4899/2030-xing-the-future-of-mobility; dubbed in English: vimeo.com/52614378; this dubbed version supplied the English text quoted here.

1. The word frequencies in these cases are of course extremely

low, limiting their significance. Among works in American English, *next-generation* surpassed *advanced technology* in 2014; among works in British English, *next-generation* pulled ahead in 2017. Google Books Ngram Viewer, books .google.com/ngrams.

Boeing was an early leader in this usage of next generation. In 1993 it introduced a new series of 737s; in 1997 it began calling them "737 Next Generation." Some in the press were reluctant to accept the then-odd name; the *Wall Street Journal* called the planes "the so-called 737 next-generation family." Charles Goldsmith, "British Airways Seeks Airbus, Boeing Bids for Jets," *Wall Street Journal*, February 24, 1998, A16.

2. American Association for the Advancement of Science, Federal R&D Budget Dashboard, www.aaas.org/programs /r-d-budget-and-policy/federal-rd-budget-dashboard.

3. Congressional Research Service, "Defense Advanced Research Projects Agency: Overview and Issues for Congress," March 17, 2020, fas.org/sgp/crs/natsec/R45088.pdf.

4. Michael Belfiore, *Department of Mad Scientists: How DARPA Is Remaking Our World, from the Internet to Artificial Limbs* (Washington, DC: Smithsonian Books, 2009), 127–66.

5. Defense Advanced Research Projects Agency, *Grand Challenge 2004 Final Report* (Arlington: DARPA, July 30, 2004); Reinhold Behringer, "The DARPA Grand Challenge: Autonomous Ground Vehicles in the Desert," *IFAC Proceedings Volumes* 37, no. 8 (July 2004): 904–909.

6. W. Wayt Gibbs, "Innovations from a Robot Rally," *Scientific American* 294, no. 1 (January 2006): 50–57.

7. Defense Advanced Research Projects Agency, *Report to Congress: DARPA Prize Authority* (Arlington: March, 2006), 12.

8. Defense Advanced Research Projects Agency, *DARPA Urban Challenge: Fiscal Year 2007 Report* (Arlington: DARPA, January 16, 2008); Belfiore, *Department of Mad Scientists*, 127–66; John Voelcker, "Autonomous Vehicles Complete DARPA

Urban Challenge," *IEEE Spectrum*, November 1, 2007, spectrum.ieee.org/transportation/advanced-cars/autonomous -vehicles-complete-darpa-urban-challenge.

9. Defense Advanced Research Projects Agency, *Report to Congress: DARPA Prize Authority* (Arlington, VA: DARPA, March, 2006).

10. Thompson Products, "Want to Build a Car That Drives Itself?," advertisement, *Fortune*, August 1958, 195.

11. Joseph L. Bower and Clayton M. Christensen, "Disruptive Technologies: Catching the Wave," *Harvard Business Review* 73, no. 1 (January–February 1995): 43–53.

12. Clayton M. Christensen, *The Innovator's Dilemma: When New Technologies Cause Great Firms to Fail* (Boston: Harvard Business School Press, 1997). In 2000 HarperBusiness reprinted the book with a new subtitle: *The Revolutionary Book That Will Change the Way You Do Business*. For the case against "disruption theory," begin with Jill Lepore, "The Disruption Machine: What the Gospel of Innovation Gets Wrong," *New Yorker* 90, no. 17 (June 16, 2014): 30–36.

13. "Aiming High," *The Economist*, July 2, 2011.

14. Bower and Christensen, "Disruptive Technologies," 43–44.

15. For disruptive innovation's debt to Joseph Schumpeter, see Jack Stilgoe, *Who's Driving Innovation? New Technologies and the Collaborative State* (London: Palgrave Macmillan, 2020), 57.

16. Charles F. Kettering, "Keep the Consumer Dissatisfied," *Nation's Business* 17, no. 1 (January 1929): 30–31, 79 (31).

17. Thrun was speaking at *Wired* magazine's annual business conference in New York. Dave Mosher, "Google's Sebastian Thrun: 3 Visions in the 'Age of Disruption.'"

18. Paul Nunes and Larry Downes, "The Five Most Disruptive Innovations at CES 2015," *Forbes*, January 9, 2015. Nunes and Downes are the authors of *Big Bang Disruption: Strategy in the Age of Devastating Innovation* (New York: Portfolio, 2014).

19. Mary Barra, "General Motors CEO Mary Barra: 'We Are Disrupting Ourselves, We're Not Trying to Preserve a Model of Yesterday,'" interview by Matthew DeBord, *Business Insider*, November 16, 2015, www.businessinsider.com/general-motors-ceo-mary-barra-were-going-to-disrupt-our-selves-we-are-disrupting-ourselves-were-not-trying-to-pres-erve-a-model-of-yesterday-2015-10.

      More recently, the Clayton Christensen Institute for Disruptive Innovation, founded by Christensen in 2007, has denied that autonomous vehicles are a "disruptive innovation" (Chandrasekar Iyer and Rich Alston, "Sorry, Autonomous Vehicles Aren't Disruptive," Christensen Institute, October 1, 2019), though in a realm where perceptions are reality, the denial hardly matters.

20. Bill Vlasic and Mike Isaac, "GM to Buy Cruise in Push for Self-Driving Cars," *New York Times*, March 12, 2016, B2.

21. *2030 Xing!* (film), by SAIC and General Motors, directed by Kuang Sheng, 2010, www.productionhub.com/vid-eo/4899/2030-xing-the-future-of-mobility; dubbed in English: vimeo.com/52614378; this dubbed version supplied the English text quoted here. I owe my acquaintance with *2030 Xing!* to Pieter van Wesemael of Eindhoven University of Technology, to whom I am profoundly indebted; he told me about it in conversation in 2017.

22. Jin Qi, in "SAIC-GM Pavilion, 'Drive to 2030' Press Conference," news release, General Motors Corporate Newsroom, December 3, 2009, www.gmchina.com/media/cn/en/gm/home.detail.html/content/Pages/news/cn/en/2009/1203.html.

23. Kevin Wale, in "GM and SAIC Begin Drive to 2030," news release, General Motors Corporate Newsroom, April 12, 2010, www.gmchina.com/media/cn/en/gm/home.detail.html/content/Pages/news/cn/en/2010/April/04021.html.

24. General Motors Corporate Newsroom, "SAIC-GM Pavilion, 'Drive to 2030' Press Conference."

25. *2030 Xing!*

26. General Motors Corporate Newsroom, "GM and SAIC Begin Drive to 2030," news release, April 12, 2010.

27. General Motors Corporate Newsroom, "SAIC-GM Pavilion Named Most Popular Enterprise Pavilion at World Expo 2010 Shanghai," news release, November 8, 2010, www.gmchina .com/media/cn/en/gm/home.detail.html/content/Pages /news/cn/en/2010/November/1108.html.

28. General Motors Corporate Newsroom, "GM and SAIC Debut World Expo 2010 Pavilion: The Road to 2030," news release, April 11, 2010, www.generalmotors.green /media/us/en/gm/home.detail.html/content/Pages/news/us /en/2010/Apr/0412_saic.html.

29. KPMG, *The Clockspeed Dilemma: What Does It Mean for Automotive Innovation?* (November 2015).

30. General Motors, *2017 Sustainability Report: Zero Crashes. Zero Emissions. Zero Congestion*, 6.

31. Since 1972, *transit-dependent* has been an official term for carless people and nondrivers (implicitly those in car-dependent places). This usage was apparently introduced by Carlos Villarreal, administrator of the Urban Mass Transit Administration (an agency in the Federal Highway Administration), in addresses of June 19 and October 3, 1972, published as "Opportunities for the Transit Dependent," in *Conference on Transportation and Human Needs in the '70s* (Washington, DC: American University, June 19, 1972), 50–55, and as "Meeting the Needs of the Transit Dependent," in *Highway and Urban Mass Transportation* (UMTA, Winter 1972), 32–34.

In 1974, as this usage proliferated (see "Los Angeles Strike Puts New Bus Riders Back into Their Cars," *New York Times*, August 17, 1974, 9), a US Department of Transportation report defined the "transportation poor" as "the elderly, the very young, the impoverished," and "the handicapped," indicating that to USDOT, every person who could drive and who could afford a car had a responsibility to buy one. "In some instances," the report added, "the transportation poor" include "even the one-car family." USDOT, *Demand-Responsive Transportation* (Washington, DC: USDOT, 1974), 1.

32. As an abbreviation, *AV* most often stands for autonomous vehicle, but sometimes for automated vehicle. Here AV is used more generally for vehicles with substantial automation, including automation short of autonomy.

33. "Cola Giants Speed Tests of Plastic Bottles," *New York Times*, July 26, 1970; Gene Smith, "Coca-Cola Trying a Plastic Bottle," *New York Times*, June 4, 1975.

34. "Tobacco Industry, Upset by Link to Cancer, Starts Own Research," *New York Times*, January 4, 1954; Tobacco Industry Research Committee, "A Frank Statement to Cigarette Smokers" (1954), published in hundreds of newspapers; see *New York Times*, January 4, 1954. Recent analogues among business groups engaged in the development and promotion of automated vehicles include the Self-Driving Coalition for Safer Streets (established 2016), the Automated Vehicle Coalition (2018), and Partners for Automated Vehicle Education (PAVE, 2019).

35. "Self-Driving Cars Take the Wheel," sponsored content from Intel, *MIT Technology Review*, February 15, 2019, www.technologyreview.com/2019/02/15/137381/self-driving-cars-take-the-wheel. See "Here's Your Definitive Guide to the Future of Mobility," sponsored content from Audi, *TechCrunch*, 2018 (precise date unspecified), techcrunch.com/sponsor/unlisted/heres-your-definitive-guide-to-the-future-of-mobility/; James Daly, "No Driver, No Problem," sponsored content from Intel, *Politico*, May 10, 2018, www.politico.com/sponsor-content/2018/05/no-driver-no-problem; Susan Penfield, Gary Labovich, and Denis Cosgrove, "Technologies That Will Change the World," *Atlantic*, 2017 (precise date unspecified), www.theatlantic.com/sponsored/booz-allen-hamilton-2017/technologies-that-will-change-the-world/1503. According to the article in *The Atlantic*, "autonomous vehicles will fundamentally change how we

live." The article originally included a disclosure only in small type at the end, noting that it was written by Booz Allen Hamilton.

36. Examples are numerous:

"Nissan today announced that the company will be ready with multiple commercially viable Autonomous Drive vehicles by 2020." "Nissan Announces Unprecedented Autonomous Drive Benchmarks," news release, *Nissan News*, August 27, 2013.

"My oldest son is eleven, and that means in four and a half years he's going to be able to get his driver's license. My team and I are committed to making sure that doesn't happen" (because autonomous vehicles will make driver's licenses unnecessary). Chris Urmson, "How a Driverless Car Sees the Road," TED Vancouver, March 17, 2015.'

Tim Adams quotes BMW's Michael Aeberhard: "We think sometime after 2020 we will be ready for the first highly automated function, which means that the driver will be actually able to do something other than monitor the system." Adams, "Self-Driving Cars: From 2020 You Will Become a Permanent Backseat Driver," *Guardian* (US edition), September 13, 2015.

Jay Ramey, "The Ultimate Self-Driving Machines Will Take Over in 2021," *Autoweek*, July 7, 2016.

Georgina Prodhan quotes BMW's senior vice president for autonomous driving, Elmar Frickenstein: "We are on the way to deliver a car in 2021 with Level 3, 4 and 5." Prodhan, "BMW Says Self-Driving Car to Be Level 5 Capable by 2021," *Automotive News*, March 16, 2017.

37. "London Robot Trains Begin Trials," *Times* (London), April 6, 1964; Anthony Rowley, "Big Strides in Automation, *Times* (London), March 7, 1969.

38. For example, "Accident rates will fall to near zero for SDCs [self-driving cars]." IHS Markit, "Self-Driving Cars Moving into the Industry's Driver's Seat," news release in IHS Markit report, January 2, 2014. This forecast was quoted as straight

news by the *Wall Street Journal* and by the *Los Angeles Times* (both on January 2, 2014).

39. "Our technology will ultimately be safer than a human driver." Chris Urmson (since 2017, CEO of Aurora), "Autonomy," *Aurora* (blog), Medium, March 8, 2019. On July 16, 2019, at the Automated Vehicles Symposium in Orlando, Urmson delivered a keynote address titled "Safer Than a Human Driver."

40. General Motors, *2017 Sustainability Report.*

41. According to the Federal Railroad Administration, in the United States in 2018, five passengers on trains were killed in "train accidents, train incidents, and nontrain incidents"; this excludes off-train fatalities at "highway-rail grade crossings." Among employees of railroads (including freight railroads) and employees of railroads' contractors, 25 were killed in rail incidents. Outside of trains, on tracks and at grade crossings, 891 persons were killed; of these, 753 were classified as "trespassers." US Department of Transportation, Bureau of Transportation Statistics, "Railroad and Grade-Crossing Fatalities by Victim Class," www.bts.gov/content/railroad-and-grade-crossing-fatalities-victim-class.

42. Cadie Thompson, "Why Driverless Cars Will Be Safer Than Human Drivers," *Business Insider*, November 16, 2016; Dou Shicong, "Autonomous Cars Will Be Safer Than Human Drivers, Robin Lee Says," Yicai Global, March 26, 2018; Jim Morrison, "Driverless Cars Will Dramatically Change Where and How We Live," *Forbes*, September 13, 2018.

43. National Transportation Safety Board, "Highway Accident Report: Collision Between Vehicle Controlled by Developmental Automated Driving System and Pedestrian, Tempe, Arizona, March 18, 2018," Accident Report NTSB/HAR-19/03 PB2019-101402, November 19, 2019, v, 1, 13–17. See Stilgoe, *Who's Driving Innovation?*, 1–6.

44. Sam Peltzman, "The Effects of Automobile Safety Regulation," *Journal of Political Economy* 83, no. 4 (August 1975): 677–726.

45. "Sam Peltzman Thinks You Should Belt Up," *Chicago Booth Review*, November 27, 2016, review.chicagobooth .edu/economics/2016/article/sam-peltzman-thinks-you -should-belt.

46. Rick Newman, "It's Time to Notice Tesla's Autopilot Death Toll," *Yahoo!Finance*, April 19, 2021, finance.yahoo.com/news /its-time-to-notice-teslas-autopilot-death-toll-195849408.html.

47. "Sam Peltzman Thinks."

48. Peltzman, "Automobile Safety Regulation," 677, 682, 717.

49. Angie Schmitt, *Right of Way: Race, Class, and the Silent Epidemic of Pedestrian Deaths in America* (Washington, DC: Island, 2020), chap. 6 (99–114); Smart Growth America and National Complete Streets Coalition, *Dangerous by Design 2021*, smartgrowthamerica.org/wp-content/uploads/2021/03 /Dangerous-By-Design-2021-update.pdf.

50. Peter Norton, *Fighting Traffic: The Dawn of the Motor Age in the American City* (Cambridge, MA: MIT Press, 2008), 95–99.

51. "Driving without Drivers?," *Time*, August 3, 1953, 50–51.

52. Al Bloom, "Parks, Honky-Tonks, and Bergen," *Record* (Hackensack), 5.

   In a 1929 article, a psychologist examined the more general problem of trancelike states among drivers and other road users. Walter Miles, "Sleeping with the Eyes Open," *Scientific American* 140, no. 6 (June 1929): 489–92.

   In 1921 the author of a letter to the *New York Herald* characterized a similar phenomenon that he diagnosed as "incursive somnipathy;" the *Herald*'s editor referred to the proposition as the "hypnotic theory of motor car mishaps." Daniel O. Skinner, letter to editor, *New York Herald*, January 30, 1921, sec. 2, 2.

53. Griffith W. Williams, "Highway Hypnosis: Our Newest Hazard," *Parade*, August 28, 1949, 6–7, in *Pittsburgh*

Post-Gazette. In the 1950s and 1960s, *turnpike hypnosis* was a common variant.

54. In the 1950s, Dr. Alvah R. Lauer, director of Iowa State College's Driving Laboratory, extensively studied highway hypnosis; see "'Highway Hypnosis,' New and Deadly Killer, Takes Dire Toll on Super Roads," *Monroe (LA) Morning World*, September 4, 1955, A3.

55. N. H. Mackworth, "The Breakdown of Vigilance during Prolonged Visual Search," *Quarterly Journal of Experimental Psychology* 1, no. 1 (1948): 6–21.

Mackworth's study still receives significant attention, including among researchers engaged in driving automation. Some have questioned the relevance of Mackworth's finding to the task of supervising a partly or fully automated car. J. C. F de Winter, a roboticist whose general assessment of automated driving systems is highly optimistic, contends that "the typical 'pitfalls of automation' narrative" (presumably including the one I have offered here) "may be exaggerated."

De Winter argues that Mackworth's study "cannot be used to prove that humans are poor at monitoring automation systems," because the signals in the study were not "salient." Citing research in which humans performed better at detecting more salient signals, he concludes that "humans are not fundamentally unable to detect targets for prolonged periods." In fact, the questioners of automated systems as the main path to safety have not argued that humans are invariably poor at supervising them. It is well known, however, that in ordinary traffic on busy city streets, or on highways at ordinary highway speeds, necessary response times to very subtle cues may be extremely brief; meanwhile, automated driving systems tend to enormously increase the salience necessary to get the driver's attention (as the circumstances culminating in the death of Elaine Herzberg illustrate).

In his argument, de Winter falls into a "pitfall" of his own—and to be fair, he is in excellent company. As he (and many others) present it, our universe of choices is limited to (1) status quo car dependency (still mostly unautomated), or (2) theoretically achievable automated car dependency. But status quo car dependency is, of course, a needlessly low standard of comparison. Were these indeed our only alternatives, option 2 might indeed be the "remedy to this public health problem," as de Winter suggests. De Winter, "Pitfalls of Automation: A Faulty Narrative?," *Ergonomics* 62, no. 4 (April 7, 2019): 505–508.

56. National Transportation Safety Board, "Highway Accident Report: Collision between Vehicle Controlled by Developmental Automated Driving System and Pedestrian, Tempe, Arizona, March 18, 2018," Accident Report NTSB/HAR-19/03 PB2019-101402, November 19, 2019, v, 1, 23.

57. De Winter, "Pitfalls of Automation," 505–508.

58. Jack Stilgoe, "Tesla Crash Report Blames Human Error: This Is a Missed Opportunity," *Guardian* (US edition), January 21, 2017.

59. Joseph Hummer, *Driverless America: What Will Happen When Most of Us Choose Automated Vehicles* (Warrendale, PA: SAE International, 2020), 37.

60. Adam Millard-Ball, "Pedestrians, Autonomous Vehicles, and Cities," *Journal of Planning Education and Research* 38, no. 1 (2018): 6–12 (6).

61. Office of the Governor, "Governor Ducey Tells Uber 'CA May Not Want You, but AZ Does,'" azgovernor.gov/governor/news/2016/12/governor-ducey-tells-uber-ca-may-not-want-you-az-does.

62. See Phil Koopman, "A Reality Check on the 94 Percent Human Error Statistic for Self-Driving Cars," *Safe Autonomy* (blog), June 5, 2018, safeautonomy.blogspot.com/2018/06/a-reality-check-on-94-percent-human.html.

63. NTSB, "Highway Accident Report," 13–16.

64. National Center for Chronic Disease Prevention and Health

Promotion, US Centers for Disease Control and Prevention, "Lack of Physical Activity," 2019, www.cdc.gov/chronicdisease /pdf/factsheets/physical-activity-H.pdf.

65. Wesley E. Marshall, Daniel P. Piatkowski, and Norman W. Garrick, "Community Design, Street Networks, and Public Health," *Journal of Transport and Health* 1 (August 8, 2014): 326–40; James Hamblin, "Do We Look Fat in These Suburbs?," *Atlantic*, August 13, 2014, www.theatlantic.com/health /archive/2014/08/blame-the-city/375888.

66. Rob McConnell et al., "Traffic, Susceptibility and Childhood Asthma," *Environmental Health Perspectives* 114, no. 5 (May 2006): 766–72; Tony Barboza and Jon Schleuss, "L.A. Keeps Building Near Freeways Even Though Living There Makes People Sick," *Los Angeles Times*, March 2, 2017.

67. Erica Burt, Peter Orris, and Susan Buchanan, *Scientific Evidence of Health Effects from Coal Use in Energy Generation* (Chicago: University of Illinois at Chicago School of Public Health, April 2013); Julia Kravchenko and H. Kim Lyerl, "The Impact of Coal-Powered Electrical Plants and Coal Ash Impoundments on the Health of Residential Communities," *North Carolina Medical Journal* 79, no. 5 (2018): 289–300.

68. KPMG, *The Clockspeed Dilemma: What Does It Mean for Automotive Innovation?* (November 2015), 12. In this thirty-seven-page report, *mobility* appears sixty-four times; *transportation* appears five times (*transport* is never used). In every instance in which *mobility* is used, mobility within vehicles (i.e., transport) is meant.

69. US Department of Transportation, National Highway Traffic Safety Administration, "Overview of Motor Vehicle Crashes in 2019," *Traffic Safety Facts*, December 2020, file:///Users /pdn2p/Downloads/Overview%20of%20Motor%20Vehicle %20Crashes%20in%202019.pdf.

70. Brian Krzanich (CEO, Intel Corporation), "Data Is the New Oil in the Future of Automated Driving," Intel Newsroom,

November 15, 2016, newsroom.intel.com/editorials/krzanich -the-future-of-automated-driving.

71. Kneebone and Holmes, "The Growing Distance between People and Jobs in Metropolitan America," Brookings Metropolitan Policy Program, March 2015.

72. Note that an AV that individuals pay for and then ride in alone, even if only for ten minutes, is not a "shared" vehicle; it is rented. If I charge you to let you use something of mine, I lose my right to claim I shared it.

73. Jevons, *The Coal Question: An Inquiry Concerning the Progress of the Nation, and the Probable Exhaustion of Our Coal-Mines* (London: Macmillan, 1865).

74. From the San Francisco County Transportation Authority, see *TNCs and Congestion,* Final Report, October 2018, and "Report Finds Transportation Network Companies Caused Approximately Half of S.F.'s Increased Congestion Since 2010," news release, October 16, 2018.

5. Data Don't Drive

Epigraph. Jack Stilgoe, *Who's Driving Innovation? New Technologies and the Collaborative State* (London: Palgrave Macmillan, 2020), 5.

1. "The BMW Group and AWS Team Up to Accelerate Data-Driven Innovation in the Automotive Industry," *Business Wire,* December 8, 2020, www.businesswire.com/news/home /20201208005443/en/The-BMW-Group-and-AWS-Team -Up-to-Accelerate-Data-Driven-Innovation-in-the -Automotive-Industry.

2. Robert J. David and David Strang, "When Fashion Is Fleeting: Transitory Collective Beliefs and the Dynamics of TQM Consulting," *Academy of Management Journal* 49, no. 2 (April 2006): 215–33.

3. Mark Joseph Zbaracki, "The Rhetoric and Reality of Total Quality Management" (PhD diss., Stanford University, 1994), 5.

4. See any of numerous CareerTrack advertisements for its TQM seminars in 1992–93, beginning with "Total Quality Management: A One-Day Management Training Program," *Miami Herald*, March 8, 1992.

5. Steven Mih, "How to Make Your Company More Data Driven," *Forbes*, October 9, 2020, www. forbes.com/sites /forbestechcouncil/2020/10/09/how-to-make-your-company -more-data-driven; Tim Stobierski, "The Advantages of Data-Driven Decision-Making," *Business Insights* (blog), Harvard Business School Online, August 26, 2019, online.hbs.edu/blog/post/data-driven-decision-making; David Waller, "10 Steps to Creating a Data-Driven Culture," *Harvard Business Review*, February 6, 2020, hbr.org/2020 /02/10-steps-to-creating-a-data-driven-culture.

6. Frederick Winslow Taylor, *The Principles of Scientific Management* (New York: Harper, 1911).

7. Biff Leland Baker, "TQM Practice and Theory: A Meta-Analysis of Empirical Studies" (PhD diss., Colorado Technical University, 2003), abstract, 1.

8. See Caroline Carruthers and Peter Jackson, *Data Driven Business Transformation: How to Disrupt, Innovate and Stay ahead of the Competition* (Hoboken, NJ: Wiley, 2019).

9. Richard Read, "Google's Autonomous Car: Now Street-Legal in California," *The Car Connection*, September 26, 2012, www .thecarconnection.com/news/1079422_googles-autonomous -car-now-street-legal-in-california.

10. "Look, No Hands," *Economist*, August 30, 2012, www.economist.com/technology-quarterly/ 2012/08/30/look-no-hands.

11. Dan Neil, "Who's Behind the Wheel? Nobody. The Driverless Car Is Coming. And We All Should Be Glad It Is," *Wall Street Journal*, September 24, 2012, www.wsj.com/articles /SB100008723963900443524904577651552635911824; Doug Aamoth and Corey Protin, "Ready or Not, Driverless Cars Are Coming," *Time*, May 7, 2014, time.com/90385 /driverless-cars.

12. Jeff Bertolucci, "Big Data Drives the Smart Car," *Informa-tionWeek*, March 18, 2014, www.informationweek.com/big -data/big-data-analytics/big-data-drives-the-smart-car/d /d-id/1127767.

13. Chris Anderson, "The End of Theory: The Data Deluge Makes the Scientific Method Obsolete," *Wired*, June 23, 2008, www.wired.com/2008/06/pb-theory.

14. Thomas Behrndt and Ben Wagner, "Seeing Like a Data Set: Reimagining Security through Big Data," *Jahrbuch für Recht und Ethik / Annual Review of Law and Ethics* 23 (2015): 129–47.

15. Thomas C. Redman, *Data Driven: Profiting from Your Most Important Business Asset* (Boston: Harvard Business Press, 2008).

16. Jenny Dearborn, *Data-Driven Leadership* (San Francisco: Jossey-Bass, 2014).

17. Jay Zaidi, *Data-Driven Leaders Always Win* (Washington, DC: AlyData, 2016).

18. Tim Phillips, *Data-Driven Business: Use Real Numbers to Improve Your Business by 352%* (Oxford: Infinite Ideas, 2016). Phillips arrived at the promised number by citing Google's revenue jump in its second year (2001) relative to its first (2000).

19. Other books exalting data-driven leadership include the following: Ontario Principals' Council, *The Principal as Data-Driven Leader* (Thousand Oaks, CA: Corwin, 2008). Paul Bambrick-Santoyo, *Driven by Data: A Practical Guide to Improve Instruction* (Hoboken, NJ: Wiley, 2010). Laura Madsen, *Data-Driven-Healthcare: How Analytics and BI Are Transforming the Industry* (Hoboken, NJ: Wiley, 2014). Carl Anderson, *Creating a Data-Driven Organization: Practical Advice from the Trenches* (Sebastopol, CA: O'Reilly Media, 2015). Amanda Datnow and Vicki Park, *Data Driven: How Performance Analytics Delivers Extraordinary Sales Results* (Hoboken, NJ: Wiley, 2015). D. J. Patil and Hilary Mason,

Data Driven: Creating a Data Culture (Sebastopol, CA: O'Reilly Media, 2015). Steve McLaughlin, *Data Driven Nonprofits* (Charleston, SC: Saltire Press, 2016). Jenny Dearborn and David Swanson, *The Data-Driven Leader: A Powerful Approach to Delivering Measurable Business Impact through People Analysis* (Hoboken, NJ: Wiley, 2017). Tom Chavez, Chris O'Hara, and Vivek Vaidya, *Data Driven: Harnessing Data and AI to Reinvent Customer Engagement* (New York: McGraw-Hill Education, 2018). Gordon Summers, *Leading a Data Driven Organization* (Gordon Summers, 2018). Mario Vanhoucke, *The Data-Driven Project Manager: A Statistical Battle against Project Obstacles* (New York: Apress, 2018). Steven L. Brunton and J. Nathan Kutz, *Data-Driven Science and Engineering: Machine Learning, Dynamical Systems, and Control* (Cambridge: Cambridge University Press, 2019). Carruthers and Jackson, *Data Driven Business Transformation*. Martin Treder, *Becoming a Data Driven Organisation: Unlock the Value of Data* (Berlin: Springer, 2019).

20. For example, Lucia Walter and Manuel Pessanha, "Synertics Is the Startup of the Week (27): Data-Driven Mobility Solutions," Innoloft, June 30, 2020, innoloft.com/public/en /2020/06/synertics-is-the-startup-of-the-week-27-data-driven -mobility-solutions.

21. Stilgoe, *Who's Driving Innovation?*, 13.

22. Oldenziel, "The Vanishing Trick: How Cyclists and Pedestrians Were Left Uncounted," keynote address, Twelfth International Conference of the Association for the History of Transport, Traffic, and Mobility, Philadelphia, 2014.

23. Hedman, "Director of Planning," in Kenneth R. Schneider, *Autokind vs. Mankind: An Analysis of Tyranny, A Proposal for Rebellion* (New York: W.W. Norton, 1971). Carlton Reid put this cartoon back into circulation in 2015 as he prepared his book *Bike Boom: The Unexpected Resurgence of Cycling* (Washington, DC, 2017). For the cartoon, see Reid, "The 1970s Kick-Back against the Almighty Motorcar," Bike Boom, March 28, 2015, www.bikeboom.info/moloch.

24. Clive Humby, "Data Is the New Oil," address to the Senior Marketers' Summit, Association of National Advertisers, Kellogg School of Management, Northwestern University, Evanston, IL, 2006, ana.blogs.com/maestros/2006/11/data_is_the_new.html.

25. Charles Arthur, "Tech Giants May Be Huge, but Nothing Matches Big Data," *Guardian* (US edition), August 23, 2013, www.theguardian.com/technology/2013/aug/23/tech-giants-data.

26. Brian Krzanich, "Data Is the New Oil," keynote address, November 2016, AutoMobility conference, Los Angeles Automobile Show, YouTube, www.youtube.com/watch?v=PjhO4e9jalo&t=125s.

27. Brian Krzanich, "Data Is the New Oil in the Future of Automated Driving," Intel Newsroom, November 15, 2016, newsroom.intel.com/editorials/krzanich-the-future-of-automated-driving.

28. Krzanich, "Future of Automated Driving."

29. Jon D. Elhai et al., "Problematic Smartphone Use: A Conceptual Overview and Systematic Review of Relations with Anxiety and Depression Psychopathology," *Journal of Affective Disorders* 207 (January 1, 2017): 251–59.

30. McKinsey and Company, *Monetizing Car Data: New Service Business Opportunities to Create New Customer Benefits*, September 2016, www.mckinsey.com/~/media/mckinsey/industries/automotive%20and%20assembly/our%20insights/monetizing%20car%20data/monetizing-car-data.ashx, 29.

31. McKinsey and Company, 29.

32. Evangelos Simoudis, *The Big Data Opportunity in Our Driverless Future* (Menlo Park, CA: Corporate Innovators, 2017).

33. Twain, letter to George Bainton, October 15, 1888, in Bainton, *The Art of Authorship: Literary Reminiscences, Methods of Work, and Advice to Young Beginners* (New York: D. Appleton, 1891), 87–88.

34. James E. Powell, "Why Gut Instinct Still Dominates Decision Making (and How to Become Data-Driven)," *Upside: Where Data Meets Business* (blog), TDWI, October 1, 2020, tdwi.org/articles/2020/10/01/biz-all-why-gut-instinct-still-dominates-decision-making.aspx.

35. See John Urry, *Sociology beyond Societies: Mobilities for the Twenty-First Century* (London: Routledge, 2000).

36. An early example of motordom's shift from *transport* to *mobility* is General Motors Corporation, *Metro-Mobility* (Detroit: GMC, 1965?), Hagley Museum and Library.

37. For example, Nissan, Aptiv, and Zoox call their AV enterprises "autonomous mobility," though all their projects under this heading are, in fact, transport in vehicles. More generally, tech and auto companies often use *mobility* as a mere substitute for *transport* or *transportation.*

38. Gosia Kung, "People Are Pedestrians by Design," DenverUrbanism, August 31, 2011 denverurbanism.com. Kung is the founder of WalkDenver.

39. KPMG, *Clockspeed Dilemma*, 12. In this thirty-seven-page report, *mobility* appears 64 times; *transportation* appears 5 times (*transport* is never used). In every instance in which *mobility* is used, mobility within vehicles (i.e., transport) is meant.

40. Allison+Partners, *The Birth of Mobility Culture: Technology's Influence on How We Get from Here to There* (2019); Allison+Partners, "New Report from Allison+Partners Uncovers a Shift from Car Culture to Mobility Culture," news release, March 13, 2019.

41. American Automobile Association, "Fact Sheet: Vehicle Technology Survey," March 2016, newsroom.aaa.com/wp-content/uploads/2019/06/Automotive-Engineering-ADAS-Survey-Fact-Sheet-FINAL-3.pdf.

42. American Automobile Association, "Fact Sheet: Vehicle Technology Survey—Phase III," January 2018.

43. American Automobile Association, "Vehicle Technology Survey."

44. James Costantino, "Overcoming an Identity Crisis: The Intelligent Transportation Industry and ITS America's National Awareness Campaign," *Public Roads* 61 no. 1 (July–August 1997): 27–29.

45. Joseph Hummer, *Driverless America: What Will Happen When Most of Us Choose Automated Vehicles* (Warrendale, PA: SAE International), 12.

46. In 2016 the Consumer Electronics Show changed its official full name to CES.

47. PAVE, "PAVE Launches at CES 2019," news release, January 7, 2019, pavecampaign.org/pave-launches-at-consumer-electronics -showcase.

　　PAVE's founding members were the National Safety Council, Audi of America, the National Federation of the Blind, Cruise, INRIX, Nvidia, Securing America's Future Energy, Toyota, Voyage, Zoox, and the Consumer Technology Association.

48. See Jack Stilgoe, "From Deficit to Dialogue: A Comment on PAVE," *Driverless Futures* (blog), January 16, 2019, driv-erless-futures.com/2019/01/16/from-deficit-to-dialogue -a-comment-on-pave.

Conclusion: Escape from Futurama

1. Deutsche Gesellschaft für Internationale Zusammenarbeit, Agora Verkehrswende, and World Economic Forum, *Transport for under Two Degrees: The Way Forward* (German Federal Foreign Office, 2020) www.t4under2.org.

2. Carlton Reid, "Bicycles and Buses Will Be Future's Dominant Modes of Urban Mobility, Predict 346 Transport Experts," *Forbes*, October 9, 2020, www.forbes.com/sites/carltonreid /2020/10/09/bikes-and-buses-will-be-futures-dominant -modes-of-urban-mobility-predict-346-transport-experts.

3. See the following: Gregory H. Shill, "Should Law Subsidize

Driving?," *New York University Law Review* 95 (May 2020): 498–579. Shill, "Americans Shouldn't Have to Drive, but the Law Insists on It," *Atlantic*, July 9, 2019, www.theatlantic .com/ideas/archive/2019/07/car-crashes-arent-always -unavoidable/592447. "Decisions, Values, and Data: Understanding Bias in Transportation Performance Measures," *ITE Journal* 84, no. 8 (August 2014): 20–25. Wesley E. Marshall and Norman Garrick, "Effect of Street Network Design on Walking and Biking," *Transportation Research Record* 2198 (January 2010): 103–115.

4. Peter Norton, "History as Motordom's Tool of Agenda Legitimation: Twentieth-Century U.S. Mobility Trajectories," in *A U-Turn to the Future: Sustainable Urban Mobility Since 1850*, ed. Martin Emanuel, Frank Schipper, and Ruth Oldenziel (New York: Berghahn, 2020), 67–90.

5. Wall-mounted sign: "What Happened to Streetcars?," *America on the Move* (exhibit), National Museum of American History, Washington, DC; photographed by the author, February 18, 2011. The sign admits that "government and corporate policies and actions" mattered, but these factors are characterized as relatively unimportant. The assertion that most commuters "prefer to drive alone" applies specifically to metropolitan Washington, DC, but the sign implies that the Washington experience is typical of the national experience.

6. Michelle J. White, "Housing and the Journey to Work in U.S. Cities," in *Housing Markets in the U.S. and Japan*, ed. Yukio Noguchi and James Poterba (Chicago: University of Chicago Press, 1994), 133–59 (152).

7. On this struggle, see Angie Schmitt, *Right of Way: Race, Class, and the Silent Epidemic of Pedestrian Deaths in America* (Washington, DC: Island, 2020).

8. See Ralph Buehler and Andrea Hamre, "The Multimodal Majority? Driving, Walking, Cycling, and Public Transportation Use among American Adults," *Transportation* 42 (October 5, 2014), 1081–1101.

9. "VisitorStats," Newsdesk, Smithsonian, www.si.edu/newsdesk/about/stats.

10. Norton, "History as Motordom's Tool," 67–90.

11. Norton, *Fighting Traffic: The Dawn of the Motor Age in the American City* (Cambridge, MA: MIT Press, 2008).

12. "Motor Killings and the Engineer," editorial, *Engineering News-Record* 89 (November 9, 1922): 775.

13. Norton, *Fighting Traffic*. Carlton Reid has documented an earlier transition, when paved roads intended for cyclists were taken over by motorists: "Roads were *not* built for motor cars. By and large, they were built for pedestrians. That roads were allowed to be colonised by cars is not something that happened by accident, nor was it inevitable." Reid, *Roads Were Not Built for Cars: How Cyclists Were the First to Push for Good Roads and Became the Pioneers of Motoring* (Washington, DC, Island, 2015), xv:

14. Gary H. Zehnpfenning, James Cromar, and Sara Jane Maclennan, *Measures to Overcome Impediments to Bicycling and Walking,* National Bicycling and Walking Study: case study 4 (Federal Highway Administration, US Department of Transportation, August 1993), 5.

15. Denver Public Works, *Moving People* (Denver Strategic Transportation Plan, October 2008), 10, 13.

16. KPMG, *Accelerating Mobility: Optimizing Transit in Response to Rapid Disruptions in Technology and Consumer Behavior* (2019), 6.

17. Norton, "History as Motordom's Tool," 67–90; Norton, "Of Love Affairs and Other Stories," in *Incomplete Streets: Processes, Practices, and Possibilities*, ed. Stephen Zavestoski and Julian Agyeman (London: Routledge, 2015), 17–35.

18. Norton, *Fighting Traffic*; Norton, "Persistent Pedestrianism: Urban Walking in Motor Age America," *Urban History* (Cambridge: Cambridge University Press, November 2019),

1–24; Norton, "The Baby Carriage Blockades," *Vision Zero Cities*, October 10, 2019.

19. Janette Sadik-Khan and Seth Solomonow, *Streetfight: Handbook for an Urban Revolution* (New York: Viking Penguin, 2016); Jason Henderson, *Street Fight: The Politics of Mobility in San Francisco* (Amherst: University of Massachusetts Press, 2013).

20. See NACTO's design guides, especially: *Urban Street Design Guide* (October 2013), *Urban Bikeway Design Guide* (2nd ed., March 2014), *Transit Street Design Guide* (April 2016), and *Global Street Design Guide* (October 2016), all published by Island.

21. Sadik-Khan and Solomonow, *Streetfight*, 109–42.

22. Sadik-Khan and Solomonow, 116–17; Javier C. Hernandez, "Car-Free Streets, a Colombian Export, Inspires Debate," *New York Times*, B6. To watch Bogotá's ciclovía in action, see Clarence Eckerson Jr., Ciclovia (video: StreetFilms, 2007, 9:40 min.; www.streetfilms.org/ciclovia).

23. Hernandez, "Car-Free Streets," B6; Sadik-Khan and Solomonow, *Streetfight*, 118–23.

24. Sergio Montero, "Worlding Bogota's Ciclovia: From Urban Experiment to International 'Best Practice,'" *Latin American Perspectives* 44, no. 2 (March 2017): 111–131.

25. Sadik-Khan and Solomonow, *Streetfight,* 117.

26. K.T. Analytics, *Lessons Learned from International Experience in Congestion Pricing: Final Report*, for the Federal Highway Administration (August 2008), 2-20, 2-22, 3-3, 3-11; Maria Börjesson et al., "The Stockholm Congestion Charges—Five Years On: Effects, Acceptability, and Lessons Learnt," *Transport Policy* 20 (2012): 1–12.

27. Sadik-Khan and Solomonow, *Streetfight*, 91–107; William Neuman, "Mayor's Plan for Broadway as a Walkway," *New York Times*, February 27, 2009, A1, A25; Michael Crowley,

28. *Una ciudad avanzada no es aquella en la que los pobres*

pueden moverse en coche, sino una en la que incluso los ricos utilizan el transporte público": Peñalosa, in EFE news agency. "Enrique Peñalosa: 'América Latina debe mirar más a Amsterdam que a Miami,'" *Semana* (Bogotá), January 13, 2011, www.semana.com/vida-moderna/articulo/enrique-penalosa-america-latina-debe-mirar-mas-amsterdam-miami/234025-3.

29. Santiago Mejía-Dugand et al., "Lessons from the Spread of Bus Rapid Transit in Latin America," *Journal of Cleaner Production* 50 (July 1, 2013): 82–90. TransMilenio passengers have endured overcrowding and poor service, though the problems are apparently due to underfunding rather than to the BRT principle. The proliferation of BRT elsewhere suggests that the technique can work well.

30. Sadik-Khan and Solomonow, *Streetfight*, 233–49. By some standards, Select Bus Service, introduced in 2008, does not qualify as full BRT service; see Michelle Young, "Why NYC's Select Bus Service Is Not a Bus Rapid Transit (BRT) System," Untapped New York, July 31, 2013, untappedcities.com/2013/07/31/why-nyc-select-bus-service-is-not-bus-rapid-transit-brt-system.

31. EFE, "Enrique Peñalosa: 'América Latina debe mirar más a Amsterdam que a Miami,'" *Semana*, January 13, 2011.

32. Derived from data for 2019 in US Environmental Protection Agency, *Draft Inventory of U.S. Greenhouse Gas Emissions and Sinks, 1990–2019* (Washington, DC: EPA, 2021), 2-38, 2-39, and from Statistics Netherlands / Centraal Bureau voor de Statistiek, www.cbs.nl.

33. According to the *World Happiness Report 2020*, ed. John F. Helliwell et al. (New York: Sustainable Development Solutions Network, 2020), among 153 nations, the Netherlands ranks 6th in happiness (p. 20).

34. Lucas Harms and Maarten Kansen, *Cycling Facts* (Netherlands Institute for Transport Policy Analysis, Ministry of Infrastructure and Water Management), 2018 (data from

Statistics Netherlands); Kennisinstituut voor Mobilite-itsbeleid, Mobiliteitsbeleid 2017 (Ministerie van Infra-structuur en Milieu, 2017; www.kimnet.nl/publicaties/rapporten/2017/10/23/mobiliteitsbeeld-2017), 46. For an overview of Dutch methods of making bicycling a practical mobility mode, see Melissa Bruntlett and Chris Bruntlett, *Building the Cycling City: The Dutch Blueprint for Urban Vitality* (Washington, DC: Island, 2018).

35. Low density is not an insuperable obstacle to transit. See Jarrett Walker, *Human Transit: How Clearer Thinking about Public Transit Can Enrich Our Communities and Our Lives* (Washington, DC: Island, 2012), 109–15.

36. David Hembrow, "The Car-Free Myth," *A View from the Cycle Path* (blog), August 24, 2019, www.aviewfromthecyclepath .com/2019/08/the-car-free-myth-netherlands-is-great.html.

37. Jonathan Chew, This Is the Best Country to Drive In, *Fortune*, September 30, 2015, fortune.com/2015/09/30/best-coun-try-drive-waze; José Santiago, "The 10 Best and Worst Coun-tries to Drive In," World Economic Forum, October 12, 2015, www.weforum.org/agenda/2015/10/the-10-best-and-worst -countries-for-drivers. Waze compared thirty-two countries.

38. Jan Ploeger and Ruth Oldenziel, "The Sociotechnical Roots of Smart Mobility: Bike Sharing since 1965," *Jour-nal of Transport History* 41, no. 2 (August 2020): 134–59. For in-depth studies revealing how cycling was marginal-ized and then recovered in Dutch cities, see the volumes of the Cycling Cities series, published by the Foundation for the History of Technology (Eindhoven): *Cycling Cities: The European Experience*, ed. Ruth Oldenziel et al. (2016): 16–75; Erick Berkers and Ruth Oldenziel, *Cycling Cities: The Arnhem and Nijmegen Experience* (2017); Eric Berkers, Frans Botma, and Ruth Oldenziel, *Cycling Cities: The Hague Expe-rience* (2018); and Eric Berkers et al., *Cycling Cities: The Rot-terdam Experience* (2019). See also Carlton Reid, *Bike Boom: The Unexpected Resurgence of Cycling* (Washington, DC: Island, 2017), 179–210, and Mark Wagenbuur, "How the

Dutch Got Their Cycling Infrastructure," with video: "How the Dutch Got Their Cycle Paths," *Bicycle Dutch* (blog), October 20, 2011.

39. Peter Norton, "Persistent Pedestrianism: Urban Walking in Motor Age America," *Urban History*, November 2019, 1–24.

40. Carlton Reid, *Bike Boom*, 179–210.

41. Norton, "History as Motordom's Tool," 67–90.

42. Rachel Carson, *Silent Spring* (Boston: Houghton Mifflin, 1962), 8.

43. Jacobs, *The Death and Life of Great American Cities* (New York: Random House, 1961), 15, 17.

44. Carson, *Silent Spring*, 8.

45. Such usage of *ecosystem* has become very common; see Jonathan Camhi, *The Autonomous Mobility Ecosystem*, *Business Insider*, March 2018, bii_autonomousmobilityecosystem_2018.pdf, and Raphaël Gindrat, "Anatomy of an Autonomous Vehicle Ecosystem," *Forbes*, October 17, 2019, www.forbes.com/sites/forbestechcouncil/2019/10/17/anatomy-of-an-autonomous-vehicle-service-ecosystem.

The term *mobility ecosystem*, to mean little more than the technology and the companies than can automate vehicles, has even been used officially by the US Department of Energy; see *The Transforming Mobility Ecosystem: Enabling an Energy-Efficient Future* (DOE, 2017; www.energy.gov/eere/vehicles/downloads/transforming-mobility-ecosystem-report), which uses the term repeatedly.

46. Arthur Tansley, who invented the word *ecosystem*, was troubled enough by its abuse to write an article to object. Tansley's specific objection was to uses that did not include "the whole system" or the "whole complex . . . in the widest sense." His condemnation applies to corporate abuses of the word. See Tansley, "The Use and Abuse of Vegetational Concepts and Terms," *Ecology* 16, no. 3 (July 1935): 284–307 (299).

47. Some corporate "ecosystems" are more inclusive than others;

for example, micromobility apps are more inclusive than AV developers.

48. Carson, *Silent Spring*, 5, 51.

49. Tansley objected to uses of *ecosystem* that did not include "the whole system" or the "whole complex . . . in the widest sense." Tansley, "Vegetational Concepts," 299, 306.

50. Hod Lipson and Melba Kurman, *Driverless: Intelligent Cars and the Road Ahead* (Cambridge, MA: MIT Press, 2016), 140.

51. The word *solutionism* was popularized by Evgeny Morozov in *To Save Everything, Click Here: The Folly of Technological Solutionism* (New York: Public Affairs, 2013).

52. Jameson M. Wetmore, "Reflecting on the Dream of Automated Vehicles: Visions of Hands-Free Driving over the Past 80 Years," *Technikgeschichte* 87 (2020): 69–94 (69).

53. Carson, *Silent Spring*, 8.

54. Jacobs, *Great American Cities*, 433 (original emphasis), 436–37, 447.

55. Federal Highway Administration, "As-Prepared Remarks for Federal Highway Administrator, Nicole R. Nason." Automated Vehicles Symposium, Orlando, July 17, 2019, cms8.fhwa.dot.gov/newsroom/prepared-remarks-federal -highway-administrator-nicole-r-nason-automated-vehicles -symposium.

56. Jacobs, *Great American Cities*, 17, 87, 223, 437.

57. Kohn, "When 'Big Data' Goes to School," *Alfie Kohn* (blog), March 7, 2018, www.alfiekohn.org/ blogs/big-data.

58. Verghese, "Treat the Patient, Not the CT Scan," *New York Times*, February 27, 2011.

59. Jack Stilgoe, *Who's Driving Innovation? New Technologies and the Collaborative State* (London: Palgrave Macmillan, 2020), 13.

60. Davidoff, "Advocacy and Pluralism in Planning," *Journal*

of the American Institute of Planners 31, no. 4 (November 1965): 331–38; Davidoff and Thomas Reiner, "A Choice Theory of Planning," *Journal of the American Institute of Planners* 28 (May 1962): 103–115 (111).

61. Yda Schreuder, "The Polder Model in Dutch Economic and Environmental Planning," *Bulletin of Science, Technology and Society* 21, no. 4 (August 2001): 237–45; "Digital Democracy: What Europe Can Learn from Taiwan," Gütersloh: Bertelsmann Stiftung, September 2020, aei.pitt.edu/103223 /1/Digital_Democracy_%2D_ What_ Europe_can_learn _from_Taiwan.pdf.

On a successful hybrid of the polder model and digital democracy in Amsterdam (called the Digital City, or De Digitale Stad), see Geert Lovink and Patrice Riemens, "A Polder Model in Cyberspace: Amsterdam Public Digital Culture," in *Shaping the Network Society: The New Role of Civil Society in Cyberspace*, ed. Douglas Schuler and Peter Day (Cambridge: MIT Press, 2004), 111–135.

62. Tony Dutzik, Benjamin Davis, and Phineas Baxandall, *Do Roads Pay for Themselves? Setting the Record Straight on Transportation Funding* (US PIRG Education Fund, January 2011), 1.

Index